"In this book Greg Beale combines a beginner's guide to the study of the use of the Old Testament in the New Testament with a detailed catalog of resource material, an illustrated exposition of the methods to be applied, and some discussion of the hermeneutical issues that arise. He himself has made notable forays into this field of study and draws on these to enrich the content of the book, making it not simply a survey of contemporary approaches but also a real personal contribution to the further development of our understanding of this crucial area of biblical studies. The volume thus compensates generously for the lack of a detailed introduction to the massive *Commentary on the New Testament Use of the Old Testament* edited by Beale and Don Carson."

—**I. Howard Marshall**, University of Aberdeen

"We have long needed a good book on the use of the Old Testament in the New. This is it. One might not agree with everything said here, but all readers will be challenged to think carefully about the issues raised. A solid work."

—**Darrell Bock**, Dallas Theological Seminary

"Greg Beale is well known for his contributions to the New Testament use of the Old Testament and the development of biblical theology. In this extremely useful handbook, we see how Beale goes about his task in terms of presuppositions, method, and the necessary reference tools for the task. The result is essential reading for anyone contemplating research in this area."

—**Steve Moyise**, University of Chichester

"No subject is more important to the interpretation of the New Testament and biblical theology than the study of the Old Testament in the New Testament. It is also one of the most technical and difficult subjects. Written by a veteran and pioneer in the field, *Handbook on the New Testament Use of the Old Testament* is a reliable guide through challenging terrain. Highly recommended to anyone who wants to work hard at appreciating the profound connections between the testaments."

—**Brian S. Rosner**, principal of Ridley Melbourne

HANDBOOK on the NEW TESTAMENT Use of the OLD TESTAMENT

EXEGESIS AND INTERPRETATION

G. K. Beale

a division of Baker Publishing Group
Grand Rapids, Michigan

Published by Baker Academic
a division of Baker Publishing Group
P.O. Box 6287, Grand Rapids, MI 49516-6287
www.bakeracademic.com

Printed in the United States of America

Library of Congress Cataloging-in-Publication Data
Beale, G. K. (Gregory K.), 1949–
Handbook on the New Testament use of the Old Testament : exegesis and interpretation / G. K. Beale.
p. cm.
Includes bibliographical references (p.) and index.
ISBN 978-0-8010-3896-9 (pbk.)
1. Bible. O.T.—Relation to the New Testament. 2. Bible—Hermeneutics. I. Title.
BS2387.B43 2012
225.6—dc23 2012013968

20 21 22 23 10 9 8 7

To the memory of S. Lewis Johnson, who first taught me about how the New Testament uses the Old Testament

Contents

Preface

My first substantive exposure to the use of the Old Testament (OT) in the New Testament (NT) was in a course I took on this subject during the mid-1970s from S. Lewis Johnson. This piqued my great interest in the subject. When I decided to do doctoral work at the University of Cambridge, Dr. Johnson suggested that one of the areas needing study was the use of the Old Testament in John's Apocalypse. So I rushed into a subject where angels fear to tread (though they do tread a lot in this book). When I finished the dissertation, I continued to write in the area of the OT in the NT and have done so since then.

This book had its birth in a class on the use of the OT in the NT, which I first taught in 1985 at Gordon-Conwell Theological Seminary. There I tried to develop further what I had learned in Dr. Johnson's class on the subject. Over the years I continued to teach the course at Gordon-Conwell on a regular basis and at Wheaton College Graduate School, and most recently I have taught it at Westminster Theological Seminary. Part of the culmination of my studies in this area over the years has been the recent publication of two major works: *Commentary on the New Testament Use of the Old Testament* (Grand Rapids: Baker Academic, 2007), which I edited together with D. A. Carson, and *A New Testament Biblical Theology: The Unfolding of the Old Testament in the New* (Grand Rapids: Baker Academic, 2011), which focused on the biblical-theological relationship of the Old Testament to the New. This handbook provides a sketch of the method lying behind the *Commentary on the New Testament Use of the Old Testament*, which Don Carson and I asked all the contributors to that volume to follow. The methodology of this handbook also lies behind much of the analysis in my *New Testament Biblical Theology*.

I have come to realize that no existing book primarily aims to set forth an approach to interpreting OT citations and allusions in the NT. Therefore, seeing this need, I have tried to fill that gap with this handbook on the subject. The purpose of this book is to provide pastors, students, and other serious readers of Scripture with a how-to approach for interpreting the use of the OT in the NT. I hope that scholars will also find the book helpful.

As with my past projects, I am indebted beyond words to my wife, Dorinda, who has discussed aspects of this book with me during the past years and remains as excited as I am about the subject. She has been one of the main instruments through which I have been able to understand this topic in more depth.

I thank Jim Kinney and his staff for accepting this book for publication. I am thankful for the careful editorial work done by the staff at Baker Academic.

I am likewise grateful to a number of churches and seminaries that over the years have asked me to speak at conferences on some of the themes of this book. I particularly want to acknowledge the following schools and organizations who invited me to speak on parts of chapters of this book in 2011 and 2012: Johaanelunds Teological Seminary (Uppsala, Sweden), Örebro Teological Seminary (Örebro, Sweden), University of Lund (Lund, Sweden), Southern Baptist Theological Seminary (Louisville, Kentucky), Theofil Conference (affiliated with the International Fellowship of Evangelical Students; Lund, Sweden), and the regional conference of the New England branch of the Evangelical Theological Society. Likewise, I am thankful to generations of students—from Gordon-Conwell Theological Seminary, Wheaton College Graduate School, and more recently, Westminster Theological Seminary—who have asked many questions about the topic, causing me to reflect more deeply and to try to clarify my perspectives.

I also want to offer appreciation to the following research students who either helped do research or double-checked and edited the manuscript of this book: Matthew A. Dudreck and Nick Owens. I am also grateful to my colleagues Vern Poythress and Brandon Crowe for reading a rough draft of this book and making many helpful comments, which I have incorporated at points. Above all, I am thankful to God for enabling me to conceive the idea for this book, building on the shoulders of others before me, and giving me the energy and discipline to write it. It is my prayer that God's glory will be more greatly manifested as a result of readers' using this book.

A few comments about some stylistic aspects of the book are in order. English translations follow the New American Standard Bible unless otherwise indicated; when a translation is different, it often represents my own translation (AT, author's trans.). With respect to all translations of ancient works, when the wording differs from standard editions, then it is my translation or someone else's (whom I indicate).

References to the Greek NT are from the Nestle-Aland *Novum Testamentum Graece*, 27th ed. (NA^{27}). I cite the Hebrew OT from the *Biblia Hebraica Stutgartensia* (MT = Masoretic Text). For the Septuagint (LXX), I use the Greek-English parallel text of *The Septuagint Version of the Old Testament and Apocrypha with an English Translation*, by Lancelot C. L. Brenton (1851;

repr., Grand Rapids: Zondervan, 1972), which is dependent on Codex B and is published by special arrangement with Samuel Bagster and Sons (London), and later under the title *The Septuagint with Apocrypha* (Peabody, MA: Hendrickson, 1986). This will enable those not knowing Greek to follow the Septuagint in a readily available English edition.

My references to the Dead Sea Scrolls (DSS) come primarily from the edition of Florentino García Martínez, *The Dead Sea Scrolls Translated* (Leiden: Brill, 1994), and sometimes I make reference to *The Dead Sea Scrolls: Study Edition*, edited by Florentino García Martínez and Eibert J. C. Tigchelaar, 2 vols. (Leiden: Brill, 2000). In addition, other translations of DSS were consulted and sometimes preferred in quotations (such as the one by A. Dupont-Sommer, *The Essene Writings from Qumran* [Oxford: Basil Blackwell, 1961]). At times variations in the translation from the primary text of García Martínez reflect my own translation.

G. K. Beale
Professor of New Testament and Biblical Theology
Westminster Theological Seminary
Philadelphia
July 2012

Abbreviations

General

AT	author's translation	p(p).	page(s)
chap(s).	chapter(s)	repr.	reprint
esp.	especially	rev.	revised
ibid.	in the same source	v(v).	verse(s)
idem	by the same author		

Divisions of the Canon

NT	New Testament	OT	Old Testament

Ancient Texts, Text Types, and Versions

DSS	Dead Sea Scrolls	MT	Masoretic Text
LXX	Septuagint	OG	Old Greek

Modern Editions

NA[27] *Novum Testamentum Graece*. Edited by [E. and E. Nestle], B. Aland, K. Aland, J. Karavidopoulos, C. M. Martini, and B. M. Metzger. 27th rev. ed. Stuttgart: Deutsche Bibelgesellschaft, 1993

USB[4] *The Greek New Testament*. Edited by B. Aland, K. Aland, J. Karavidopoulos, C. M. Martini, and B. M. Metzger. 4th rev. ed. Stuttgart: Deutsche Bibelgesellschaft / United Bible Societies, 1993

Modern Versions

KJV	King James Version
NIV	New International Version
NRSV	New Revised Standard Version

Hebrew Bible / Old Testament

Gen.	Genesis
Exod.	Exodus
Lev.	Leviticus
Num.	Numbers
Deut.	Deuteronomy
Josh.	Joshua
Judg.	Judges
Ruth	Ruth
1–2 Sam.	1–2 Samuel
1–2 Kings	1–2 Kings
1–2 Chron.	1–2 Chronicles
Ezra	Ezra
Neh.	Nehemiah
Esther	Esther
Job	Job
Ps./Pss.	Psalms
Prov.	Proverbs
Eccles.	Ecclesiastes
Song	Song of Songs
Isa.	Isaiah
Jer.	Jeremiah
Lam.	Lamentations
Ezek.	Ezekiel
Dan.	Daniel
Hosea	Hosea
Joel	Joel
Amos	Amos
Obad.	Obadiah
Jon.	Jonah
Mic.	Micah
Nah.	Nahum
Hab.	Habakkuk
Zeph.	Zephaniah
Hag.	Haggai
Zech.	Zechariah
Mal.	Malachi

New Testament

Matt.	Matthew
Mark	Mark
Luke	Luke
John	John
Acts	Acts
Rom.	Romans
1–2 Cor.	1–2 Corinthians
Gal.	Galatians
Eph.	Ephesians
Phil.	Philippians
Col.	Colossians
1–2 Thess.	1–2 Thessalonians
1–2 Tim.	1–2 Timothy
Titus	Titus
Philem.	Philemon
Heb.	Hebrews
James	James
1–2 Pet.	1–2 Peter
1–3 John	1–3 John
Jude	Jude
Rev.	Revelation

Apocrypha and Septuagint

Bar.	Baruch
1–2 Esd.	1–2 Esdras
1–4 Macc.	1–4 Maccabees

Secondary Sources

AB	Anchor Bible
BECNT	Baker Exegetical Commentary on the New Testament
BZAW	Beihefte zur Zeitschrift für die alttestamentliche Wissenschaft
BZNW	Beihefte zur Zeitschrift für die neutestamentliche Wissenschaft
EBC	Expositor's Bible Commentary
HNT	Handbuch zum Neuen Testament
ICC	International Critical Commentary
JETS	*Journal of the Evangelical Theological Society*
JSNT	*Journal for the Study of the New Testament*
JSNTSup	Journal for the Study of the New Testament: Supplement Series
JSOT	*Journal for the Study of the Old Testament*
JSOTSup	Journal for the Study of the Old Testament: Supplement Series
NAC	New American Commentary
NICNT	New International Commentary on the New Testament
NIGTC	New International Greek Testament Commentary
NovTSup	Novum Testamentum Supplements
NTM	New Testament Monographs
NTS	*New Testament Studies*
PNTC	Pillar New Testament Commentary
SNTSMS	Society for New Testament Studies Monograph Series
SSEJC	Studies in Scripture in Early Judaism and Christianity
TOTC	Tyndale Old Testament Commentaries
WBC	Word Biblical Commentary
WTJ	*Westminster Theological Journal*
WUNT	Wissenschaftliche Untersuchungen zum Neuen Testament

Introduction

The purpose of this handbook is to provide a short guide to the use of OT citations and allusions in the NT. The intended audience is serious-minded Christians, students, and pastors, with the hope that even scholars might benefit. The way the OT is used in the NT has been a topic of many, many books and scholarly articles since the mid-twentieth century. No one, however, has yet attempted to produce a handbook that can help guide interpreters through the process of analyzing the multitude of OT references. There will never be a perfect handbook for this topic. Nevertheless, the present project is an attempt to provide more help in this endeavor than previously available.

This book does not try to give thorough discussions of the various issues that it addresses. Rather, the focus is on methodological approaches and sources to aid in the task of understanding how the NT writers refer to the OT. The main guidelines covered in this book lie behind the work done in the *Commentary on the New Testament Use of the Old Testament*.[1]

Chapter 1 begins with a brief discussion of some of the most important debates about the use of the OT in the NT. The purpose here is to alert readers to some of the challenging issues confronting interpreters in this area before they begin the interpretative work themselves.

After reviewing some of the difficult problems confronting interpreters in this field, chapter 2 begins to focus on the first step in analyzing the OT in the NT: how does one know when a NT writer is actually referring to an OT passage? In particular, this chapter discusses the criteria for recognizing quotations and especially allusions. The criteria for discerning allusions have been the subject of much debate over the last few decades.

1. G. K. Beale and D. A. Carson, eds., *Commentary on the New Testament Use of the Old Testament* (Grand Rapids: Baker Academic, 2007).

Chapter 3 addresses the main concern of this handbook: what method should be used for interpreting how the NT uses the OT? A ninefold procedure is offered for analyzing OT references. Some scholars do not like the suggestion that a "method" or "procedure" can be offered that is adequate for any interpretative enterprise in the Bible. Naturally, no procedure can be used as a strict formula that, when followed, guarantees finding the "true interpretation" or "exhaustive" meaning. This is because interpretation is not only a science but also a literary art. Furthermore, no interpretation can exhaust the full meaning of a text, though good interpretation can uncover meaning so that readers can obtain a sufficient understanding of a passage. Accordingly, the guidelines offered in this chapter are just that—guides—not formulas that inevitably lead to correct interpretations. The approaches analyzed in this chapter offer various angles from which readers can view the biblical text, angles that cumulatively help readers to better understand the way the NT uses the OT. Other angles of reflection can certainly be added to the ones covered here. The goal is to better grasp the way the two Testaments are related at the particular points where OT references are found. Our ultimate aim is to hear and understand more clearly the voice of the living God as he has spoken and continues to speak in his "living words" (Acts 7:38 NIV) and accordingly to know and encounter God increasingly, to know his will, and so to honor him.[2]

Chapter 4 elaborates on one of the elements of the approach mentioned in chapter 3: the kinds of interpretative uses of the OT in the NT. This certainly is not an exhaustive list. Instead, it is an effort to discuss the main ways NT writers have interpreted OT passages. This section is based partly on the work of past scholars in their studies of this subject.

Chapter 5 further develops another aspect of the central discussion from chapter 3: the theological and hermeneutical presuppositions underlying the NT authors' use of the OT. Not all agree about what these presuppositions are.

Chapter 6 likewise expands on yet one more aspect of the central discussion in chapter 3: How does one discover the various ways Judaism has interpreted a particular OT passage referred to in the NT? What primary sources in Judaism are important in this task? How does one use these sources to discover how they interpret OT passages? Tracing such an interpretative tradition in Judaism can sometimes shed light on the way a NT writer uses an OT passage. Such Jewish interpretations may positively illuminate the meaning or may show how unique the NT's use is in contrast to that of Judaism.

The last chapter provides a fleshing out of the preceding chapters on methodology. There is a case study illustrating a typical use of the OT in the NT.

A select bibliography appears at the end of the book.

2. Although I realize that not everyone in the academic guild shares this goal.

1

Challenges to Interpreting the Use of the Old Testament in the New

Before proceeding to suggest guidelines for studying the OT in the NT, readers should be generally aware of several classic debates that have arisen over the way the NT writers and Jesus use the OT.

How Much Continuity or Discontinuity Is There between the Old Testament and the New?

The most important debate is about whether the NT interprets the Old in line with the original OT meaning. Does the NT show awareness of the contextual meaning of the OT references to which it appeals? How much continuity or discontinuity is there between the original meaning of the OT passages and their use in the NT? Scholars give conflicting answers to these questions.

The Debate about the Influence of Jewish Interpretation on the New Testament Writers

One widely held position is that Jesus and the writers of the NT used noncontextual hermeneutical methods that caused them to miss the original meaning of the OT texts that they were trying to interpret. In doing so, they were influenced by their Jewish contemporaries, whether in earlier rabbinic midrashic exegesis, Qumran scrolls, or Jewish apocalyptic literature. Today we generally regard noncontextual methods as illegitimate. While they refer to the OT, they do not interpret it in a way consistent with the original meaning of the OT passage.[1] For example, it is held that the NT allegorizes various OT texts, reading in foreign meanings that completely miss the earlier meaning of the OT author. Some scholars conclude that such uncontrolled interpretations are but one of the many ways the NT bears the mark of human fallibility.

Others agree that at certain places the NT writers missed the meaning of the OT yet believe that they were guided in their interpretation by the example of Christ and by the Spirit. Thus, while their interpretative procedure was flawed, the meaning they wrote down was inspired. Accordingly, though we cannot imitate their interpretative methods today, we can trust their conclusions and believe their doctrine.[2] It is comparable to listening to preachers whose interpretation of a particular passage is clearly off the mark, but what they say is good theology and found elsewhere in the Bible, though not in the passage they are expounding.

Thus many would conclude that an inductive study reveals an oft-occurring disconnection of meaning between NT writers' interpretations of the OT and the original meaning of that OT text. Examples of such alleged misinterpretations include:[3]

1. Ad hominem argumentation: the role of angels in revealing the law in Gal. 3:19; the exodus "veil" theme in 2 Cor. 3:13–18; and the "seed" of Gen. 12:7 (KJV) and 22:17–18 in Gal. 3:16.
2. Noncontextual midrashic treatments: the understanding of baptism and the "following rock" in 1 Cor. 10:1–4; Deut. 30:12–14 in Rom. 10:6–8; Gen. 12:7 (KJV) and 22:17–18 in Gal. 3:16; Ps. 68:18 in Eph. 4:8; Hosea 11:1 in Matt. 2:15.
3. Allegorical interpretations: Deut. 25:4 in 1 Cor. 9:9; the use of the OT in Gal. 4:24; Gen. 14 in Heb. 7.
4. Atomistic interpretations, uncontrolled by any kind of interpretative rules: Isa. 40:6–8 in 1 Pet. 1:24–25.

However, some scholars are more optimistic about the NT authors' ability to interpret the OT.

1. Yet in light of postmodern influence, I am aware that some scholars claim that the uncontrolled Jewish hermeneutic was a legitimate approach then but perhaps not for us, though some would say it may be a guide for modern interpreters too.

2. For a clear and sympathetic presentation of this sort of view, see the writings of R. N. Longenecker, including his article "'Who Is the Prophet Talking About?' Some Reflections on the New Testament's Use of the Old," *Themelios* 13 (1987): 4–8.

3. Here for the most part I am using R. N. Longenecker's examples from his "Can We Reproduce the Exegesis of the New Testament?" *Tyndale Bulletin* 21 (1970): 3–38; and idem, *Biblical Exegesis in the Apostolic Period* (Grand Rapids: Eerdmans, 1975).

It is not at all clear that noncontextual midrashic exegesis was as central to earlier Pharisaic and Qumran exegesis as is suggested by scholars favoring the approach we have described above. First, it may not be appropriate to speak of a noncontextual *rabbinic* method before AD 70 since most examples come from later, and earlier ones that can be dated with probability do not appear to reflect such an uncontrolled interpretative approach.[4] Second, concern for contextual exegesis is characteristically found in both Qumran scrolls and Jewish apocalyptic.[5] This analysis has far-reaching negative implications for the argument of those who believe that early Christian interpreters were influenced by a prevalent Jewish hermeneutic that was not concerned about the original meaning of OT passages.

But even this assumption of Jewish influence on NT exegesis of the Old may be questioned. It sounds a priori plausible that the interpretative procedures of the NT would resemble those of contemporary Judaism. And yet, since early Christianity had a unique perspective in comparison with early Judaism, one should not assume that first-century Jewish and Christian exegetical approaches are mostly the same.[6] To assess the issue, it is necessary to look at the NT itself without prejudice about methodological continuity or discontinuity. Though this is a debated assessment, it is not unusual. For example, along these same lines, Richard Hays has declared:

> Rabbinic Judaism, no less than early Christianity, represents (along with the Qumran community and Philo's scholastic Alexandrian Judaism, inter alia), one of several different adaptations of the religious and cultural heritage represented by Israel's Scriptures. These different adaptations should be studied, at least initially, as parallel phenomena, related but distinct dispositions of that heritage. To argue that one of these phenomena represents a source of influence for another is likely to be misleading unless some documentable line of historical dependence can be demonstrated. One thing that is clearly documentable is

4. On this latter point, David Instone-Brewer has identified all the exegetical examples representing this early period (about 100) of purported pre-AD 70 protorabbinic exegesis. He has tried to demonstrate how every example shows that, although these Jewish exegetes may not always have succeeded, they tried to interpret the OT according to its context and never supplanted the primary meaning by a secondary or allegorical one. Even if his conclusions are judged to be overstated, as some have affirmed, they nevertheless reveal an early concern for context to varying significant degrees, a concern previously not sufficiently acknowledged. See his *Techniques and Assumptions in Jewish Exegesis before 70 C.E.*, Texte und Studien zum Antiken Judentum 30 (Tübingen: Mohr Siebeck, 1992).

5. In Qumran, e.g., 1QM 1; in Jewish apocalyptic, e.g., *1 Enoch* 36–72; *4 Ezra* (= 2 Esd.) 11–13; *2 Baruch* 36–42; *Testament of Joseph* 19:6–12. See G. K. Beale, *The Use of Daniel in Jewish Apocalyptic Literature and in the Revelation of St. John* (Lanham, MD: University Press of America, 1984); L. Hartman, *Prophecy Interpreted* (Lund: C. W. K. Gleerup, 1966).

6. As, e.g., Longenecker surprisingly seems to assume ("New Testament's Use," 7), since he points out the same kind of presuppositional fallacy on the part of others (ibid., 1). See further on Longenecker's view at note 10 below.

that all of them deliberately regard Scripture as source and authority for their own quite different theological developments. Thus, we are undertaking a valid and necessary (even if preliminary) task when we inquire independently into the way in which any one of them uses scriptural texts.[7]

This is not a conclusion reached only by more conservative American or English scholars. For example, Hans Hübner in his *Biblische Theologie des Neuen Testaments* concludes that the key to Paul's interpretation of the OT is not found by seeing Judaism as the determinative influence on him. Rather, the way NT authors handle their Scripture should be analyzed first from their own writings, independent of Jewish methods of interpretation.[8]

Furthermore, it is not certain that the typical examples of noncontextual exegesis adduced above are really conclusive. A number of scholars have offered viable and even persuasive explanations of how they could well be cases of contextual exegesis.[9] In addition, even if it were granted that they are convincing examples of noncontextual hermeneutics, it does not necessarily follow that they are truly representative of a wider hermeneutical pattern in the NT.[10] They may be exceptional rather than typical.

7. R. Hays, *Echoes of Scripture in the Letters of Paul* (New Haven: Yale University Press, 1989), 11.

8. H. Hübner, *Biblische Theologie des Neuen Testaments* (Göttingen: Vandenhoeck & Ruprecht, 1990), 1:258–59, where he also cites other German scholars in agreement, even though he ends up concluding that the NT's christological focus caused a significant discontinuity between a text's meaning in the OT and its use in the NT.

9. On 1 Cor. 10 and Gal. 3–4 see E. E. Ellis, *Paul's Use of the Old Testament* (1957; repr., Grand Rapids: Baker, 1981), 51–54, 66–73; R. M. Davidson, *Typology in Scripture* (Berrien Springs, MI: Andrews University Press, 1981), 193–297; and D. A. Hagner, "The Old Testament in the New Testament," in *Interpreting the Word of God: Festschrift in Honor of S. Barabas*, ed. S. J. Schultz and M. A. Inch (Chicago: Moody, 1976), 101–2, who sees a broad contextual and typological approach in these texts.

On 2 Cor. 3 see W. J. Dumbrell, *The Beginning of the End* (Homebrush West, Australia: Lancer, 1985), 107–13, 121–28; and on 2 Cor. 3:6–18 see S. J. Hafemann, *Paul, Moses, and the History of Israel*, WUNT 81 (Tübingen: Mohr Siebeck, 1995); for further argument claiming a noncontextual use of the OT in the same passage, see L. L. Belleville, *Reflections of Glory: Paul's Polemical Use of the Moses-Doxa Tradition in 2 Corinthians 3.1–18*, JSNTSup 52 (Sheffield: JSOT Press, 1991).

On 1 Cor. 9:9 see R. E. Ciampa and B. S. Rosner, *The First Letter to the Corinthians*, PNTC (Grand Rapids: Eerdmans, 2010), 404–7; cf. A. T. Hanson, *Studies in Paul's Technique and Theology* (London: SPCK, 1974), 161–66; S. L. Johnson, *The Old Testament in the New* (Grand Rapids: Zondervan, 1980), 39–51; D. J. Moo, "The Problem of *Sensus Plenior*," in *Hermeneutics, Authority, and Canon*, ed. D. A. Carson and J. D. Woodbridge (Grand Rapids: Zondervan / Academie Books, 1986), 179–211.

On Rom. 10, cf. M. A. Seifrid, "Paul's Approach to the Old Testament in Romans 10:6–8," *Trinity Journal* 6 (1985): 3–37, who sees a contextual and typological use.

10. But Longenecker has contended that among NT writers we can find only "some literalist, straightforward exegesis of biblical texts"; that the pesher method (which he defines as an atomistic approach and which includes typology) "dominates" Matthew, John, and the early chapters

A substantial and sometimes neglected argument against the view that the NT uses the OT differently from its original meaning is C. H. Dodd's classic work *According to the Scriptures*.[11] In brief, Dodd observes that throughout the NT are numerous and scattered quotations that derive from the same few OT contexts. He asks why, given that the same segment of the OT is in view, there are so few identical quotations of the same verse; and second, why different verses are cited from the same segments of the OT. *He concludes that this phenomenon indicates that the NT authors were aware of broad OT contexts and did not focus merely on single verses independent of the segment from which they were drawn.* Single verses and phrases are merely signposts to the overall OT context from which they are cited. Furthermore, he concludes that this was a *unique hermeneutical phenomenon* of the day, in contrast to Jewish exegesis. He goes on to assert that since this hermeneutical phenomenon can be found in the very earliest strata of the NT traditions, and since such innovations are not characteristic of committees, then Christ was the most likely source of this original, creative hermeneutic, and from him the NT writers learned their interpretative approach.[12]

Some disagree with Dodd, and indeed many scholars in this field generally affirm that the NT writers often employ a noncontextual exegetical method.[13] Nevertheless, others have confirmed Dodd's thesis about the NT's unique and consistent respect for the OT context.[14]

---

of Acts and 1 Peter; and that midrashic interpretation (which he also views as a noncontextual method) "characterizes" Paul and Hebrews ("New Testament's Use," 6–8; cf. his *Biblical Exegesis*, 218–19). He does qualify this by saying that NT authors employed a "controlled atomistic exegesis" ("New Testament's Use," 7), but this is unclear, and he never explains what he means by this.

11. C. H. Dodd, *According to the Scriptures* (London: Nisbet, 1952).

12. Ibid., 110, 126–27.

13. Thus, e.g., B. Lindars, *New Testament Apologetic* (London: SCM, 1961); S. V. McCasland, "Matthew Twists the Scripture," *Journal of Biblical Literature* 80 (1961): 143–48; S. L. Edgar, "Respect for Context in Quotations from the Old Testament," *NTS* 9 (1962–63): 56–59; A. T. Hanson, *The Living Utterances of God* (London: Darton, Longman & Todd, 1983), 184–90; M. D. Hooker, "Beyond the Things That Are Written? St. Paul's Use of Scripture," *NTS* 27 (1981–82): 295–309; B. Lindars, "The Place of the Old Testament in the Formation of New Testament Theology," *NTS* 23 (1977): 59–66. For other references in this respect, consult Longenecker's bibliography in *Biblical Exegesis*, 223–30; C. D. Stanley, *Arguing with Scripture* (New York: T&T Clark, 2004); S. Moyise, *The Old Testament in the Book of Revelation*, *JSNT* 115 (Sheffield: Sheffield Academic Press, 1995); idem, "The Old Testament in the New: A Reply to Greg Beale," *Irish Biblical Studies* 21 (1999): 54–58; idem, "Does the New Testament Quote the Old Testament out of Context?" *Anvil* 11 (1994): 133–43, which tries to take a both-and view on the issue in the light of intertextual theory, though still leaning toward the noncontextual approach.

14. In addition to the sources cited above in this regard, see also, e.g., S. Kistemaker, *The Psalm Citations in the Epistle to the Hebrews* (Amsterdam: Van Soest, 1961); R. Rendell, "Quotation in Scripture as an Index of Wider Reference," *Evangelical Quarterly* 36 (1964): 214–21; Hartman, *Prophecy Interpreted*; R. T. France, *Jesus and the Old Testament* (Grand Rapids: Baker, 1971); idem, "The Formula-Quotations of Matthew 2 and the Problem of Communication," *NTS*

The Testimony Book Debate

Additionally, some scholars have contended that the NT writers took their OT quotations from a so-called testimony book, which contained various kinds of proof texts (*testimonia*) commonly used for apologetic reasons.[15] If this were the case, then the NT authors would not have been using these OT references with the literary context of the OT in view. Others have qualified the hypothesis of one testimony book and have proposed that there were excerpts of Scripture texts on various topics made by individuals and used either privately or circulated more generally.[16]

This qualified view of excerpted Scripture lists, if true, would still point to the likelihood that the NT writers were not interpreting OT passages holistically in the light of their literary context, but were merely using texts from an abstracted list of selected OT verses. Some argue for the existence of such lists because similar lists were found with the Qumran scrolls and among the writings of the later church fathers; they claim that these findings point to the existence of such excerpts among apostolic writers like Paul. In addition, such lists appear to be the more likely source of the NT writers' OT references, since whole manuscripts of OT books would have been expensive and not easily available. Accordingly, someone like Paul would presumably have made his own anthological lists from such manuscripts possessed by more wealthy Christians in the various places where he traveled.[17]

---

27 (1980–81): 233–51; D. Seccombe, "Luke and Isaiah," *NTS* 27 (1980–81), 252–59; Johnson, *Old Testament in the New*; D. J. Moo, *The Old Testament in the Gospel Passion Narratives* (Sheffield: Almond, 1983); W. C. Kaiser, *The Uses of the Old Testament in the New* (Chicago: Moody, 1985); Moo, "Problem of *Sensus Plenior*"; G. K. Beale, "The Influence of Daniel upon the Structure and Theology of John's Apocalypse," *JETS* 27 (1984): 413–23; idem, "The Use of the Old Testament in Revelation," in *It Is Written: Scripture Citing Scripture; Festschrift in Honour of Barnabas Lindars*, ed. D. A. Carson and H. Williamson (Cambridge: Cambridge University Press, 1988), 318–36; idem, "The Old Testament Background of Reconciliation in 2 Corinthians 5–7 and Its Bearing on the Literary Problem of 2 Corinthians 6:14–7:1," *NTS* 35 (1989): 550–81; R. Hays, *Echoes of Scripture in Paul*; idem, *The Conversion of the Imagination: Paul as Interpreter of Israel's Scripture* (Grand Rapids: Eerdmans, 2005); J. R. Wagner, *Heralds of the Good News: Isaiah and Paul "in Concert" in the Letter to the Romans* (Boston: Brill, 2003).

15. The classic formulation of such a testimony book was first given by J. R. Harris, with V. Burch, *Testimonies*, 2 vols. (Cambridge: Cambridge University Press, 1916–20).

16. See, e.g., C. D. Stanley, *Paul and the Language of Scripture: Citation Technique in the Pauline Epistles and Contemporary Literature*, SNTSMS 69 (Cambridge: Cambridge University Press, 1992), 73–79, 341–42, 349, 351; M. C. Albl, *"And Scripture Cannot Be Broken": The Form and Function of the Early Christian* Testimonia *Collections*, NovTSup 96 (Boston: Brill, 1999), who says, e.g., the "core of all *testimonia* hypotheses is the claim that early Christians did not use the Jewish Scriptures as an undifferentiated whole, but rather selected, shaped, and interpreted certain passages in support of emerging Christian beliefs" (65; see also his overall view on 65–69, 286–90). Albl holds that Paul, e.g., made his own list of Scriptures or inherited such a list from Christian tradition, from which he drew in his various epistles.

17. For other reasons offered in favor of Paul's making such lists, see Stanley, *Paul and Scripture*, 69–78.

Since C. H. Dodd believed that his conclusions about the NT authors' awareness of the context of OT references show that *a* testimony book did not exist, some have said his arguments do not have as much force against the idea that there were multiple testimony books or especially excerpted Scripture lists of different kinds. Other scholars have concluded, however, that Dodd's arguments still hold, even if several testimony books or excerpted testimony lists also existed.

The most balanced view appears to be that such excerpted lists did exist but that the NT writers also had access to actual OT scrolls containing whole books. In addition, they would likely have committed a number of OT books or segments thereof to memory, which to some extent would also have naturally occurred through their having been saturated with liturgical readings of Scripture sections in synagogue worship. The probability that authors like Paul were not limited to accessing excerpts is indicated by a spate of works appearing since Dodd's *According to the Scriptures*, works showing that NT writers were aware of the broader OT contexts from which they cited specific verses. A good example of such works most recently is by Richard B. Hays, *Echoes of Scripture in the Letters of Paul*, and others have followed in his wake.[18] But even if NT writers were often dependent on such testimony books, since they would also have been familiar with the OT and memorized portions of the OT, as we have posited just above, would it not be that such individual testimony quotations would invoke for them the wider context of that cited verse? In this respect David Lincicum's conclusion is on target: "The more convincing such readings [with contextual awareness of the OT] may be shown to be, the less likelihood there is that Paul was solely reliant upon a collection of excerpta."[19]

The Christocentric Debate

The influence of contemporary Jewish interpretation and dependence on lists of excerpted Scripture verses are not the only reasons that certain scholars see NT writers as interpreting the OT contrary to its original meaning. Some believe that the apostolic writers were so christocentric in their understanding of the OT that they read Christ into passages that had nothing to do with the coming Messiah. In so doing, they (allegedly) distorted the meaning of the

18. See, e.g., Wagner, *Heralds of the Good News*; C. A. Beetham, *Echoes of Scripture in the Letter of Paul to the Colossians*, Biblical Interpretation 96 (Leiden: Brill, 2008); Beale and Carson, *Commentary on the New Testament Use*; B. L. Gladd, *Revealing the* Mysterion*: The Use of Mystery in Daniel and Second Temple Judaism with Its Bearing on First Corinthians*, BZNW 16 (Berlin: de Gruyter, 2009); S. Mihalios, *The Danielic Eschatological Hour in the Johannine Literature*, Library of New Testament Studies 436 (New York: T&T Clark, 2011).

19. D. Lincicum, "Paul and the *Testimonia*: *Quo Vademus?*" *JETS* 51 (2008): 307. See the entirety of the article (297–308), providing a good, balanced perspective, with which my conclusion is in line, and discussing more scholars on both sides of the issue.

OT writer by reading in their presupposition that all of OT Scripture points to Christ.[20] Similarly, others believe that many of the NT authors were so caught up in defending Christ as Messiah that they twisted OT passages to support their viewpoint about the truth of the gospel.[21]

On the one hand, according to traditional exegetical criteria, this christocentric misreading of the OT is counted by some as mistaken interpretation. On the other hand, those of a more postmodern bent (see below), while acknowledging that the OT meaning has been distorted, would merely say that modern interpreters have no right to impose their standards of interpretation on the ancient writers and judge them by those standards. Still others of a more conservative persuasion, while agreeing with the postmodern assessment, claim that what we moderns might view as a defective interpretative approach of the NT authors resulted in a divinely inspired doctrinal conclusion. That is, the apostolic writers preached the right doctrine but from the wrong texts, though the interpretations they wrote down were done so with divine authority.

But does a christocentric presupposition necessitate a misreading of the OT? It certainly could, but must it? The answer to the question depends to a large degree on how one defines what is a christocentric hermeneutic. Some prefer to call this a "christotelic" approach, but this faces the same problem of finding a precise definition. In addition to the vagueness of definition, a christocentric or christotelic approach is one of a number of presuppositions that the apostles held in their understanding of the OT. A later chapter discusses this presupposition in the light of other presuppositions in order to obtain a more precise and balanced perspective of it. Then we can further address the question about whether such an interpretative assumption reads into the OT a foreign idea that distorts the original meaning.

In addition, a case-by-case study of each instance of a purported christocentric or christotelic interpretation of OT passages would need to include careful exegetical examination before one could determine whether distortion of the OT's meaning has taken place. Even after such thorough investigations, however, scholars will still disagree. There is one criterion, however, that can eventually point us in the right direction for solving this difficult issue: Do such analyses show that these christocentric readings reveal an awareness of the broader OT context and provide satisfying rhetorical and insightful

20. P. Enns, *Inspiration and Incarnation: Evangelicals and the Problem of the Old Testament* (Grand Rapids: Baker Academic, 2005), 113–66; idem, "Apostolic Hermeneutics and an Evangelical Doctrine of Scripture: Moving beyond the Modern Impasse," *WTJ* 65 (2003): 263–87, who prefers to call this approach a "christotelic" perspective: the NT writers viewed the OT as designed to point toward Christ. Enns admits that the NT writers' hermeneutic may be viewed as a distortion of the OT meaning from the vantage point of what many have considered traditionally to be a correct exegetical method. He says that, according to first-century standards of acceptable Jewish exegesis, the apostles' approach should be viewed as legitimate.

21. Lindars, *New Testament Apologetic*.

interpretative and theological readings of both the OT and NT contexts? Or do these readings reveal significant discontinuity between the OT and NT contexts? This will not be an absolute guarantee of deciding the issue, since interpretation is a subjective enterprise whereby what satisfies and appears insightful to one interpreter will not be so to another interpreter. Nevertheless, I believe that there is sufficient corroborating and cumulative hard evidence in this task that can provide us a way forward in debating this in the public domain, which involves comparing one's presuppositions with the assumptions of others who disagree.[22]

The Rhetorical Debate

Still others affirm that writers like Paul were not primarily concerned to use the OT to convey its contextual import but rhetorically to persuade readers to obey their exhortations. Thus only the wording of the OT is appealed to without consideration for its sense—in order to enhance the NT writer's apostolic authority in a "power move" to make the readers submit.[23] Some contend that NT writers would not care about what an OT verse means in its context since the majority of the readers/hearers in churches would have been gentiles, lacking the educational background to read the OT and appreciate its significance. Furthermore, such a view likely entails that even if many had possessed such an educational preparation to be able to read Greek, since they were recently converted pagans, they would not have had any exposure to the Greek OT. Consequently, in either case they would not understand Paul's contextual use of the OT.

According to some scholars, such considerations make it unlikely that NT writers would have expected the majority of their readers to understand the OT contextual ideas of the verses that they cite in their writings. Therefore, according to this perspective, the upshot of the preceding considerations makes it unlikely that these writers referred to the OT with its contextual sense in mind.

Were the apostolic writers primarily concerned to use the OT only for its rhetorical force to persuade readers to obey them, so that they were unconcerned about what the OT originally meant? Were the majority of Paul's readers uneducated and unable to read the Greek (much less the Hebrew) OT? Furthermore, since the majority of the readers/hearers in the early churches were recently converted gentiles, does that mean that they would not have been in a position to appreciate the intended meaning of the OT writings cited by NT writers?

22. In this respect, one should decide whether the presuppositions of the NT writers (laid out in chap. 5) are true for today's interpreters or are culturally relative.

23. See, e.g., C. D. Stanley, *Arguing with Scripture: The Rhetoric of Quotations in the Letters of Paul* (New York: T&T Clark, 2004).

In response to these questions, one should remember that, for the most part, apostolic writings were first read by someone like a lector, and the rest of the church heard what was read (cf. Acts 13:15; Col. 4:16; Rev. 1:3). One does not need education in Greek and Hebrew to *hear* what was read, whether that be letters from Paul or readings from the OT Scriptures, which was the Bible of the first-century churches (cf. Rom. 15:4; 1 Cor. 10:11; 2 Tim. 3:14–17; 2 Pet. 1:20–21). On the one hand, it is true that the majority of the first hearers of apostolic missives in the churches would have been recently converted gentiles, which means that they would not have much understanding of the meaning of the OT references that they heard as the apostles' writings were read aloud. On the other hand, as is acknowledged by most, there were at least three levels of hearers in the earliest churches: (1) A small group of Jewish Christians understood and appreciated the context of the OT references to which appeal was made. (2) A group of gentiles (perhaps God-fearers) had continued contact with the Jewish synagogue and growing acquaintance with the Jewish Scriptures. They had some appreciation of the OT references, though not as much as the Jewish hearers. (3) The third group, the majority, were recently converted gentiles and did not understand much about the OT quotations on a first hearing.

Yet from the NT itself, it is apparent that letters were to be read and reread not only in different churches but probably also in the same churches. Furthermore, new believers would have been increasingly exposed to the content of the OT: we know that part of the early church's meetings and instruction included the reading and teaching of the OT Scriptures (e.g., cf. Rom. 15:4; 1 Cor. 10:6, 11; 1 Tim. 4:13–16; 5:17–18; 2 Tim. 2:15; 3:16–17). In addition, we also know that letter carriers likely explained part of the meaning of the letters,[24] which probably would include at least some OT references. These last three considerations point to the plausibility, if not probability, that ultimately most would have sufficiently apprehended the meaning of OT references read from the apostles' works (esp. with the letter carrier's explanations). The new gentile believers would not have gathered as much out of these quotations as the first two groups on a first hearing, but they would have understood better on second, third, and subsequent readings. The richness of the NT writers' theology (e.g., Paul), including their views of eschatology and the power of the gospel, are such that from the beginning they speak truth in depth even to those who understand very imperfectly at first. Authorial communication is not exhausted by the immediate reader/listener uptake.[25] This is the reason,

24. P. M. Head, "Named Letter-Carriers among the Oxyrhynchus Papyri," *JSNT* 31 (2009): 279–99; idem, "Letter Carriers in the Ancient Jewish Epistolary Material," in *Jewish and Christian Scripture as Artifact and Canon*, ed. C. A. Evans and H. D. Zacharias, SSEJC 13, Library of Second Temple Studies 70 (London: T&T Clark / Continuum, 2009), 203–19.

25. I am grateful to a private communication from my colleague Vern Poythress, who has made these points.

together with the fact that these letters became regarded as Scripture, that the letters were to be read again and again.

While many of the ancient common people may not have been educated through their own reading of the textual traditions of the Romans, Greeks, and Hebrews, they were more likely to have been orally and culturally literate. They doubtless heard the reading and telling of some of the great works of the ancient world and committed some passages to memory. Therefore, they were capable of doing the same thing with the OT Bible.

Another point fuels the idea that appeals to the OT carried with them the broader OT context: the rhetorical impact is heightened when the broader contextual meaning is taken into consideration. Naturally, such a conclusion about this heightening is an interpretative decision, which needs substantial analysis on a case-by-case basis and may be more persuasive in some cases than in others. Thus we are not skeptical that NT writers use the OT rhetorically but believe that when this happens, the OT contextual meaning of the passage cited enhances the rhetorical impact.

The Postmodern Debate

A postmodern approach, which is a more recent development in biblical studies, has contributed further to the pessimism that the NT has continuity with the meaning of the OT references cited there. "Hard postmodernists" (or hard reader-response critics) hold that it is impossible for an ancient (or modern!) reader to be able to understand the earlier meaning of a text that is being read. All readers have presuppositions, and it is impossible for readers "objectively" to interpret the writings of others. Rather, their presuppositions distort or change the original authorial meaning so much that the intended meaning is obscured. This is equally true of NT writers themselves in trying to understand the OT. "Soft postmodern" interpreters would acknowledge some significant distortion on the part of readers' presuppositions but allow that some of the intended meaning is apprehended, and they would make the same conclusion about the NT writers' view of the OT.

If it is true that no one interprets without their own presuppositions, does that mean it is impossible for anyone to sufficiently understand the oral and written speech acts of others? Was this the case with NT writers' interpreting the OT, and is it the case with modern readers in their attempt to understand the Bible? Such a major hermeneutical and philosophical problem certainly cannot be adequately addressed in this short section. The conclusions one reaches about this particular issue depend on one's own philosophical and theological assumptions about epistemology. Those who presuppose that there is an inability for humans to know the intentions of other humans, whether in written or spoken communication, will be skeptical that NT writers could sufficiently understand what OT authors intended to communicate.

Alternatively, others presuppose that God has designed human minds and imparted to them an ability to be able to function in such a way as to produce true beliefs.[26] This includes being able to perceive authorial communications sufficiently and reliably but not exhaustively. Such a perspective makes it possible to consider the plausibility of NT authors' being able to perceive what OT authors wanted to convey and to cite them in line with their intentions.[27] Here we cannot elaborate further on this thorny philosophical and theological problem of epistemology. Whole books have been written on this issue and will continue to be written as the debate persists.[28]

Conclusion

The issue of how much continuity there is between the OT and the NT will continue to be debated. My own overall judgment is that NT authors display varying degrees of awareness of literary contexts, as well as perhaps historical contexts, although the former is predominant. Texts with a low degree of correspondence with the OT literary context can be referred to as semicontextual since they seem to fall between the poles of what we ordinarily call contextual and noncontextual usages.[29] Indeed, there are instances where NT writers handle OT texts in a diametrically opposite manner to that in which they appear to function in their original contexts. Upon closer examination, such uses often reveal an ironic or polemical intention.[30] In such examples it would be wrong to conclude that an OT reference has been interpreted noncontextually. Indeed, awareness of context must be presupposed in making such interpretations of OT texts. On the one hand, caution should be exercised in labeling usages of the OT merely either as contextual or noncontextual since

26. On which see, e.g., J. H. Sennett, *The Analytic Theist: An Alvin Plantinga Reader* (Grand Rapids: Eerdmans, 1998), 162–86, though this is an optimistic reading of Plantinga in support of the above point. For a summary and qualifications of Plantinga's epistemology from a Reformed presuppositional perspective, see K. S. Oliphint, "Plantinga on Warrant," *WTJ* 57 (1995): 415–35; idem, "Review Essay: Epistemology and Christian Belief," *WTJ* 63 (2001): 151–82.

27. On which see further G. K. Beale, *The Erosion of Inerrancy in Evangelicalism* (Wheaton: Crossway, 2008), 251–59, amid a discussion of issues concerning whether NT authors could understand the intentions of OT authors living hundreds of years earlier; e.g., "The enduring foundation for 'an absolute transcendent determinant meaning to all texts' is the presupposition of an omniscient, sovereign, and transcendent God, who knows the exhaustive yet determinant and true meaning of all texts because he stands above the world he has constructed and above all the social constructs his creatures have constructed; yet he has created them as his analogue to reflect his attributes, so that they may have some determinant meaning of the communicative acts of others" (257 [though some wording is changed here]).

28. See, e.g., K. Vanhoozer, *Is There a Meaning in This Text?* (Grand Rapids: Zondervan, 2001), and the works cited therein on various perspectives about this issue.

29. Cf. Beale, "Old Testament in Revelation," 318–36, here 322.

30. Cf. ibid., 330–32.

other more precisely descriptive interpretive categories may be better. On the other hand, my position lies on the side of those who affirm that the NT uses the OT in line with its original contextual meaning.[31]

The point of this section is to inform the reader briefly about the debates on this issue and not to make a sustained argument for any viewpoint. Indeed, a substantial book could be written only on this topic. In fact, the 1,200-page *Commentary on the New Testament Use of the Old Testament* has done just this: the vast majority of discussions in it have concluded that, to varying degrees, the context of the OT is important for understanding its use in the NT. The approach of this handbook will continue this perspective and will assume that the NT refers to OT passages, at least to one degree or another, with awareness of the wider literary context. This debate about how much NT references show awareness of OT contexts will surely continue.

The Debate over Typology

The definition and nature of typology has been one of the thorniest issues to face in OT-in-the-NT studies in the twentieth and early twenty-first centuries. Part of this debate concerns the topic of the directly preceding section since some see the NT's typological interpretation of the Old to be close to allegory, an approach that reads foreign NT meanings into OT passages. Accordingly, some see typological interpretation to have no continuity with the original meaning of OT texts and to be reading Christ into OT passages that have nothing to do with the Messiah or the church.

Therefore this issue of the NT's continuity versus noncontinuity with the OT will continue to be addressed in the remainder of this chapter, though the question about typology tackled here is broader and will go beyond this and touch other concerns and issues as well.

The Definition and Nature of Typology

One major question at issue here is whether typology[32] essentially indicates an analogy between the OT and NT[33] or whether it also includes some kind

31. See, e.g., G. K. Beale, ed., *The Right Doctrine from the Wrong Texts? Essays on the Use of the Old Testament in the New Testament* (Grand Rapids: Baker, 1994), esp. its last chapter, which is my early attempt at a programmatic article on this subject.

32. This section has been shaped by class notes from the unpublished lectures of S. Lewis Johnson on typology delivered in a class on "The Use of the Old Testament in the New" at Dallas Theological Seminary in 1974. To a significant degree the notes have been revised in the light of my further studies in this field.

33. So D. L. Baker, "Typology and the Christian Use of the Old Testament," in Beale, *Right Doctrine from the Wrong Texts?*, 313–30.

of forward-looking element or foreshadowing.[34] Even among those who may include the notion of the forward-looking element, most hold that it is so only from the NT writer's viewpoint and *not from the OT vantage point*.[35] Many would qualify this further by saying that, although the OT author did not consciously intend to indicate any foreshadowing sense, the fuller divine intention did include it. Some who also hold to a retrospective prophetic view from the NT writer's viewpoint, however, may not see this as even part of the fuller divine intention in the OT, but a completely new meaning given under inspiration.[36] The last two positions, especially the last, view the NT's typological interpretation not to be in line with the meaning of the OT passage. Some other scholars do not hold to any form of divine inspiration of Scripture and view the NT's typological interpretation of the OT to be a distortion of the OT intention.

A definition of typology that includes both analogy and a prophetic element is the following: *the study of analogical correspondences among revealed truths about persons, events, institutions, and other things within the historical framework of God's special revelation, which, from a retrospective view, are of a prophetic nature and are escalated in their meaning*.[37] According to this definition, the essential characteristics of a type are (1) analogical correspondence, (2) historicity, (3) a pointing-forwardness (i.e., an aspect of foreshadowing or presignification), (4) escalation, and (5) retrospection.

The latter two elements need some explanation. By "escalation" is meant that the antitype (the NT correspondence) is heightened in some way in relation to the OT type.[38] For example, John 19:36 views the requirement of not breaking the bones of the Passover lamb in the OT epoch to point to the greater reality of the bones of Jesus not being broken at his crucifixion (for this prophetic nuance, note the phrase "that the Scripture might be fulfilled" [NRSV]). By "retrospection" is meant the idea that it was after Christ's resurrection and under the direction of the Spirit that the apostolic writers understood certain OT historical narratives about persons, events, or institutions to be indirect prophecies of Christ or the church. A qualification, however, needs to be made about how the retrospective view is understood. Recent ongoing research is

34. See, e.g., L. Goppelt, *Typos: The Typological Interpretation of the Old Testament* (Grand Rapids: Eerdmans, 1982); F. Foulkes, "The Acts of God: A Study of the Basis of Typology in the Old Testament," in Beale, *Right Doctrine from the Wrong Texts?*, 342–71; Davidson, *Typology in Scripture*.

35. France, *Jesus and the Old Testament*, 38–43.

36. See, e.g., this view apparently in R. N. Longenecker, *Biblical Exegesis in the Apostolic Period*, 2nd ed. (Grand Rapids: Eerdmans, 1999), e.g., 124–34.

37. For example, escalation would be the correspondence of God providing literal manna from heaven for physical sustenance and providing the manna of Christ from heaven for spiritual sustenance—though physical resurrection of believers is the final escalation of Christ providing spiritual sustenance (on which see John 6:31–40).

38. From here on it is important to remember that the OT element is called the "type," and the NT correspondence is the "antitype."

finding that in the context of some of these OT passages viewed as types by the NT, there is evidence of the foreshadowing nature of the OT narrative itself, which then is better understood after the coming of Christ.[39]

But even when the immediate context of a passage does not indicate that something is being viewed typologically from the OT author's conscious vantage point, the wider canonical context of the OT usually provides hints or indications that the passage is typological. I will argue later that the portrayal of Eliakim as a ruler in Isaiah 22:22 is viewed typologically in Revelation 3:7: Christ is the one "who has the key of David, who opens and no one will shut, and who shuts and no one opens." I will argue further that the immediate context of Isaiah 22 provides clues that this OT passage was intended originally by Isaiah as a type that points forward (on which see chap. 8). But even if there were no such contextual intimations within the book of Isaiah itself, one can plausibly say that Isaiah had generally understood the prior biblical revelation about Israel's coming eschatological ruler and David's heir, so that even if messianic nuances were not in his mind when he wrote that verse, he would not have disapproved of the use made of his words in Revelation 3:7. Thus, Isaiah supplied a little part of the revelation unfolded in the course of salvation history about kingship, but he himself perceived that part to be a pictorial representation of the essence of Davidic kingship.[40] In this respect D. A. Carson affirms with respect to the NT writers' use of typology,

> The NT writers insist that the OT can be rightly interpreted only if the entire revelation is kept in perspective as it is historically unfolded (e.g., Gal. 3:6–14). Hermeneutically this is not an innovation. OT writers drew lessons out of earlier salvation history, lessons difficult to [completely] perceive while that history was being lived, but lessons that retrospect would clarify (e.g., Asaph in Ps 78; cf. on Matt 13:35). Matthew [for example] does the same in the context of the fulfillment of OT hopes in Jesus Christ. We may therefore legitimately speak of a "fuller meaning" than any one text provides. But the appeal should be made, not to some hidden divine knowledge, but to the pattern of revelation up to that time—a pattern not yet adequately [or fully] discerned. The new revelation may therefore be truly new, yet at the same time capable of being checked against the old [and thus clarifying the older revelation].[41]

Therefore, NT writers may interpret historical portions of the OT to have a forward-looking sense in the light of the whole OT canonical context. For

39. See, e.g., G. K. Beale and S. M. McDonough, "Revelation," in Beale and Carson, *Commentary on the New Testament Use*, 1096–97, on the use of Isa. 22:22 in Rev. 3:7, which is expanded further in chap. 7 below.

40. In these last two sentences, I have adopted the wording applied to another typological passage, the use of Hos. 11:1 in Matt. 2:15, by D. A. Carson, *Matthew*, vol. 1, *Chapters 1 through 12*, EBC (Grand Rapids: Zondervan, 1995), 92.

41. Ibid., 92–93.

example, the portrayal by various eschatological prophecies about a coming king, priest, and prophet throughout OT revelation were so intrinsically similar to the historical descriptions of other kings, priests, and prophets elsewhere in the OT that the latter were seen to contain the same pattern of the former (except for the historical failure) and thus to point forward to the ideal end-time figures, who would perfectly carry out these roles.

There are other kinds of typological anticipation of which OT authors and their readers may have been conscious. A later OT author may style some historical character being narrated about according to the pattern of an earlier OT character in order to indicate that the earlier historical person is a typological pointer to the later person in focus. For example, there is abundant evidence that Noah is patterned after the first Adam and that the intention for this patterning is to indicate that Noah is a typological fulfillment of Adam.[42] Noah, for example, is given the same commission as is the first Adam (cf. Gen. 1:28 with Gen. 9:1–2, 7). It becomes quite apparent, however, that Noah as a second Adam figure does not accomplish the commission given to the first Adam (Gen. 1:26–28; 2:15–17), just as the first Adam failed in the same way. Thus, the completion of fulfilling God's commission to Adam remained unfulfilled even in the semi-typological fulfillment in Noah, so that both the first Adam and Noah, as a secondary Adamic figure, pointed to another Adam to come, who would finally fulfill the commission.

A similar kind of typology involves OT prophets who issued prophecies that were to be fulfilled in the short term, at least at some point within the OT epoch itself. When the prophecy is fulfilled, it is clear that the full contours of the prophecy have not been consummately fulfilled. Then the partial historical fulfillment itself becomes a foreshadowing of or points to a later complete fulfillment in the latter days. Good examples of this are prophecies of the "day of the Lord," which predict judgment on a catastrophic scale. Although these "day of the Lord" prophecies are fulfilled in various events of judgment within the OT period itself (such as parts of the prophecy of Joel, where the phrase occurs five times), all the details of the predicted destruction are not. Consequently, the nature of the fulfillment within the OT itself contains a pattern that points yet forward to the climactic period of such fulfillment when the pattern is fully filled out[43] (the "day of the Lord" *par excellence*).[44]

42. For example, see W. A. Gage, *The Gospel of Genesis: Studies in Protology and Eschatology* (Winona Lake, IN: Carpenter Books, 1984), 3–72.

43. Note that the "day of the Lord" occurs seventeen times in the OT with reference to some historical destruction coming within the OT era and five times in the NT with respect to the final end-time day, two of which specify eschatological destruction.

44. I am following here an example given by D. Bock, "Scripture Citing Scripture," 272. It is possible to categorize some of these kinds of typological uses as examples of a "first fulfillment and second fulfillment" or a "double fulfillment" or a "semi-fulfillment and complete fulfillment" of direct verbal prophecy. For example, the prophecy of a young woman (or virgin) giving birth to a child named "Immanuel" in Isa. 7:13–14 finds its first provisional fulfillment in the birth of

That typology is more than the drawing of a mere analogy is apparent from the numerous examples where a fulfillment formula or the equivalent introduces or is connected to the OT reference, whether that be reference to a historical person, event, or institution. Matthew's famous quotation of Hosea 11:1, "Out of Egypt I called my son," is a classic example. The specific verse in Hosea is clearly an allusion to Israel's exodus from Egypt and not a prophecy. Matthew, however, quotes it and prefixes to it the formula "to fulfill what had been spoken by the Lord through the prophet" (2:15). Jesus's going to Egypt and then later out from Egypt is the fulfillment in some way of the historical portrayal of Hosea 11:1. The same or similar prophetic fulfillment formulas accompany similar kinds of historical descriptions from the OT elsewhere in the Gospels; hence it is hard to deny that the NT writers viewed such historical events as prophetic (e.g., see Matt. 1:22–23; 13:35; 27:9–10; John 13:18; 19:24, 28, 36; Acts 2:16–21).

In this light many scholars conclude that typology is more than mere analogy but includes some kind of prophetic sense, as viewed from the NT perspective. If this is a correct conclusion, then what is the difference between fulfillment of verbal prophecy and typology? Both are prophetic. Verbal prophecy, however, is seen to be directly fulfilled, whereas typological foreshadowings are viewed to be indirectly fulfilled. On the one hand, for example, Matthew 2:4–6 understands the straightforward verbal prophecy in Micah 5:2, that the Messiah would be born in Bethlehem, to be directly fulfilled in Jesus's birth there. On the other hand, as we saw above, John 19:36 views the historical narrative about the requirement of not breaking the Passover lamb's bones in Exodus 12:46 and Numbers 9:12[45] to be fulfilled in the soldiers' not breaking Jesus's bones at the cross. Since these OT references are not prophecies but historical narratives and John sees them as prophecy being fulfilled, it would appear best to say that this is an *indirect fulfillment* of what John considered to be foreshadowed by the historical event involving the Passover lamb. There is another way to describe

---

Isaiah's son (Isa. 8:3–4; cf. 8:8, 10, 18). Yet the greater fulfillment is predicted in Isa. 9:1–7, where the prophesied Davidic king is called "Mighty God, Eternal Father, Prince of Peace," and Matt. 1:22–23 shows this is fulfilled climactically in Jesus. I think this is best explained as fulfillment of prophecy within the OT itself that contains a typological pattern that points yet forward to the climactic period of such fulfillment when the pattern is fully filled out in Jesus. That Isaiah himself was aware that Isaiah's child was a typological pointer to Jesus is evident in his prophecy in 9:1–7. However, it is possible to see this also as an example of "first fulfillment and second fulfillment" or a "semi-fulfillment and complete fulfillment" or a "double fulfillment" of direct verbal prophecy (the latter terminology is preferred in this case by C. Blomberg, "Matthew," in *Commentary on the New Testament Use of the Old Testament*, edited by G. K. Beale and D. A. Carson [Grand Rapids: Baker Academic, 2007], 3–5). Throughout the church's tradition, there have also been those who have seen Isa. 7:13–14 as a direct verbal prophecy of Jesus and fulfilled only in him (which is less likely in light of the above discussion), while many modern commentators see no predictive element at all in Isa. 7:13–14, which denies the authority of the text (for sources of both of these last two views, see Blomberg, "Matthew," 3–5).

45. Cf. also Ps. 34:20, which may also be part of the allusion, though there is not space here to elaborate on its significance. Brief comment will be made on this in chap. 4.

the distinction between the two types of prophecy: one as direct prophecy by word, the other as indirect prophecy by foreshadowing event.

A number of scholars have understandably concluded that such typological fulfillments drawn by the apostolic authors read foreign meanings into the OT passage.[46] It is obvious, for example, that the Exodus 12 description of the Passover lamb and the Hosea 11 reference to Israel's coming out of Egypt are part of a historical narrative and not specific prophecies. What could be more of a misreading of the OT than this? Would not interpreting an OT text to be a prophecy when in reality it is a historical description seem to be the epitome of misinterpretation? Would this not be a supreme example of what many consider to be a violation of a historical-grammatical interpretative approach, which has been the traditionally accepted modern standard of a proper interpretative method?[47]

Others, however, affirm that there are other viable approaches to interpreting the OT than that of the historical-grammatical method. Such other approaches do not have to entail an allegorical or atomistic interpretative approach, which pays no attention to what an OT text originally meant. Some hold that typological interpretation is an example of a viable method and does not need to involve reading into the OT completely new meanings foreign to it.[48] Like any proper interpretative method, however, typological interpretation can be and often has been used to read foreign meanings into the OT, thus twisting and distorting the meaning.

Though my own assessment is that typological interpretation is a viable approach when used cautiously, others obviously disagree. The purpose of this section is not to try to argue for one view over another but to lay out the options and debates concerning typology. Part of this debate also involves one's perspective on the hermeneutical and theological presuppositions underlying Jesus's and the apostles' interpretative approach to the OT. These presuppositions, as we will see, are also debated. One's perspective on the typological debate will depend on what one views these hermeneutical and theological presuppositions to be and whether they are counted as viable presuppositions.[49] These presuppositions are discussed in chapter 5 below.

46. On which, e.g., see Enns, *Inspiration and Incarnation*, 113–66; idem, "Apostolic Hermeneutics," 263–87; and sources cited in these.

47. Now in the wake of postmodernism, some say there is no traditional standard of what can be considered a "correct" interpretative approach, but every interpretative community determines its own approach; each community's approach, no matter how different from others, is to be considered just as legitimate as the others.

48. On which, e.g., see Goppelt, *Typos*; Foulkes, "Acts of God"; France, *Jesus and the Old Testament*, 365–71; G. K. Beale, "Did Jesus and His Followers Preach the Right Doctrine from the Wrong Texts? An Examination of the Presuppositions of Jesus' and the Apostles' Exegetical Method," *Themelios* 14 (1989): 89–96.

49. Some would say that even if modern interpreters judge the first-century Jewish or apostolic presuppositions not to be valid according to today's standards, we should not consider

The Criteria for Determining What Is a "Type"

Scholars propose different criteria for discerning types. Part of the problem in even beginning to formulate criteria is to recall that the basic definition of typology is debated. We saw above that there is debate concerning whether typology is essentially analogical or whether it also includes an implicit prophetic-fulfillment element in the NT use. Our following discussion will assume that types include both analogy and some kind of foreshadowing sense that is seen to be fulfilled in the NT antitype.

Some have been so narrow as to identify types only as being in passages that actually contain the word *type* (Greek, *typos*, e.g., as in Rom. 5:14; 1 Cor. 10:6).[50] Most scholars do not agree with this strict criterion. Others identify types to occur only where the immediate NT context directly connects a textual feature to some kind of a "fulfillment" formula (e.g., "that it might be fulfilled") or indicates fulfillment[51] of the OT reference (of a person, place, event, institution, etc.). Accordingly, commentators may differ over identifying types: when there is no clear fulfillment formula, there may be disagreement over whether the immediate context conveys a sense of fulfillment for the OT reference. When the NT context gives no indication of a sense of fulfillment, then the OT reference should not be considered a "type" but merely an analogy.

Despite varying definitions of types, we have proposed above that for something to be recognized as a type in the NT, it must meet the definition of a type: (1) close analogical correspondence of truths about people, events, or institutions; (2) historicity; (3) a pointing-forwardness; (4) escalation in meaning between correspondences; (5) and retrospection. We have seen that types in the NT are not always easy to identify through interpretative examination, though it is clearest when there are fulfillment formulas and other similar indicators attached to the citations of or allusions to OT persons, events, things, or institutions.

Some other criteria for a prophetic type, though not widely recognized, should be kept in mind. Is there evidence in the immediate context of the focus OT passage itself that the reference was already conceived to be part of a foreshadowing pattern? If so, then there would be some grounds in the OT context itself that would lead a NT writer to understand such a reference to

---

them to be "wrong" but to be "correct" according to the ancient standards of their own day. In my own view, this is a postmodern perspective, to which I do not adhere.

50. This includes forms based on the root *typos* that, e.g., are found in 1 Cor. 10:11 and 1 Pet. 3:21. Such a restrictive view, however, was unusual in the history of the study of typology (on which see the discussion of G. P. Hugenberger, "Introductory Notes on Typology," in Beale, *Right Doctrine from the Wrong Texts?*, 339.

51. Note such formulas mentioned earlier: Matt. 1:22–23; 13:35; 27:9–10; John 13:18; 19:24, 28, 36; Acts 2:16–21. Such fulfillment formulas may vary, as with "therefore it is necessary that" in Acts 1:15–22. Even without formulas, a fulfillment sense may be deducible from other features in the nearby NT context.

be a typological fulfillment, even if there is not a fulfillment formula or some clear indication of fulfillment in the nearby NT context.[52]

There can be various kinds of evidence in OT contexts themselves that a narration about a person, event, or institution was already understood as having a foreshadowing sense.[53] One such indication was formulated by Gerhard von Rad. He observed that in certain sections of the OT are repeated narrations of Yahweh's commissioning people to fill certain offices (like that of the judges, prophets, priests, or kings). In these clusterings of narrations are the repeated descriptions of a commission, the failure of the one commissioned, and judgment—and then the same cycle is repeated.[54] Von Rad proceeds to draw the following typological significance of these narratives:

> [The] range of OT saving utterances is that which tells of the calls of charismatic persons and of people summoned to great offices. . . . In the case of certain descriptions of the call and the failure of charismatic leaders (Gideon, Samson, and Saul), we are dealing with literary compositions which already show a typological trend, in that the narrators are only concerned with the phenomenon of the rise and speeding failure of the man thus called. Here, too, in each case there is a fulfillment, the proof of the charisma and victory. Suddenly, however, these men are removed, Jahweh can no longer consider them, and the story ends with the reader feeling that, since Jahweh has so far been unable to find a really suitable instrument, the commission remains unfulfilled. Can we not say of each of these stories that Jahweh's designs far transcend their historical contexts? What happened to the ascriptions of a universal rule made by Jahweh to the kings of Judah (Pss. II, LXXII, CX)? It is impossible that the post-exilic readers and transmitters of these Messianic texts saw them only as venerable monuments of a glorious but vanished past. . . . These men [the judges, Saul, David, etc.] all passed away; but the tasks, the titles and the divine promises connected with them, were handed on. The Shebna-Eliakim pericope [Isa. 22:15–25] is a fine example of such transmission. . . . The almost Messianic full powers of the unworthy Shebna will fail. Thus, the office of "the key of David" remained unprovided for until finally it could be laid down at the feet of Christ (Rev. III. 7).

52. See also Foulkes, "Acts of God," who likewise says that a NT writer's recognition of a type does not mean "that the [OT] writer was conscious of presenting a type or foreshadowing of the Christ, although we have seen that there was sometimes in the OT the consciousness that the acts of God in the past pointed forward to similar but much more glorious acts in the future" (370). Similarly, Moo, "Problem of *Sensus Plenior*," who says the "'anticipatory' element in these typological experiences may sometimes have been more or less dimly perceived by the participants and human authors," though he says at other times it could be seen only retrospectively after Christ's death, resurrection, and coming of the Spirit (106–7). Cf. also J. E. Alsup, "Typology," in *The Anchor Bible Dictionary*, ed. D. N. Freedman (New York: Doubleday, 1992), 6:684.

53. See chap. 7 with respect to the use of Isa. 22:22 in Rev. 3:7; for discussion of the use of Hosea 11:1 in Matt. 2:15, see G. K. Beale, *A New Testament Biblical Theology: The Unfolding of the Old Testament in the New* (Grand Rapids: Baker Academic, 2011), 406–12.

54. Thus note the book of Judges and Isa. 22:15–25, as well as the rise and fall of the many kings in the northern and southern kingdoms, as narrated in Kings and Chronicles.

> It is in this sense—*i.e.*, in the light of a final fulfillment and of the ceaseless movement towards such a fulfillment—that we can speak of a prophetic power resident in the OT prototypes. . . .
>
> No special hermeneutic method is necessary to see the whole diversified movement of the OT saving events, made up of God's promises and their temporary fulfillments, as pointing to their future fulfillment in Jesus Christ. This can be said quite categorically. The coming of Jesus Christ as a historical reality leaves the exegete no choice at all; he must interpret the OT as pointing to Christ, whom he must understand in this light.[55]

Thus von Rad contends that the literary clustering of repeated commissions and failures is evidence of a type within the OT itself. Furthermore, the forward-looking nature of these cyclic narratives of people and events can be discerned within the OT itself and often within each of the narratives themselves. Accordingly, if von Rad is correct, and I believe he is, this would mean that we can recognize OT types as having a prophetic element even before the fuller revelation of their fulfillment in the NT.

There is another criterion for discerning OT types. If it can be shown in the OT itself that a later person is seen as an antitype of an earlier person, who is clearly viewed as a type of Christ by the NT, then this later OT person is also likely a good candidate to be considered to be a type of Christ. An example would be the case of Joshua in renewing the covenant and leading the people of God into the promised land. "Since the original reader/observer would have been justified in interpreting Joshua as a second Moses figure (cf. Deut. 31, Josh. 1; 3:7), and since Jesus may also be viewed as a second Moses, it is possible to correlate the significance of Joshua's acts of salvation and conquest of the promised land to the work of Christ."[56] Or consider the relation of Adam, Noah, and Christ—an example discussed briefly earlier in this chapter. Significant OT commentators view Adam to be a type of Noah in the Genesis narrative itself. Nowhere in the NT, however, does it say that Noah is a type of Christ.[57] Nevertheless, if Noah is a partial antitype of the first Adam but does not fulfill all to which the typological first Adam points, then Noah also can plausibly be considered a part of the Adamic type[58] of Christ in the OT.

55. G. von Rad, *Old Testament Theology* (New York: Harper & Row, 1965), 2:372–74; see also 384–85.

56. Hugenberger, "Notes on Typology," 341.

57. There are NT passages saying that the climax of the age will resemble the apostate days of Noah (see Matt. 24:37–39), that baptism is an antitype of Noah's flood (1 Pet. 3:20–21), or that the flood is a precursor of the universal destruction of the world by fire (2 Pet. 3:5–7), though none of these passages say that Noah himself is a type of Christ; nevertheless, these passages further point to the above observation being made about Adam and Noah in relation to Christ. Noah is called "a preacher of righteousness" in 2 Pet. 2:5. While it is possible to see Noah as a type here, it is more probable that he is to be viewed only as an analogy for the present time.

58. See E. D. Hirsch, *Validity in Interpretation* (New Haven: Yale University Press, 1967), 44–67, for explanation of a "willed type," which helps to explain the idea that we have in mind

Candidates for types may also be those major redemptive-historical events that in some fashion are repeated throughout the OT and share such unique characteristics that they are clearly to be identified with one another long before the era of the NT. For example, OT commentators have noticed the following: (1) The emergence of the earth out of the water of Noah's flood has a number of affinities with the emergence of the first earth from the chaos waters described in Genesis 1. (2) In several ways the redemption of Israel from Egypt is patterned after the creation in Genesis 1. (3) Israel's return from Babylonian exile is pictured as a new creation, modeled on the first creation. Likewise, it is commonly recognized that second-generation Israel's crossing of the Jordan is depicted like the first generation's crossing through the Red Sea, as likewise is Israel's restoration from Babylonian exile portrayed as another exodus like the first out of Egypt. Israel's tabernacle, the Solomonic temple, and Israel's second temple are all uniquely patterned in many ways after essential features in the garden of Eden. In each of the three above examples of creation, exodus, and temple repetitions, the earlier events may not only correspond uniquely to the later events but within the OT itself may also be designed to point forward to these later events. Accordingly, these earlier OT references that are linked together also typologically point to these same escalated realities in the NT's reference to Christ and the church as the beginning of the new creation, the end-time exodus, and the latter-day temple. But even when key redemptive-historical events are not repeated, a candidate for a type can still be discerned. It should, however, not be found among the minute details of a passage but in the central theological message of the literary unit, and it should concern God's acts to redeem a people[59] or in his acts to judge those who are faithless and disobedient.

There are other interpretative ways to discern OT types from the OT itself, but these must suffice for the purposes of the present discussion.[60]

Debate on Recognizing Types in the Old Testament

The question here is this: Should modern interpreters follow the typological approach of the apostles as a model for interpreting other parts of the OT not addressed as types by the NT? As we have already seen, some commentators do not see typology as a legitimate approach to be used by contemporary Christians in understanding OT passages typologically, which NT writers have

here between Adam, Noah, and Christ, yet it also goes beyond the concept of typology discussed so far in this chapter.

59. Sidney Greidanus, *Preaching Christ from the Old Testament* (Grand Rapids: Eerdmans, 1999), 257.

60. For a good selective bibliography on typology, see esp. Davidson, *Typology in Scripture*, 426–96; and D. L. Baker, *Two Testaments, One Bible: A Study of Some Modern Solutions to the Theological Problem of the Relationship between the Old and New Testaments* (Downers Grove, IL: InterVarsity, 1976), 239–70; cf. also Alsup, "Typology," 682–85.

not addressed. Others affirm that while typological interpretation is a viable interpretative approach, it was proper only for the apostles, who did so under divine inspiration. Others trying to use the approach would too often go astray since they do not operate under divine influence, which would restrain their eisegetical tendencies. Such caution is borne out by the checkered history of the church's misuse of typology, which sometimes was outright allegory. Another perspective views the apostolic typological method as prescriptive for Christian interpreters today. For the most part the reasons supporting such an approach have been given in the preceding section, especially with respect to how one may discern types in OT texts not mentioned by Jesus and the NT writers.[61] Here we especially have in mind the criteria of (1) discerning an OT type as exegetically discerned from the OT writer's authorial perspective, (2) the clustered narratival principle cited by von Rad, (3) discerning OT people modeled on other earlier well known and established OT types,[62] (4) observing major redemptive-historical events that are repeated (e.g., the repeated new creation narratives throughout Scripture), (5) being aware that types may be discernible in the central theological message of the literary unit and not in the minute details of a particular verse, and (6) being aware of OT prophecies that are only partially fulfilled within the OT epoch itself and that contain patterns that still point forward to a complete fulfillment (e.g., the "day of the Lord" prophecies).

Therefore typology by nature does not necessitate a noncontextual approach (although like any method it can be misused in that way), but it is an attempted identification of OT contextual features with similar escalated NT correspondences. Whether an interpreter has made a legitimate typological connection is a matter of interpretive possibility or probability. One may not reply that this is an inappropriate method on the basis that the authorial intention of OT writers, especially of historical narratives, would never have included such forward-looking identifications. Furthermore, one should also take into consideration the divine intention discernible from a retrospective viewpoint (after Christ's death and resurrection and the coming of the Spirit). That is, can a divine meaning, consistent with the OT writer's human intent, be discerned subsequently to grow out of and be fuller than the original human meaning? The larger context of canonical-redemptive history reveals how such narrow human OT intentions are legitimately and consistently developed by other biblical writers (and ultimately the divine author) to include wider meaning, so that the whole canon of Scripture becomes the ultimate context for interpreting any particular passage.[63] Nevertheless, these are only general parameters and will not be infallible

61. See, e.g., Foulkes, "Acts of God," 371.

62. Such as Noah in Genesis being modeled on the well known type of Adam, so that Noah himself can be considered an Adamic type.

63. On this point see the discussion in chap. 6 (below) of the fifth presupposition of early Christian exegesis of the OT, that later parts of biblical history function as the broader context for interpreting earlier parts.

guards against misuse and misinterpretation. We must also remember that the conclusions of all biblical interpretation are a matter of degrees of possibility and probability; the conclusions of typology must be viewed in the same way.

Some dispute that typology should be referred to as an exegetical method since exegesis is concerned with deriving a human author's original intention and meaning from a text.[64] But this question is also bound up with the prior question of whether typology is looking forward from the OT vantage point itself.[65] If typology is classified as partially prophetic even from the OT human author's viewpoint, then it can be viewed as an exegetical method. This is true because such an anticipatory aspect of an OT passage can be discerned by a historical-grammatical approach. There are likely several types in the NT that were not consciously intended by OT authors. In such cases, the NT correspondence would be retrospectively drawing out the fuller prophetic meaning of the OT type that was originally included by the divine author but apparently outside the conscious purview of that human author. We have qualified this earlier in this chapter by saying that such OT authors likely would not have disapproved of the later prophetic use of their historical descriptions made by NT writers. One's presuppositions also can determine how typology is classified. For example, if we concede that God is also the author of OT Scripture, then we are concerned not only with discerning the intention of the human author but also with the ultimate and wider divine intent of what was written in the OT, which could well transcend and organically grow out of the immediate written speech act of the writer but not contradict it.[66] The attempt to draw out the forward-looking typological aspect of the human and/or the divine intention of an OT text is certainly part of the interpretative task. And above all, if we assume the legitimacy of an inspired canon, then we should seek to interpret any part of that canon within its overall canonical context (given that one divine mind stands behind it all and expresses its thoughts in logical fashion). In fact, should not divine authorship of all OT passages in relation to the NT be a part of even "grammatical-historical interpretation"? An affirmative answer should be given to this question, since OT writers were themselves writing with an awareness of divine inspiration and, for interpreters who accept this claim, part of interpreting such OT passages is to obtain both the human and divine authors' intention. But, even if interpreters do

64. See, e.g., France, *Jesus and the Old Testament*, 40–41; and Baker, "Typology," 149.

65. Ibid.

66. On the fallacy of equating meaning exhaustively with authorial intention, see P. B. Payne, "The Fallacy of Equating Meaning with the Human Author's Intention," *JETS* 20 (1977): 243–52, in contrast to the more extreme position of W. Kaiser, "The Eschatological Hermeneutics of 'Epangelicalism': Promise Theology," *JETS* 13 (1970): 94–95; idem, "The Present State of Old Testament Studies," *JETS* 18 (1975): 71–72. Kaiser thinks that discerning only the human author's intention exhausts the *full meaning* of an OT text and that the NT provides no fuller meaning of OT texts that the OT authors would not also have been completely cognizant of; the somewhat unusual interpretations that result from this view can be seen in Kaiser's *Uses of the Old Testament*.

not believe in divine inspiration of OT authors, if they believe that a prophet like Jeremiah thought that he wrote God's Word, that intention has to be projected onto the process of interpreting the texts in Jeremiah in terms of how the prophet would likely have perceived the authorial implications of writing under such inspiration.[67]

In this regard, typology can be called contextual exegesis within the framework of the canon since it primarily involves the interpretation and elucidation of the meaning of earlier parts of Scripture by later parts. If one instead wants to refer to such canonical contextual exegesis as the doing of biblical or systematic theology, or as theological interpretation of Scripture, or even as scriptural application, that would seem to be a purely semantic distinction. Rather than interpreting a text only in the light of its immediate literary context within a book, we are now merely interpreting the passage in view of the wider canonical context. The canonical extension of the context of a passage being interpreted does not by itself transform the interpretative procedure into a noninterpretative one. Put another way, the expansion of the database being interpreted does not mean that we are no longer interpreting but only that we are doing so with a larger block of material. Even those rejecting typology as exegesis employ exegetical language to describe typology.[68]

The suggestion is plausible that typological interpretation is normative and that we may seek for more OT types than the NT actually states for us; in support, we observe that this method is not unique to the NT writers but pervades the OT, some examples of which we have given above.[69] The fact that later OT writers understand earlier OT texts typologically also dilutes the claim that the NT writers' typological method is unique because of their special charismatic stance.[70] It is nevertheless still true that we today cannot reproduce the inspired *certainty* of our typological interpretations as either the OT or NT writers could, but the consistent use of such a method by biblical authors throughout hundreds of years of sacred history suggests strongly that it is a viable method for all saints to employ today.

67. I am grateful to Vern Poythress for communicating these points to me.

68. Thus, e.g., Baker, "Typology," says, "Although it is not a method of exegesis, typology supplements exegesis by throwing further light on the text in question" (155); cf. Goppelt, *Typos*: although referring to typology as not "a systematic exposition of Scripture, but as a spiritual approach," he says it "is the method of interpreting Scripture that is predominant in the New Testament" (152, 198).

69. See further Foulkes, *Acts of God*, passim, also 371, stating that observation of types in the OT is not limited to cases listed in the NT but that typological interpretation is a normative interpretative approach for Christians even today.

70. See Foulkes, *Acts of God*; M. Fishbane, *Biblical Interpretation in Ancient Israel* (Oxford: Clarendon, 1985), 350–79, and sources cited therein for discussion of such typological exegesis within the OT itself; H. G. Reventlow, *Problems of Biblical Theology in the Twentieth Century* (Philadelphia: Fortress, 1986), 28–29; H. D. Hummel, "The OT Basis of Typological Interpretation," *Biblical Research* 9 (1964): 38–50.

Conclusion

The significance of this chapter so far should not be limited to interpretative method; it also has a bearing on theology and a theological approach to Scripture. This is true because the use of the OT in the NT is the key to the theological relation of the Testaments, which many scholars have acknowledged.[71] If we are limited to understanding this relation only by the explicit conclusions concerning particular OT passages given by NT writers, vast portions of the OT are lost to us. We can use the contextual method of interpreting these portions, but we must remember, according to some scholars, that this was not the dominant hermeneutical approach of the NT writers. Therefore a hiatus remains between the way they linked the Testaments both interpretatively *and* theologically and the way we should link them. If the contemporary church cannot interpret and do theology as the apostles did, how can it feel corporately at one with them in the theological enterprise? If a radical hiatus exists between the interpretive method of the NT and our method today, then the study of the relationship of the OT and the NT from the apostolic perspective is something to which the church has little access. Furthermore, if Jesus and the apostles were impoverished in their exegetical and theological method, and if only divine inspiration salvaged their conclusions, then the intellectual and apologetic foundation of our faith is seriously eroded. What kind of intellectual or apologetic foundation for our faith is this? Moisés Silva is likely correct in stating, "If we refuse to pattern our exegesis after that of the apostles, we are in practice denying the authoritative character of their scriptural interpretation—and to do so is to strike at the very heart of the Christian faith."[72] Indeed, the polemical and apologetic atmosphere of early Christian interpretation also points to an intense concern for correctly interpreting the OT (e.g., Acts 17:2; 18:24–28; 1 Tim. 1:6–10; 2 Tim. 2:15).

Thus I believe a positive answer can and must be given to the question "Can we reproduce the exegesis of the NT?" Yes. Yet we must be careful in distinguishing between the normative and descriptive (in this area evangelicals have various disagreements), but in the case of the NT's method of interpreting the OT, the burden of proof rests on those who are trying to deny its normativity.

Does this mean that there is a one-to-one exact correspondence of meaning between an OT passage and the NT use of that passage? Sometimes yes and sometimes no. Much of the time the latter is the case. Accordingly, this

71. See, e.g., G. Hasel, *Current Issues in New Testament Theology: Basic Issues in the Current Debate* (Grand Rapids: Eerdmans, 1978); D. L. Baker, *Two Testaments, One Bible* (3rd rev. ed., 2010); Reventlow, *Problems of Biblical Theology*. So also Longenecker, "New Testament's Use," 1.

72. M. Silva, "The New Testament Use of the Old Testament: Text Form and Authority," in *Scripture and Truth*, ed. D. A. Carson and J. D. Woodbridge (Grand Rapids: Zondervan, 1983), 164, though he does slightly qualify this assertion; so likewise Johnson, *Old Testament in the New*, 67.

means that in the light of progressive revelation, OT passages do not receive brand-new or contradictory meanings but undergo an organic expansion or development of meaning, such as the growth of an "acorn to an oak tree, a bud to a flower, or a seed to an apple."[73] Another way to say this is that OT passages contain thick descriptive meanings that are unraveled layer after layer by subsequent stages of canonical revelation. This means that OT passages can be understood more deeply in the light of the developing revelation of later parts of the OT and especially of the NT. The OT authors had a true understanding of what they wrote but not an exhaustive understanding. This means that a NT text's contextual understanding of an OT text will involve some essential identity of meaning between the two, but often the meaning is expanded and unfolded, growing out of the earlier meaning. Chapter 5, "Hermeneutical and Theological Presuppositions of the New Testament Writers," will elaborate further on this notion of how OT passages are to be understood in the light of the entire canon.

The purpose of this first chapter has been briefly to introduce readers to some of the most significant debates among scholars in the area of how the NT uses the OT. I have laid out my own position on these issues, though readers can consult much literature that elaborates further on both sides of the debate (indeed, the purpose of my *Right Doctrine from the Wrong Texts?* was to lay out for readers both sides of the various debates). No matter on which side of these debates readers find themselves, the methodological approach elaborated in the rest of the book will be of use to all. The reason for this utility is that one must go through the process laid out in the rest of the book to determine whether an OT passage has been used or misused by a NT writer. I have repeatedly found that this methodological approach reveals the depth, beauty, interpretative richness, and unity of Scripture, including wonderful ways in which these uses help modern Christians understand their own relationship to Christ and his church within the context of the unfolding redemptive-historical story line of Scripture.

73. See J. M. Compton, "Shared Intentions? Reflections on Inspiration and Interpretation in Light of Scripture's Dual Authorship," *Themelios* 33 (2008): 23–33, esp. 30–31nn43–47, http://andynaselli.com/themelios-333, and the bibliography throughout the notes. The entire article is a good explanation of the concept entailed in how OT passages can be seen to expand in meaning in the light of the progressive revelation of the whole canon.

2

Seeing the Old Testament in the New

Definitions of Quotations and Allusions and Criteria for Discerning Them

One must start somewhere in studying the use of the OT in the NT. The obvious starting point is first to identify where the NT quotes and alludes to the OT. This is fairly easy in the case of quotations but more difficult with allusions. First we will look at the definition of a quotation and criteria for recognizing one and then address the thorny problem of allusions.

Recognizing Quotations in the New Testament

A quotation is a direct citation of an OT passage that is easily recognizable by its clear and unique verbal parallelism. Many of these quotations are introduced by a formula, such as "that what was spoken by the Lord through the prophet might be fulfilled" (Matt. 2:15 AT), "it is written" (Rom. 3:4), or another similar expression. Other citations without such introductory indicators are so obviously parallel to an OT text that clearly a quotation is being made (e.g., see Gal. 3:6; Eph. 6:3). Most commentators agree on the vast majority of what should be recognized as quotations from the OT.[1]

1. See B. L. Gladd, *Revealing the* Mysterion*: The Use of Mystery in Daniel and Second Temple Judaism with Its Bearing on First Corinthians*, BZNW 160 (New York: de Gruyter, 2009), 2–3; and C. A. Beetham, *Echoes of Scripture in the Letter of Paul to the Colossians*, Biblical Interpretation

Yet there is debate about whether writers like Paul adapt quotations and intersperse their own wording or merely quote various OT texts in unaltered form.[2] It is likely that he does both at various points. It may sometimes be difficult to know when there is a direct unaltered quotation from the Hebrew or Greek OT, since there is room for debate about when a Greek translation is "literal" or not and thus at times virtually identical to the Hebrew. Accordingly, a NT writer may be quoting from the Greek OT when it is virtually the same as the Hebrew. It often is impossible to translate a word or expression in an exactly equivalent way from the source language into the receptor language. When the Greek Septuagint is the source of citations, it is still hard to know how much Paul, for example, may be altering the reference, since he may be citing from different forms, protorevisions, or variant textual traditions of the Septuagint, some of which may no longer be extant. Nevertheless, that he sometimes does alter his quotations is highly probable.

One writer has counted 295 separate quotations of the OT in the NT (including quotations with and without formulas). These make up about 4.5 percent of the entire NT, about 352 verses. Thus 1 out of 22.5 verses in the NT incorporates a quotation.[3] In Paul, for example, there are about 100 quotations, the majority of which, to one degree or another, come from an OT text most resembling the Greek Septuagint.[4]

---

96 (Boston: Brill, 2008), 15–17, for discussion by various scholars on the nature and definition of a quotation. See S. E. Porter, "The Use of the Old Testament in the New Testament: A Brief Comment on Method and Terminology," in *Early Christian Interpretation of the Scriptures of Israel*, ed. C. A. Evans and J. A. Sanders, JSNTSup 148, SSEJC 5 (Sheffield: Sheffield Academic Press, 1997), 79–96, who also reviews the different perspectives on the nature of quotations, allusions, and echoes while offering his own recommendations. Also see S. E. Porter, "Further Comments on the Use of the Old Testament in the New Testament," in *The Intertextuality of the Epistles: Explorations of Theory and Practice*, ed. T. L. Brodie, D. R. MacDonald, and S. E. Porter, NTM 16 (Sheffield: Sheffield Phoenix, 2007), 107–9, who categorizes direct references to the OT as formal quotation (with an introductory formula), informal quotation (which must have a minimum of three words in common with the OT reference), and "paraphrase" (which has enough unique words that a recognizable link with the OT text can be observed). Porter's "paraphrase" is what most in the field would consider to be an "allusion," but he restricts "allusion" to what "may not be consciously intentional"; he is less focused on language and more concerned with making a link to a "person, place, or literary work" and applying it to "the contemporary material" (109). He defines "echo" as "invocation by means of thematically related language of some more general notion or concept" (109).

2. See a summary of the debate in K. D. Litwak, "Echoes of Scripture? A Critical Survey of Recent Works on Paul's Use of the Old Testament," *Currents in Biblical Research* 6 (1998): 280–83.

3. These statistics are from R. Nicole, "The New Testament Use of the Old Testament," in *The Right Doctrine from the Wrong Texts? Essays on the Use of the Old Testament in the New Testament*, ed. G. K. Beale (Grand Rapids: Baker, 1994), 13. For a different count of 401 quotations together with allusions (and a breakdown book by book) on the basis of the United Bible Societies' first (1966) edition of the Greek NT, see K. Snodgrass, "The Use of the Old Testament in the New," in Beale, ed., *Right Doctrine from the Wrong Texts?*, 35.

4. See D. M. Smith, "The Pauline Literature," in *It Is Written: Scripture Citing Scripture; Essays in Honor of Barnabas Lindars*, ed. D. A. Carson and H. G. M. Williamson (Cambridge:

Recognizing Allusions in the New Testament

In contrast to quotations, there is greater debate about the definition of an allusion and the criteria by which one can discern an allusion. Accordingly, commentators differ about how many allusions there are in the entire NT. The count goes anywhere from about 600 allusions to 1,650 and even up to about 4,100.[5] In the book of Revelation, for example, where there are no formal quotations, the tally of allusions goes anywhere from 394 (UBS³) to 635 (NA²⁶) and up to 1,000.[6] The wide disparity in the calculation is due to differences in how scholars define an allusion. To make matters more complicated, most commentators acknowledge that the validity of allusions must be judged along a spectrum of being virtually certain, probable, or possible, the latter being essentially equivalent to "echoes."[7]

Some books on the NT's use of the OT produce elaborate criteria for validating whether something is an allusion; others set out briefer and more basic criteria. This discussion will try to steer a course between these two extremes.

An "allusion" may simply be defined as a brief expression consciously intended by an author to be dependent on an OT passage. In contrast to a quotation of the OT, which is a direct reference, allusions are indirect references (the OT wording is not reproduced directly as in a quotation). Some believe that an allusion must consist of a reproduction from the OT passage of a unique combination of at least three words. Though this may be a good rule of thumb, it remains possible that fewer than three words or even an idea may be an allusion. The telltale key to discerning an allusion is that of recognizing an *incomparable or unique parallel in wording, syntax, concept, or cluster of motifs in the same order or structure*.[8] When both unique wording

Cambridge University Press, 1988), 267–76; and M. Silva, "Old Testament in Paul," in *Dictionary of Paul and His Letters*, ed. G. F. Hawthorne, R. P. Martin, and D. G. Reid (Downers Grove, IL: InterVarsity, 1993), 630–33, who cites a few more than Smith.

5. See Nicole, "New Testament Use," 14, who cites this statistic from counting the allusions found in E. Hühn, *Die alttestamentlichen Citate und Reminiscenzen im Neuen Testament* (Tübingen: Mohr Siebeck, 1900).

6. For the various statistics in Revelation in this respect, see G. K. Beale, "Revelation," in Carson and Williamson, *It Is Written*, 333.

7. The determination of a spectrum of clearer to less clear allusions is made harder to determine at times by the fact that a NT writer may sometimes be alluding to an OT theme found in several OT texts, without being more precise about which single text in the OT is the definitive source for his use. In such cases, one must be content that merely an OT theme found in multiple OT texts is being alluded to.

8. For this latter criterion, see R. Alter, *The Art of Biblical Narrative* (New York: Basic Books, 1981), 47–62, who gives such examples in the OT as repeated betrothal scenes that follow the same basic pattern and allude to prior betrothal scenes, such as Gen. 24; 29; Exod. 2:15b–21; the book of Ruth; see also further G. D. Miller, "Intertextuality in Old Testament Research," *Currents in Biblical Research* 9 (2010): 296–98. This occurs also in the NT, e.g.,

(verbal coherence) and theme are found, the proposed allusion takes on greater probability. Recognizing allusions is like interpretation: there are degrees of probability and possibility in any attempt to identify an allusion.[9]

Some commentators speak of "echoes" in distinction to "allusions." For a number of reasons, this distinction may ultimately not be that helpful. First, some scholars use the two terms almost synonymously.[10] Second, those who clearly make a qualitative distinction between the terms view an echo to contain less volume from the OT or verbal coherence with the OT than an allusion. Thus the echo is merely a subtle reference to the OT that is not as clear a reference as an allusion. Another way to say this is that an echo is an allusion that is possibly dependent on an OT text in distinction to a reference that is clearly or probably dependent. Therefore I will not pose criteria for discerning allusions in distinction to criteria for recognizing echoes.[11] It is fine to propose specific criteria for allusions and echoes; thus readers can know how an interpreter is making judgments. However, the fact that scholars differ over specifically what criteria are best has led me to posit more general and basic criteria for allusions and echoes. At the end of the process, it is difficult to produce hard and fast criteria that can be applicable to every OT-in-the-NT allusion or echo. A case-by-case study must be made.

Probably the most referred-to criteria for validating allusions is that offered by Richard Hays.[12] He discusses several criteria that have an overall cumula-

---

between Luke and Acts (on which see M. Goulder, *Type and History in Acts* [London: SPCK, 1964]), and it can be found elsewhere in the NT (e.g., see G. K. Beale, *The Use of Daniel in Jewish Apocalyptic Literature and in the Revelation of St. John* [Lanham, MD: University Press of America, 1984], 178–228).

9. For discussion of the nature of allusion and perspectives on the subject by various scholars, see Gladd, *Revealing the* Mysterion, 3–4nn5–9; and Beetham, *Echoes of Scripture in Colossians*, 17–20. There is much literature on the literary and philosophical nature of allusion, but the nature of this handbook does not allow in-depth survey and interaction with this material (nevertheless, for a good evaluative overview, see M. Dudreck, "Literary Allusion: A Hermeneutical Problem of Theory and Definition in Biblical Studies," *WTJ* [forthcoming]). Thus, while the present discussion of "allusion" in this chapter could be more nuanced, we shall have to rest content with our more general analysis.

10. See, e.g., R. Hays, *Echoes of Scripture in the Letters of Paul* (New Haven: Yale University Press, 1989), 18–21, 30–31, 119. Yet Hays at other times clearly distinguishes between quotation, allusion, and echo, viewing them to represent OT references on a descending scale, respectively, of certain, probable, and possible (20, 23–24, 29).

11. Echoes may also include an author's unconscious reference to the OT, though such references are more subtle and more difficult to validate. See, e.g., Beale, "Revelation," 319–21; and Beetham, *Echoes of Scripture in Colossians*, 20–24, 34–35; Beale and Beetham discuss the possibility of distinguishing conscious from unconscious allusions and echoes, though Beetham sees a clear distinction between "allusion" and "echo." His argument for such a distinction is the best that I have seen.

12. Hays, *Echoes of Scripture in Paul*, 29–32, on which Hays elaborates further in *The Conversion of the Imagination* (Grand Rapids: Eerdmans, 2005), 34–44; I have added a few of

tive effect in pointing to the presence of an allusion. These criteria may be summarized in the following way:

1. *Availability*. The source text (the Greek or Hebrew OT) must be available to the writer. The writer would have expected his audience on a first or subsequent reading to recognize the intended allusion.
2. *Volume*. There is a significant degree of verbatim repetition of words or syntactical patterns.
3. *Recurrence*. There are references in the immediate context (or elsewhere by the same author) to the same OT context from which the purported allusion derives.
4. *Thematic Coherence*. The alleged OT allusion is suitable and satisfying in that its meaning in the OT not only thematically fits into the NT writer's argument but also illuminates it.
5. *Historical Plausibility*. There is plausibility that the NT writer could have intended such an allusion and that the audience could have understood the NT writer's use of it to varying degrees, especially on subsequent readings of his letters. Nevertheless, it is always possible that readers may not pick up an allusion intended by an author (this part of the criterion appears to have some overlap with the first). Also, if it can be demonstrated that the NT writer's use of the OT has parallels and analogies to other contemporary Jewish uses of the same OT passages, then this may enhance the validity of the allusion.
6. *History of Interpretation*. It is important to survey the history of the interpretation of the NT passage in order to see if others have observed the allusion. Yet this is one of the least reliable criteria in recognizing allusions. Though a study of past interpretation may reveal the possible allusions proposed by others, it can also lead to a narrowing of the possibilities since commentators can tend to follow earlier commentators and since commentary tradition always has the possibility of distorting or misinterpreting and losing the fresh and creative approach of the NT writers' intertextual collocations.
7. *Satisfaction*. With or without confirmation from the preceding six criteria, does the proposed allusion and its interpretative usage make sense in the immediate context? Does it illuminate the surrounding context? Does it enhance the rhetorical punch of the point being made by the NT writer? Does the use of the allusion result in a satisfying account of how the author intended the allusion and how this use of the allusion would have made its effect upon the reader?

---

my own explanatory comments to Hays's criteria, and I have revised some. See also Beetham, *Echoes of Scripture in Colossians*, 28–34, who also follows and expands somewhat on Hays's criteria.

Hays's approach is one of the best ways to discern and discuss the nature and validity of allusions (though he likes the term "echoes"), despite the fact, as we have seen, that some scholars have been critical of his methodology.[13]

Excursus on the Criteria for Validating Allusions and Echoes

For a review of those supporting Hays and those criticizing his view, see Kenneth Litwak, "Echoes of Scripture?" For discussion of the nature of allusions and echoes see Stanley Porter, "Allusions and Echoes."[14] Porter has been one of the foremost critics of Hays's criteria, contending that they are contradictory and some are mutually exclusive of others. It is true that Hays does sometimes appear to contradict himself and leaves himself open to such criticisms. Nevertheless, Porter's criticisms at times reflect a too-narrow understanding of Hays's criteria (including Hays's qualified embracing of a multiple hermeneutical scheme for where meaning is to be located).[15] Porter makes some valid criticisms of Hays's sevenfold criteria for discerning allusions, but again they sometimes go too far. For example, Hays's first criterion ("availability") asks whether the source of the allusion or echo was available to the author and/or the readers. Porter rightly criticizes this and asks, if sources were not available to the audience, does that mean the text is different or just that the audience was different? However, this is still an excellent and basic criterion from the authorial standpoint, so the entire criterion should not be discarded.

Porter also contends that Hays's second criterion of volume is wrongly defined as "explicit repetition," which Porter says is "a separate issue from verbal coherence."[16] Yet this is a pedantic criticism since it is fairly evident that Hays has in mind a criterion of the same unique wording that coheres between the OT and NT texts. In addition, Porter says that the last four criteria are not so much about establishing the validity of OT references as they are for interpreting those references. Porter therefore concludes that only Hays's first three criteria deal with validating the presence of allusions.[17] But why does Porter put the fourth criterion of "thematic coherence" as purely interpretative, since one of the basic criteria for

13. For a sampling of scholars favorable and unfavorable to Hays's approach, see the following excursus and Gladd, *Revealing the* Mysterion, 3n5, 4n9, the latter specifically discussing those who generally follow Hays's above criteria for discerning and interpreting allusions.

14. S. E. Porter, "Allusions and Echoes," in *As It Is Written: Studying Paul's Use of Scripture*, ed. S. E. Porter and C. D. Stanley, SBL Symposium Series 50 (Atlanta: Society of Biblical Literature, 2008), 29–40.

15. Ibid., 36–37. Here Porter responds specifically to the hermeneutical theory of Hays (*Echoes of Scripture*, 26–28).

16. Porter, "Allusions and Echoes," 38.

17. Ibid., 38–39.

judging the validity of an allusion is that of a unique thematic link between an OT text and a NT text? Although this criterion does shade into interpretation, it still has relevance as an important criterion for validating an allusion.

It is true that the last three criteria ("historical plausibility," "history of interpretation," and "satisfaction") are less reliable guides to validating allusions. Indeed, "thematic coherence" and "satisfaction" are so overlapping that they could be combined into one criterion. They both focus on how the theme from the OT context functions in the NT context and how much that OT theme illuminates the NT author's argument in the context. Likewise, the first and fifth criteria have some overlap. Thus one could reduce Hays's seven criteria to five.

Thus I find that Porter makes some valid criticisms of Hays's criteria, but these do not entirely invalidate the various criteria concerned. Hays himself admits that some of the criteria ("history of interpretation" and "satisfaction") are not very strong evaluative standards. This topic of criteria for the validity of allusions deserves further discussion, but further elaboration here is not possible because of space constraints.[18]

Sources for Recognizing Quotations and Allusions in the New Testament

Several published sources indicate where quotations and allusions occur in the NT. The following is a list of the most helpful sources and some annotated comments about them.

The first source to turn to is the twenty-seventh edition of the Nestle-Aland *Novum Testamentum Graece*.[19] The editors have placed in the outer margins of each page an OT reference where they think a quotation or allusion occurs in the corresponding part of the body of this Greek NT text. Quotation references are in italics, and allusions are in regular font. In addition, in an appendix of the NA[27] is a complete listing of all the quotations and allusions in their OT canonical order that are found throughout the margins of this Greek edition. Interpreters must decide whether the references to allusions meet the criteria for being valid. One must also remember that there may well be valid allusions not listed in the margins beside the NT passage in the NA[27]. In other words, the NA[27] does not give an exhaustive listing of allusions. Parallels to other NT texts in the NA[27] are also found in the outer margins.

18. Readers should consult the sources cited and discussed in this excursus in order to fully benefit from it.

19. Edited by B. Aland, K. Aland, J. Karavidopoulos, C. M. Martini, and B. M. Metzger (Stuttgart: Deutsche Bibelgesellschaft, 1993).

The same setup is also found in the fourth edition of the United Bible Societies' *Greek New Testament*,[20] though one will notice that this Greek edition lists far fewer allusions than does the NA[27]. In contrast to the NA[27], this UBS edition also includes an appendix of quotations that occur in the canonical order of the NT. The UBS[4] also lists various kinds of parallels (literary and otherwise) along with allusions.[21] Very helpfully, in contrast to the NA[27], the UBS[4] cites a quotation by giving the first and last principal words of the citation at the bottom of the page. Similarly, at the bottom it also cites the principal words for proposed allusions.

Reference may also be made to the second edition of the *H KAINH ΔIAΘHKH* [*THE NEW TESTAMENT*],[22] where OT references are also found in the outer margins, but there is no distinction among quotations, allusions, and parallels.

Readers should also consult the full (not abbreviated) editions of the various standard English translations of the NT,[23] where also in the margins are references to quotations, allusions, and general parallels. Except for quotations, readers will need to judge for themselves whether such marginal references are valid allusions or are merely general parallels. Such marginal references in the English translations are also a veritable gold mine of possible references to the OT.

A few important caveats must be made about the use of the English translations. First, they will not be as precise as a Greek NT when comparing their wording with the Hebrew or Greek OT. However, it is still a useful exercise to compare the English translation of the Greek NT with the English translation of the Hebrew OT or the English translation of the Greek OT. A second qualification is important in the use of English-only translations. Comparing formally equivalent NT English translations with formally equivalent OT English translations will yield more precise comparisons than in the case of comparing dynamically equivalent translations. And sometimes there will be differences because of a different preference by the various translations in dealing with text-critical problems and because NT writers sometimes produce their own interpretative paraphrases of OT texts.

Other important tools for identifying and/or discussing quotations and allusions are the following:

20. Edited by B. Aland, K. Aland, J. Karavidopoulos, C. M. Martini, and B. M. Metzger (Stuttgart: Deutsche Bibelgesellschaft / United Bible Societies, 1993).

21. At the bottom of each page of Greek text are listed first quotations and then allusions. Parallels to other OT texts, NT texts, and other kinds of texts are found listed under the section headings for the Greek text.

22. *H KAINH ΔIAΘHKH* (London: British and Foreign Bible Society, 1958).

23. Among the less interpretative or formally equivalent translations are the following: New American Standard Bible, English Standard Version, New King James Version, Revised Standard Version, New Revised Standard Version, the Holman Christian Standard Bible, New English Translation Bible, and so forth. Among the more interpretative or dynamic equivalent translations are the following: New International Version, the New Living Translation, the New English Bible, the New Jerusalem Bible, and so forth.

Archer, G., and G. Chinichigno. *Old Testament Quotations in the New Testament: A Complete Survey*. Chicago: Moody, 1983.

Beale, G. K., and D. A. Carson, eds. *Commentary on the New Testament Use of the Old Testament*. Grand Rapids: Baker Academic, 2007.

Bratcher, R. G. *Old Testament Quotations in the New Testament*. London: United Bible Societies, 1984.

Dittmar, W. *Vetus Testamentum in Novo: Die alttestamentlichen Parallelen des Neuen Testament im Wortlaut der Urtexte und der Septuaginta*. 2 vols. Göttingen: Vandenhoeck & Ruprecht, 1899. Vol. 1 on the Gospels through Acts is online at Google Books.

Evans, C. A. *Ancient Texts for New Testament Studies: A Guide to the Background Literature*. Peabody, MA: Hendrickson, 2005. See 342–409.

Fairbairn, P. *Hermeneutical Manual*. Edinburgh: T&T Clark, 1876. See 354–460. Online at Google Books.

Gough, H. *The New Testament Quotations Collated with the Scriptures of the Old Testament*. London: Walton & Maberly, 1855. Online at Google Books.

Hübner, H. *Vetus Testamentum in Novo*. Vol. 1.2, *Johannesvangelium*. Vol. 2, *Corpus Paulinum*. Göttingen: Vandenhoeck & Ruprecht, 1997–. Designed to be a revision of the earlier work of Dittmar (above).

Hühn, E. *Die alttestamentlichen Citate und Reminiscenzen im Neuen Testament*. Tübingen: Mohr Siebeck, 1900.

McLean, B. *Citations and Allusions to Jewish Scripture in Early Christian and Jewish Writings through 180 C.E.* Lewiston, NY: Edwin Mellen, 1992.

Toy, C. H. *Quotations in the New Testament*. New York: Scribner's, 1884. Online at Google Books.

Turpie, D. M. *The Old Testament in the New*. London: Williams & Norgate, 1868.[24] Online at Google Books.

Some of the above sources treat only quotations (Archer/Chinichigno, Bratcher, Toy, and Turpie), while others include allusions and sometimes even parallels (Beale/Carson, Dittmar, Hübner, Hühn, and McLean). Some of these sources not only provide lists of quotations and allusions but also offer significant discussion of them (Beale/Carson, Toy, Turpie, and Fairbairn).[25] Evans's

24. The above work by Hühn is no longer in print and cannot be found online but may be obtained at various online used bookstores and may also be found in a number of university or seminary libraries, as can the works by Gough, Toy, Turpie, and Dittmar.

25. Archer and Chinichigno have brief discussion typically of textual comparisons of the Hebrew, Septuagint, and the NT. Other works like those of Toy and Turpie, though perhaps not quite as helpful, are the following: H. Maclachlan, *Notes on References and Quotations in the New Testament Scriptures from the Old Testament* (Edinburgh: W. Blackwood & Sons, 1872);

work includes quotations, allusions, and parallels not only from the OT but also from the Apocrypha, the Pseudepigrapha, classical and Hellenistic pagan writings, Philo, Josephus, targums, Qumran, rabbinic literature, papyri, and gnostic writings.

Other helpful lists of quotations may be found in various books and articles on the use of the OT in the NT.[26] Those who do not know Greek can still benefit from the above-cited Greek sources to a significant degree. They can refer to their English Bibles for a representation of what the Hebrew text has said and to a Greek-English Septuagint edition for what the Greek OT has said.[27] English readers without knowledge of the biblical languages should remember to make use of the margins of the various standard English translations of the Bible.

Naturally, NT commentaries will propose additional allusions that the above sources may lack, though again, readers will need to judge the validity of such proposals.

In my opinion, the most useful of the above tools are the NA[27], UBS[4], Beale and Carson, and Hübner. The work by Beale and Carson, however, is the only one among these that also gives substantial analysis of the quotations and clear allusions. Though this book does not provide a list of quotations and allusions in summary form, it is a commentary that covers each quotation and many of the allusions that can be found in the canonical order of the entire NT.

Gough's book is particularly helpful since, unlike all the other above sources, he gives the OT quotations and many of the allusions in the NT in the order of the canonical OT. In addition, this is the first work (of which I am aware) that cites subsequent places in the OT where the initial quotation or allusion is referred to. For example, Gough cites Exodus 20:6, "showing mercy unto thousands of them that love me and keep my commandments" (KJV), and then cites subsequent references or close verbal parallels to this passage in Deuteronomy 5:10; 7:9; Nehemiah 1:5; and Daniel 9:4. Next he shows where he believes the NT alludes to this particular Exodus passage (or to the other OT passages that reiterate it): John 14:15, 21; 15:10; 1 John 5:2–3. Gough's work, however, lists only the parallels and does not discuss

---

E. Böhl, *Die alttestamentlichen Citate im Neuen Testament* (Vienna: W. Braumüller, 1878); and F. Robinson, *The Quotations of the New Testament from the Old Considered in the Light of General Literature* (Philadelphia: American Baptist Publication Society, 1896). Böhl's work may also be found online at Google Books.

26. Among such lists, see the useful registers of OT quotations in Paul offered by Smith, "The Pauline Literature," 267–76; Silva, "Old Testament in Paul," 630–33; and S. Moyise, *Paul and Scripture* (Grand Rapids: Baker Academic, 2010), 126–32.

27. There are two standard English translations of the Greek OT: L. C. L. Brenton, *The Septuagint Version of the Old Testament and Apocrypha with an English Translation* (Grand Rapids: Zondervan, 1972), depending on Codex B (Vaticanus), reprinted by arrangement with Samuel Bagster & Sons of London, originally published in 1844; and A. Pietersma and B. G. Wright, eds., *A New English Translation of the Septuagint* (New York: Oxford University Press, 2007).

how these OT passages are related to one another, nor does he discuss the way they are used in the NT.[28]

Finally, in addition to the above works, concordances are very important sources. Here one should search for unique word combinations that perhaps can be found only in one's focus text and one or two other OT texts.[29]

If such unique combinations are found, they are good candidates to consider as either quotations or allusions to the OT text.

Since chapter 1 above has surveyed some of the major debates in the field of the OT in the NT and this chapter has tried to clarify what is meant by "quotation," "allusion," and "echo," it is now time to focus on the heart of this book: after an OT quotation or allusion has been identified, how does one approach a study of the way the NT uses this OT reference? The next chapter will strive to answer this question.

Excursus: Shall We Understand Quotations and Allusions as "Intertextuality"?

One more issue involving quotations and allusions still needs comment. It is not unusual in the field of biblical studies today to hear the word *intertextuality* used to refer to how later parts of Scripture refer to earlier parts. This applies to quotations, allusions, and so-called echoes, though the term is used more often with respect to allusions and echoes. The term "intertextuality," however, is fuzzy. The word's original meaning and its ongoing typical definition is the synchronic study of multiple linkages among texts that are not the result of authorial intent but are considered often only from the readers' viewpoint. Accordingly, intertextuality associates at least two texts (and their contexts), which creates a new context in which to understand a text (often the earlier text); this also means that texts are open to the influence of past texts and to the contexts of present readers.[30] According to many, intertextuality entails that the reader and the reader's new context are what give the most meaning to these linkages.[31] Others see

28. Gough also has concluding sections on quotations and allusions from the Apocrypha and Judaism in the NT.

29. Here electronic concordances have special search functions to determine whether unique combinations of words occur between various OT books (or within such books), such as Accordance for Apple OS X; and Bibleworks, GRAMCORD, or Logos, all for Microsoft Windows. These are usually somewhat sophisticated search operations, so students may want to consult the technicians of the software programs they are using for advice.

30. For this definition, see K. J. Vanhoozer, *Is There a Meaning in This Text?* (Grand Rapids: Zondervan, 1998), 132–33.

31. For a sampling of only a few works on intertextuality, see S. Draisma, ed., *Intertextuality in Biblical Writings: Essays in Honour of Bas van Iersel* (Kampen: J. H. Kok, 1989); M. A. Fishbane, *Biblical Interpretation in Ancient Israel* (Oxford: Clarendon, 1985); D. Boyarin, *Intertextuality and the Reading of Midrash* (Bloomington: Indiana University Press, 1990); R. L. Schultz, *The Search for Quotation*, JSOTSup 180 (Sheffield: Sheffield Academic Press, 1999), with

a fusion of the author's and reader's meanings being combined to produce a new meaning, often a completely new and different meaning.

In biblical studies, as noted above, "intertextuality" is sometimes used merely to refer to the procedure by which a later biblical text refers to an earlier text, how that earlier text enhances the meaning of the later one, and how the later one creatively develops the earlier meaning.[32] In this respect, "intertextuality" may be seen as a procedure of inner-biblical or intrabiblical exegesis, which is crucial to doing biblical theology[33] and for understanding the relation of the OT to the NT.

However, "intertextuality" is used and understood in various ways. The above are the primary uses. Debates in this area often revolve around whether meaning lies with readers of earlier texts, or whether the intention or speech act of an author has the power to inform later readers of that original meaning, and whether such later readers have the ability to perceive that earlier meaning.[34] This debate involves philosophical and epistemological issues, which cannot be taken up further here. Therefore it may be better to use the phrase "inner-biblical exegesis" or "inner-biblical allusion" instead of "intertextuality," since the former two nomenclatures are less likely to be confused with postmodern reader-oriented approaches to interpretation, where the term "intertextuality" had its origin.[35]

---

the accompanying bibliography; idem, "The Ties That Bind: Intertextuality, the Identification of Verbal Parallels and Reading Strategies in the Book of the Twelve," in *Thematic Threads in the Book of the Twelve*, ed. P. L. Redditt and A. Schart, BZAW 325 (Berlin: de Gruyter, 2003), 27–45; Paul E. Koptak, "Intertextuality," in *Dictionary for Theological Interpretation of the Bible*, ed. K. J. Vanhoozer (Grand Rapids: Baker Academic, 2005), 332–34, and the accompanying bibliography.

32. This is how the word is typically used by Hays, *Echoes of Scripture in Paul*, and in his later work *Conversion of the Imagination*. This is also how the term is understood in G. K. Beale and D. A. Carson, eds., *Commentary on the New Testament Use of the Old Testament* (Grand Rapids: Baker Academic, 2007), which provides numerous examples of this kind of phenomenon, as defined above. Likewise, see further Schultz, *Search for Quotation*.

33. Though this inner-biblical exegesis already begins with later OT authors' alluding to and interpreting earlier OT texts (on which, e.g., see Fishbane, *Biblical Interpretation in Ancient Israel*).

34. For the nature of the debate on the OT, see Miller, "Intertextuality in Old Testament Research"; and for the NT, see G. K. Beale, "Questions of Authorial Intent, Epistemology, and Presuppositions and Their Bearing on the Study of the Old Testament in the New: A Rejoinder to Steve Moyise," *Irish Biblical Studies* 21 (1999): 1–26, which builds on Vanhoozer, *Is There a Meaning in This Text?* and on E. D. Hirsch, *Validity in Interpretation* (New Haven: Yale University Press, 1967), in arguing that later readers can understand earlier authors' meaningful speech acts that are written down.

35. Following Miller, "Intertextuality in Old Testament Research," 305. See Porter, "Use of the Old Testament in the New Testament," 84–85, who considers the use of the term "intertextuality" in biblical studies to be a fad and an unnecessary intrusion into the field of biblical studies, since the term is typically used differently than in postmodern literary studies.

3

An Approach to Interpreting the Old Testament in the New

Introduction

This chapter is the core of the book. Once an OT reference has been identified in the NT, one can begin to work on how the NT writer is interpreting the reference. This chapter offers a ninefold approach to understanding the Old in the New.

As mentioned in the introduction to this book, there is no airtight method that can be followed in interpreting the Bible that will guarantee a true or exhaustive meaning. The reasons for this are manifold. First, interpreters are fallible creatures: despite whatever procedure they are following, their fallibility extends to their ability to interpret. Second, the task of interpretation is not merely a science but also a literary art, which defies the following of strict rules. Third, no one person can exhaustively understand what another has said, whether that be understanding what someone has said or written in the modern setting or in the ancient world. An authorial speech act is "thick," and it is impossible for any one interpreter to unravel all the layers of meaning in it.

Nevertheless, this does not mean we can retrieve nothing from what has been said or written. Good interpretations can uncover layers of meaning that result in sufficient understanding of a biblical passage. In this respect, the guidelines offered below are not prescriptions that will ultimately lead to correct interpretations. Rather, the procedures discussed here suggest different angles from which we can look at a passage. When all these approaches are put together, they will provide a cumulatively better understanding of the way the NT interprets the OT. Certainly additional angles of viewing a text can be added to the ones covered here, angles that will result in further understanding. To analyze an OT reference by following the ninefold approach of this chapter will take some work, but I believe it will enable the researcher to better understand the passage at hand.

The aim of this chapter, and indeed of this entire handbook, is to obtain a better understanding of the way the NT is related to the OT at just those points where the New refers to the Old. The ultimate purpose in this exercise is more clearly to hear and apprehend the living word of the living God (cf. Acts 7:38), so that we may encounter God increasingly and know him more deeply, and so think and do those things that honor God.[1]

Overview

Here I elaborate on the following ninefold approach to interpreting the use of the OT in the NT. First, it will be helpful to see an overview of the approach before elaborating on each of the nine steps.[2]

1. Identify the OT reference. Is it a quotation or allusion? If it is an allusion, then there must be validation that it is an allusion, judging by the criteria discussed in the preceding chapter.
2. Analyze the broad NT context where the OT reference occurs.
3. Analyze the OT context both broadly and immediately, especially thoroughly interpreting the paragraph in which the quotation or allusion occurs.
4. Survey the use of the OT text in early and late Judaism that might be of relevance to the NT appropriation of the OT text.
5. Compare the texts (including their textual variants): NT, LXX, MT, and targums, early Jewish citations (DSS, the Pseudepigrapha, Josephus, Philo). Underline or color-code the various differences.
6. Analyze the author's textual use of the OT. (Which text does the author rely on, or is the author making his own rendering, and how does this bear on the interpretation of the OT text?)
7. Analyze the author's interpretative (hermeneutical) use of the OT.

1. As noted earlier, I realize that this purpose is not shared by all in the academic guild.

2. I first encountered the essence of this approach in a class on the OT in the NT taught by S. L. Johnson in the mid-1970s at Dallas Theological Seminary. Johnson later put this approach into print in *The Old Testament in the New* (Grand Rapids: Zondervan, 1980), though the passages that he discussed were different from the earlier class lectures. Likewise, see K. Snodgrass, "The Use of the Old Testament in the New," in *The Right Doctrine from the Wrong Texts?* ed. G. K. Beale (Grand Rapids: Baker, 1994), 48–49, whose approach is very similar to the one independently developed in this chapter, though his is only briefly set forth.

8. Analyze the author's theological use of the OT.
9. Analyze the author's rhetorical use of the OT.

Elaboration

Here each of the nine steps listed above will be elaborated.

Identify the OT reference. Is it a quotation or allusion? If it is an allusion, then there must be validation that it is an allusion, judging by the criteria discussed in the preceding chapter.

Since chapter 2 has addressed this step, I will proceed to the next step.

Analyze the broad NT context where the OT reference occurs.

1. *Overview of the broad NT context.* Try to discover the occasion for the particular NT book in which the OT quotation occurs. Why was it written? To whom? These questions are easier to answer in epistolary literature but harder in the Gospels and Acts. Next, gather an overview of the outline of the entire NT book in which the OT reference occurs. Try as best as possible to discern the way the argument develops logically throughout the book, paying special attention to the main themes of the paragraphs and how they appear to be related. Since this is a massive task in itself, it is advisable that after a reading of the entire biblical book and reflection on how the argument develops, the introductions of two or three substantive commentaries on the biblical book should be consulted. Pay special attention to those introductory sections where these commentaries outline the book (and how they break down the major literary units) and how they trace the progress of thought throughout the book. Combine your own views with what you consider to be the best views of the commentaries and construct a tentative working outline of the book, showing how its argument develops.

2. *Overview of the immediate NT context.* Then pay special attention to how the chapter in which your quotation occurs appears to fit into the overall argument of the biblical book. More specifically, how does the paragraph in which the quotation occurs fit into the argument of the chapter itself? Is it a basis or purpose for what has preceded or for what follows? Is it a detailed explanation or interpretation of what has gone before or perhaps a summary of what is to follow? Is it an inference or result of what has preceded? Is it a response to a preceding narration of an event or conversation between two parties? Does it indicate the means by which something in the surrounding context is accomplished? Is it a contrast or comparison to something in the context? Does the paragraph answer a preceding question? Is it perhaps part of a series of statements in the chapter that have no logical relationship to

one another? At a later point in the procedure, more in-depth interpretation of the paragraph itself will take place.

After doing this study, one is ready to move on to the next step.

Analyze the OT context both broadly and immediately, especially thoroughly interpreting the paragraph in which the quotation or allusion occurs.

This is crucial! It may provide significant insights into the OT citation or allusion that may not have been seen before. One should go into the exegetical depths of the Hebrew text (or English text, if the researcher does not know Hebrew). Here one should interpret the OT on its own grounds and within its own redemptive-historical context, without allowing the NT text to influence the interpretation, since it represents a later stage of redemptive history.

1. *Overview of the broad OT context.* First, analyze the broad OT context from where the NT draws its reference. In this respect, the researcher should go through the same process as discussed in the preceding step concerning the NT context, though now applying this to the broad and immediate OT context from which the NT draws its reference.

2. *Overview of the immediate OT context.* One now focuses on the very OT paragraph from which the NT has taken its reference. Here one tries to employ all the angles of OT exegetical practice when studying the literary unit that contains the OT quotation. Accordingly, the interpreter should be aware of how the focus paragraph logically fits into the flow of thought in the chapter, and the same questions asked just above for the NT context apply here also. Then the flow of thought within the paragraph should be traced, especially to ascertain how the part that is quoted fits into that flow. Here again, the various questions just asked above for the NT should be asked about how each of the verses (or propositions) relate to one another in the paragraph under focus. How does the quotation fit into the logical development of thought in the paragraph?

Other interpretative questions should be asked about the paragraph, especially since they may have potential bearing on the material providing the NT quotation: is there a major textual, grammatical, syntactical, lexical, theological, genre, historical-background (in the ancient Near East), or figure-of-speech problem in the paragraph? In this regard, the student should consult Douglas Stuart's *Old Testament Exegesis*[3] for an elaboration of these interpretative problems and how to go about addressing them.

3. *Relate the OT quotation to what comes earlier and later in the canonical Scripture.* First, how does the historical and redemptive epoch of this OT passage relate to the earlier or later stages of redemptive history within the OT itself?

3. D. K. Stuart, *Old Testament Exegesis: A Primer for Students and Pastors* (Philadelphia: Westminster, 1980).

Second, try to determine if the quotation in its original literary context is itself a quotation of or allusion to an earlier written OT text (or even to an earlier passage in the book in which it occurs). Or is the quotation repeated or alluded to later in the OT (or even by a later passage in the book in which it occurs)? In either case, the interpreter would need to go to the earlier or later text and analyze it in the same way as described above for the focus text in order to try to determine how the focus text is using the earlier text or being used by the later OT text. There are some aids in trying to discover whether the focus quotation is a development of or being developed by another OT passage. First, check the margins of the Hebrew text.[4] Second, check the margins of the English translations (e.g., refer to the translations discussed in chap. 2 above). Finally, use concordances to search for unique word combinations that perhaps can be found only in the focus text and one or two other OT texts.[5]

If such unique word combinations are found elsewhere in the OT, they are good candidates to consider as either allusions to the OT focus text or as being alluded to by the focus passage. If we find that two or three other later OT texts allude to the focus text, for example, then there is the possibility of tracing the interpretative or theological trajectory of its use. This is an important exercise to conduct since there is always the possibility that a NT writer may refer to an earlier OT text but understand it through the interpretative lens of a later OT passage that alludes to the earlier one. Or it is possible that a NT writer could refer to a later OT text but understand it through the interpretative lens of an earlier OT text to which the later text alludes. In such cases, if the interpreter is unaware of such connections, the NT writer's interpretation of the OT quotation or allusion may be hard to understand. In this respect, we are entering into the realm of biblical theology and face some key questions: How are several OT passages literarily and interpretatively linked? How do such linkages relate to the NT author's use of a particular OT passage? It is also possible that a NT writer might be influenced by some OT theme (found

4. Here the researcher needs to check the outer and bottom margins of the *Biblia Hebraica Stuttgartensia*, containing the Masorah Parva and the Masorah Magna (for help and explanation of the marginal references, consult P. H. Kelly, D. S. Mynatt, and T. G. Crawford, *The Masorah of the Biblia Hebraica Stuttgartensia* [Grand Rapids: Eerdmans, 1998]). These marginal notes give the frequency of unique forms of words and phrases occurring elsewhere in the OT so that they function as an abbreviated concordance. These references, esp. when they indicate that a unique word or phrase is used only a few times elsewhere, may help in detecting that a later passage has alluded to or been influenced by an earlier passage. When these marginal notes do not give all the occurrences of a phrase, then one may consult A. Even-Shoshan, ed., *A New Concordance to the Old Testament*, 2nd ed. (Grand Rapids: Baker, 1990), who also gives the occurrences of common expressions in the introduction to each root or word.

5. Here electronic concordances have special search functions to determine whether unique combinations of words occur between various OT books (or within such books). Some available ones are *Accordance Bible Software* (Altamonte Springs, FL: Oaktree Software, 1994–2011) and *Logos Bible Software* (Bellingham, WA: Logos Research Systems, 1992–2011). These can be somewhat sophisticated search operations, so students may want to consult the technicians of the software programs they are using for advice.

in multiple passages) through which he understands the OT text to which he is making reference.

Tentatively apply the findings from this step to the NT quotation: Are there similarities in theme, argument, problems between the OT and NT quotation or allusion, and so on?

Survey the use of the OT text in early and late Judaism that might be of relevance to the NT appropriation of the OT text.

1. *Explain the relevance of Jewish background for the use of the OT in the NT*. One must become acquainted with the various primary sources in early and late Judaism in English translation. An annotated bibliography of the relevant Jewish sources is found in chapter 6. Some of the Hebrew and Greek editions of these sources will be cited for those who know the biblical languages.

The purpose of this section is to discover how Judaism independently understood the very same OT passages that the NT has cited. Therefore one should consult Scripture indexes in these various Jewish works. The indexes will direct the reader to the particular page in the Jewish source where the specific OT passage is discussed. In addition, there are commentaries on historical backgrounds that the researcher may consult to see if a NT passage contains a Jewish or Greco-Roman background. These commentaries will often be helpful in showing where there is an independent Jewish interpretation of the same OT references that appear in the NT. These background commentaries are also in the annotated bibliography in chapter 6.

This is a threefold task. First, the researcher needs to collect all of the citations and discussions in Judaism of the specific OT text under focus. Second, summarize any patterns, trends, or similar uses or similar ideas observable in these Jewish uses of the OT text. Third, compare these Jewish uses in their own Jewish contexts to the way the OT text is used in the NT and its context. Here it is important to evaluate whether the non-Christian Jewish uses are similar to the NT use. If so, does the Jewish use give a better understanding of the NT use? Sometimes looking at a NT employment of the OT through the lens of a non-Christian Jewish use brings new vistas of perspective.

In this respect, one would not necessarily conclude that the NT text is literarily dependent on the earlier or contemporary Jewish use, though this is possible.[6] Both Judaism and the NT could be drawing on a common stock

6. Here I invoke the warning of S. Sandmel, "Parallelomania," *Journal of Biblical Literature* 81 (1962): 1–13, who warns of the temptation too often to see dependence by one writer on an earlier writer. See also T. L. Donaldson, "Parallels: Use, Misuse, and Limitations," *Evangelical Quarterly* 55 (1983): 193–210, who elaborates further on Sandmel's position. See also R. Bauckham, *The Jewish World around the New Testament* (Grand Rapids: Baker Academic, 2010), 207–20, for discussion of the relevance of extracanonical Jewish works to the study of the NT.

of understandings of OT texts that was in general circulation at the time. In such cases, primarily Jewish writings contemporaneous with or earlier than the NT are crucial for consideration, since the perspectives they express would have had opportunity to circulate in first-century Palestinian culture and reflect a common stock of tradition that was potentially available for a NT writer to be aware of. Later Jewish interpretations (sources from the second century and later) may still be relevant to one degree or another, especially when corroborating but not directly dependent on earlier Jewish interpretations, since they may reflect earlier traditions existing at the time of the first century. Nevertheless, when there is only later evidence, it must be treated very cautiously and not viewed as having significant bearing on the way the NT has understood an OT reference.

More typical, in my view, is that both Judaism and the NT writers are going back to some of the same OT texts and interpreting them for their own communities. The different segments of early Judaism (e.g., Qumran, Palestinian Judaism, Alexandrian Judaism, apocalyptic Judaism) did not primarily learn their interpretative approach to the OT from one another, nor was early Christianity primarily dependent on any of these segments of Judaism for their understanding of how to approach the OT.[7] Rather, it is more likely that both the NT writers and early Jewish interpreters patterned their interpretation of the OT after the model of the way later OT writers interpreted earlier OT passages.[8]

Accordingly, it is beneficial to look at Jewish interpretations of the same OT texts as those found cited in the NT in the same way that we look at modern commentaries. There are very good commentaries, some that are so-so, and others that are not very insightful. I am sure that many readers have consulted a commentary on an OT passage and had an "aha" moment. The commentary discussion provided an interpretation that we had never thought of before, and the new perspective caused us to look at the biblical passage in a new way and to see what was really there in the first place. Obviously it is absurd to think that the OT passage is dependent on a contemporary commentary. Nevertheless, the commentary provides insight into the original meaning of the passage. Once given the new perspective, the interpretation

7. Again, note the warning of Sandmel, "Parallelomania," about the temptation of too quickly or too often seeing dependence between writers on other near-contemporary writers or religious parties.

8. Compare E. E. Ellis, *The Old Testament in Early Christianity* (Grand Rapids: Baker, 1992), 87–91, who mentions Rabbi Hillel's (ca. early first century AD) seven rules of interpretation that were generally practiced in early Judaism and the NT. These rules primarily concern three broad hermeneutical principles: (1) making *inferences* from or (2) *analogies* between OT passages, and (3) interpreting an OT passage in the light of its *context*. These hermeneutical approaches likely were modeled on the use of the OT by later OT writers. The next chapter will elaborate on specific interpretative uses of the OT in the NT, which in various ways reflect the above three general hermeneutical principles.

may be demonstrated really to lie in the ancient biblical text. The same is true with Jewish interpretations of OT texts, whether they come from early or late Judaism. They can serve as very helpful commentaries in fostering a better understanding of the way Christian writers interpreted the same OT passages. Indeed, if we find value in consulting modern commentaries, why would we not avail ourselves of ancient commentaries, which are closer to the time when the NT writings were composed and may have been privy to patterns of thinking in common with the NT writers themselves. References in early Judaism (second century BC–second century AD) are more relevant than those in later Judaism (third century AD–sixth century AD and onward). The obvious reason for this is that a first-century NT writer could have been familiar with or influenced by ideas from early Jewish references and not those that were created after the first century AD. Nevertheless, it is possible that notions found in post–first century Jewish references existed in earlier oral sources or traditions with which a NT author could have been familiar.

There surely will be Jewish interpretations of the OT that are the opposite of the NT's use of the same passage. In such cases the Jewish use shows how unique the early NT writers and Judaism itself were, especially where several early Jewish sources have interpretations antithetical to those of the NT. In such cases we can grow to appreciate the uniqueness of the NT witness in the context of its Jewish environment. Yet it is always possible that the Jewish parallels may be unclear in how they relate to the NT use. There may be cases where Jewish interpretations offer neither positive nor contrasting interpretations that contribute to any useful understanding of the NT reference.

Therefore, at the conclusion of this analysis, there should be a *tentative* comparison of the way the OT text is used by Jewish writers with the way it is used in the NT text.

2. *Illustration of the relevance of Jewish background for the use of the OT in the NT*. Here we could adduce many examples of how Jewish interpretations of OT texts have shed interesting light on the same texts cited in the NT. A number of examples may be found in *Commentary on the New Testament's Use of the Old Testament* (ed. Beale and Carson); in treating OT quotations, there is often a section dealing with how Judaism understood the quotation and what bearing this may or may not have on the NT use.[9] However, we shall wait until chapter 6 to elaborate in some detail on an illustration of such usage. Chapter 6 will also offer a partially annotated bibliography designed to help the researcher find and survey OT passages in Jewish literature that are also used in the NT.

9. Reference may also be made to other works on the use of the OT in the NT, on which see the representative bibliography at the end of this handbook. Likewise, the more technical commentaries on NT books will sometimes include discussion of relevant Jewish backgrounds to the OT references found in the book. Samples are presented throughout G. K. Beale, *The Book of Revelation*, NIGTC (Grand Rapids: Eerdmans, 1999).

Compare the texts (including their textual variants): NT, LXX, MT, and targums, early Jewish citations (DSS, the Pseudepigrapha, Josephus, Philo). Underline or color-code the various differences.

For example,[10] note the following textual comparisons of Isaiah 6:9–10 in John 12:40:[11]

Isaiah 6:9–10 MT	Isaiah 6:9–10 LXX	John 12:40
9 וַיֹּאמֶר לֵךְ וְאָמַרְתָּ לָעָם הַזֶּה שִׁמְעוּ שָׁמוֹעַ וְאַל־תָּבִינוּ וּרְאוּ רָאוֹ וְאַל־תֵּדָעוּ 10 הַשְׁמֵן לֵב־הָעָם הַזֶּה וְאָזְנָיו הַכְבֵּד וְעֵינָיו הָשַׁע פֶּן־יִרְאֶה בְעֵינָיו וּבְאָזְנָיו יִשְׁמָע וּלְבָבוֹ יָבִין וָשָׁב וְרָפָא לוֹ	9 *καὶ εἶπεν Πορεύθητι καὶ εἰπὸν τῷ λαῷ τούτῳ* Ἀκοῇ ἀκούσετε *καὶ* οὐ μὴ συνῆτε *καὶ* βλέποντες βλέψετε *καὶ* οὐ μὴ ἴδητε. 10 ἐπαχύνθη γὰρ ἡ καρδία *τοῦ λαοῦ τούτου, καὶ τοῖς ὠσὶν αὐτῶν* βαρέως ἤκουσαν καὶ τοὺς ὀφθαλμοὺς αὐτῶν ἐκάμμυσαν, μήποτε ἴδωσιν τοῖς ὀφθαλμοῖς *καὶ τοῖς ὠσὶν ἀκούσωσιν* καὶ τῇ καρδίᾳ συνῶσιν καὶ ἐπιστρέψωσιν καὶ *ἰάσομαι αὐτούς*.	Τετύφλωκεν αὐτῶν τοὺς ὀφθαλμοὺς καὶ ἐπώρωσεν αὐτῶν τὴν καρδίαν, ἵνα μὴ ἴδωσιν τοῖς ὀφθαλμοῖς καὶ νοήσωσιν τῇ καρδίᾳ καὶ στραφῶσιν, καὶ *ἰάσομαι αὐτούς*.

Note: Triple agreement is portrayed as regular text. Double agreement is portrayed in italics. Unique elements (grammar, terminology) are underlined. Change in word order is portrayed with double underlining.

Isaiah 6:9–10 MT	Isaiah 6:9–10 LXX	John 12:40
9 *And he said, "Go, and say to this people:* 'Hear continually, *but* do not understand; *and* see continually, *but* do not perceive.'	9 *And he said, "Go, and say to this people:* 'With hearing you shall hear *but* shall by no means understand; *and* seeing you shall see *but* shall by no means perceive.'	

10. It would be helpful if researchers were familiar with using the textual apparatus of the *Biblia Hebraica Stuttgartensia*, the NA[27], and for the Septuagint, *The Old Testament in Greek according to the Text of Codex Vaticanus, Supplemented from Other Uncial Manuscripts, with a Critical Apparatus Containing the Variants of the Chief Ancient Authorities for the Text of the Septuagint*, ed. A. E. Brooke, N. McLean, and H. Thackeray, 3 vols. in 9 (Cambridge: Cambridge University Press, 1940); and *Septuaginta: Vetus Testamentum Graecum*, Auctoritate Academiae Scientiarum Göttingensis editum, 16 vols. (Göttingen: Vandenhoeck & Ruprecht, 1931–). See chap. 6 for sources to find Greek and Hebrew texts from Qumran, in the Pseudepigrapha, Philo, and Josephus, as well as other Jewish sources.

11. Hebrew and Greek fonts are used here instead of English transliteration in order to make clear the differences in the textual comparisons. This illustration, including the English version of the chart below, is taken from the forthcoming dissertation of Dan Brendsel at Wheaton College Graduate School, "'Isaiah Saw His Glory': The Use of Isaiah 52–53 and Isaiah 6 in John 12."

Isaiah 6:9–10 MT	Isaiah 6:9–10 LXX	John 12:40
[10] Make the heart *of this people* fat, *and* make *their ears* unresponsive, and stick their eyes shut, lest they see with their eyes, *and with their ears hear*, and with their heart understand, and turn and be healed." [AT]	[10] For the heart *of this people* has become fat, *and with their ears* they hear with difficulty, and they have closed their eyes, lest they should see with the eyes, *and with the ears hear*, and with the heart understand, and turn and *I heal them*." [AT]	He has blinded their eyes and hardened their heart, in order that they might not see with the eyes and understand with the heart, and turn and *I heal them*. [AT]

Note: Triple agreement is portrayed as regular text. Double agreement is portrayed in italics. Unique elements (grammar, terminology) are underlined. Change in word order is portrayed with double underlining. Not every minute change can be shown according to this fourfold scheme in the above Greek, Hebrew, or English comparisons, but the significant ones are exhibited.

Analyze the author's textual use of the OT. (Which text does the author rely on, or is the author making his own rendering and how does this bear on the interpretation of the OT text?)

In this section major changes among the Hebrew, LXX, and NT text should be noted. In light of those changes, one should try to ascertain on what OT text the author is dependent or if the author is making his own interpretative paraphrase. How this bears on the interpretation of the OT text will be discussed in the next section.

Analyze the author's interpretative (hermeneutical) use of the OT.

Study the immediate NT context, especially thoroughly interpreting the paragraph in which the quotation or allusion occurs. At the conclusion of this part of the study, it is important to survey the possible categorical uses of the OT in the NT (discussed in the next chapter) to decide which may be in mind.

1. *Overview of the immediate context*. The broad context of the quotation in the NT has already been explored in step 2 above. Now, as in the OT analysis section (step 3 above), one focuses on the very paragraph in which the NT quotation is found. Here one tries to employ all the angles of NT exegetical practice when studying the literary unit that contains the OT quotation. Accordingly, after the interpreter has determined how the focus paragraph logically fits into the flow of thought in the chapter, the flow of thought within the paragraph should be traced, especially with a view to how the quoted part fits into that flow. Here again, the various questions asked in the above section on the NT (see step 2 under the heading "Analyze the broad NT context where the OT reference occurs") should be asked about how each of the verses (or propositions) relates to one another in the paragraph under focus. How does the quotation fit into the development of thought in the paragraph?

Other interpretative questions should be asked about the paragraph, especially since they may have potential bearing on the material providing the

NT quotation: Is there a major problem in the paragraph concerning issues of textual criticism, grammar, syntax, word meanings, theology, genre, historical background (any helpful Jewish interpretation of the OT passage), or figures of speech? In this regard, the student should consult Gordon D. Fee's *New Testament Exegesis*[12] for elaboration of many of these interpretative problems and how to go about addressing them.

2. *Relate the quotation to other quotations from or allusions to the same OT passage elsewhere in the NT*. There are several aids to help one become aware of other NT quotations or allusions to the same OT text outside the passage of focus. These have already been mentioned and discussed in chapter 2. If other parallel uses within the NT are found, the interpreter would need to go to those other texts and analyze them in the same way as described above for the focus text; the goal is to determine how the use in the focus text is to be compared with the other interpretative uses elsewhere in the NT. The time spent in analyzing these other uses will likely be less than the time already spent researching the use of the OT in the focus text, since a number of the steps will have already been accomplished. The practical demands of time (whether of pastoral ministry or the limits of a scholarly project) will impose certain limitations on how much further exploration of these other texts can be done.

If there are differences of interpretation or of interpretative emphasis between the focus text and the other parallel OT uses, then these need to be spelled out clearly. Do the other uses shed any light on the use in the focus text? Do the other NT uses pose difficult questions or pose problems for how the focus text is related to them? In this respect, we are entering into the realm of biblical theology: How are several NT uses of the same OT texts interpretatively and theologically linked? How do such linkages relate to the NT author's use of a particular OT passage?

3. *Relate the quotation to other quotations from or allusions to the same OT passage elsewhere in post–NT literature*, primarily the NT Apocrypha[13] and the church fathers (esp. of the second century AD). There are two main sources for finding where the church fathers quote or allude to the OT. First, the most thorough source is Biblia patristica,[14] which gives both references to the OT and the NT. A second source, though less exhaustive, is the massive set of *The Ante-Nicene Fathers*[15] and *The Nicene and Post-Nicene Fathers*

12. G. D. Fee, *New Testament Exegesis*, 3rd ed. (Philadelphia: Westminster, 2002).

13. See E. Hennecke and W. Schneemelcher, eds., *New Testament Apocrypha*, 2 vols. (Philadelphia: Westminster, 1963–65).

14. J. Allenbach et al., eds. Biblia patristica: Index des citations et allusions bibliques dans la littérature patristique, 7 vols. + supplement, Centre d'analyse et de documentation patristiques (Paris: Centre national de la recherche scientifique, 1975–2000). This source also indexes apocryphal references. For the particular church fathers covered in these volumes, see chap. 6 below. The index is available online at http://www.biblindex.mom.fr/.

15. A. C. Coxe, A. Robertson, and J. Donaldson, eds., *Ante-Nicene Fathers*, 10 vols. repr. (1885–96; repr., Peabody, MA: Hendrickson, 1999); vol. 10 contains a Scripture index; all volumes

(Series 1[16] and Series 2[17]). At the end of each volume is a Scripture index, which allows one easily to find references to the OT in the particular fathers found translated in each volume (though vols. 2 and 14 of *The Nicene and Post-Nicene Fathers* do not contain a Scripture index).[18]

4. At the conclusion of this part of the study, *survey the possible categorical uses of the OT in the NT* (to be discussed in the next chapter) to decide which may be in mind. How do the conclusions reached so far in this part of the study point to or indicate which categorical use is intended? All of the conclusions reached so far in the steps of this chapter (up through the present step) should be brought to bear in attempting to answer this question.

Analyze the author's theological use of the OT.

After determining the interpretative use of the OT passage, a question should be asked: To what part of theology does this use of the OT passage contribute? Here is where the categories of systematic theology, biblical theology, and so-called constructive theology are surveyed in order to reflect on the theological use. One can consult the table of contents of some of the standard systematic theologies to recognize the categories of systematic theology that may be relevant to the passage in question.[19] For example, in almost all systematic theologies are the categories of Christology, ecclesiology, and pneumatology. Some uses of the OT in the NT pertain to each of these particular categories.[20]

One should also be aware of the categories of biblical theology. One source that will make one more aware of the relevant categories of biblical theology

---

online at http://www.ccel.org/fathers.html. A very helpful aid is *The Apostolic Fathers: Greek Texts and English Translations*, ed. and rev. Michael W. Holmes (Grand Rapids: Baker, 1999), with the Greek text on the left and the corresponding English translation on the facing page. Also helpful for studying the meaning of words in the Apostolic Fathers are the following: the lexicon of Henry Kaft, *Clavis Patrum Apostolicorum* (Munich: Kösel, 1963); and Edgar J. Goodspeed, *Index Patristicus* (Naperville, IL: Allenson, 1907).

16. P. Schaff, ed., *The Nicene and Post-Nicene Fathers*, Series 1, 15 vols. (1886–99; repr., Peabody, MA: Hendrickson, 1994). Online at http://www.ccel.org/fathers.html.

17. P. Schaff and H. Wace, eds., *The Nicene and Post-Nicene Fathers*, Series 2, 14 vols. (1890–1900; repr., Peabody, MA: Hendrickson, 1994). Online at http://www.ccel.org/fathers.html.

18. See also W. Jurgens, *The Faith of the Early Fathers*, 3 vols. (Collegeville, MN: Liturgical Press, 1970–79), which has both topical and Scripture indexes.

19. See, e.g., H. Bavinck, *Reformed Dogmatics*, vols. 1–4 (Grand Rapids: Baker Academic, 2003–8); L. Berkhof, *Systematic Theology*, 11th ed. (Grand Rapids: Eerdmans, 1969); C. Hodge, *Systematic Theology*, 3 vols. (1871–73; repr., Grand Rapids: Eerdmans, 1973); F. Turretin, *Institutes of Elenctic Theology*, 3 vols. (Phillipsburg, NJ: P&R, 1992–97); W. Grudem, *Systematic Theology* (Grand Rapids: Zondervan, 1994).

20. Thus with respect to Christology, there are some cases where an OT passage describing God is applied to Christ (e.g., see Matt. 3:3; John 1:23); with regard to ecclesiology, many NT passages take OT prophecies about Israel and apply them to the church (e.g., Rom. 9:26; 10:13); concerning pneumatology, several NT passages cite the OT (e.g., Luke 4:18–19; Acts 2:17–21).

is *The New Dictionary of Biblical Theology*.[21] For example, among important biblical-theological categories to which OT-in-the-NT uses may contribute are the "restoration of Israel," "inaugurated eschatology," "the second exodus," recapitulations of Eden, the temple, the image of God, and so on.

Another important aspect of considering the theological use is to try to discern what theological presuppositions might underlie the interpretative use. Certain uses may appear strange or hard to understand in relation to the original meaning of the OT passage. In some of these cases, a NT writer may be understanding the OT text through the lens of a NT presupposition. In the light of the writers' presuppositions, their use of the OT may become more understandable and explainable. The main presuppositions that are relevant for consideration are the following, though the validity of some of these are debated:

1. Corporate solidarity or representation is assumed.
2. On the basis of point 1 above, Christ is viewed as representing the *true Israel* of the OT *and* the true Israel—the church—in the NT.
3. *History is unified* by a wise and sovereign plan so that the earlier parts are designed to correspond and point to the later parts (cf. Matt. 11:13–14).
4. The age of *eschatological fulfillment* has come but has not been fully consummated in Christ.
5. As a consequence of point 4, it may be deduced that the later parts of biblical history function as the broader context to interpret earlier parts because they all have the same, ultimate divine author, who inspires the various human authors. One deduction from this premise is that Christ and his glory as the end-time center and goal of redemptive history are the *key to interpreting the earlier portions of the OT and its promises*.

These presuppositions need further explanation and substantiation, which we will try to do in chapter 5, where we will also try to show that these presuppositions have their roots in the OT itself. Again, keep in mind that all of the conclusions reached so far in the various steps of this chapter will contribute to a better understanding of the theological use of the OT.

Analyze the author's rhetorical use of the OT.

What was the author's purpose in referring to the OT? What is the final intended force of the statement, especially with respect to its goal to move the readers in a particular direction theologically or ethically? This may be

21. T. D. Alexander and B. S. Rosner, eds., *The New Dictionary of Biblical Theology* (Downers Grove, IL: InterVarsity, 2001). See also W. A. Elwell, ed., *Evangelical Dictionary of Biblical Theology* (Grand Rapids: Baker, 1996); and X. Léon-Dufour, ed., *Dictionary of Biblical Theology* (New York: Desclée, 1967).

harder to discern in the Gospels and Acts but a bit easier in epistolary literature, where the occasion for writing and the problems being addressed by the NT writers are more explicitly stated. As before, remembering that the conclusions reached in all of the various steps of this chapter will help toward a better understanding of the rhetorical use of the OT.

Conclusion

This chapter has laid out the heart of the book. While chapters 1–2 have anticipated some aspects of the approach set forth here (esp. see chap. 2, "Identify the OT Reference," which fleshes out the first step of our approach), the following chapters will give further elaboration of some of the above steps. In particular, chapter 4 will explain the primary possible ways that the NT writers may interpret the OT (see step seven above, "Analyze the author's interpretative [hermeneutical] use of the OT"). These possible categories of interpretation are crucial in making us aware of how a specific OT text is being used in the NT. Chapter 5 will discuss in more detail the possible theological and hermeneutical presuppositions underlying the NT writer's use of the OT (which is essential to step eight above, "Analyze the author's theological use of the OT"). Chapter 6 will address how one goes about surveying the use of the OT text under study in texts of early and late Judaism that might be of relevance to the NT employment of the OT passage (step four above, "Survey the use of the OT text in early and late Judaism that might be of relevance to the NT appropriation of the OT text"). Chapter 7 will then give a case study of a specific quotation of the OT in the NT. This case study will utilize every one of the nine steps set forth in this chapter. The purpose of chapter 7 is to see an example of how the method can be applied in an actual case of a quotation. At the end of chapter 7, I will direct readers to resources they may consult for other case studies that utilize the approach set forth in this handbook. Finally, a select bibliography on the use of the OT in the NT can be found at the end of the book.

4

Primary Ways the New Testament Uses the Old Testament

The preceding chapter gave an overview of a method for studying the OT in the NT. One of the crucial steps in that approach is to analyze the NT writer's interpretative use of the OT (step seven, "Analyze the author's interpretative [hermeneutical] use of the OT"). This chapter elaborates on that particular step. In what variety of ways does the NT use the OT? If students at the outset are generally aware of the various primary ways NT writers interpret the OT, then they are in a better position to narrow down what use may be in mind in a particular passage under study. When one knows the possible options of use, one can try these on for size in a specific case being analyzed. It is mainly consideration of the OT context, reuse within the OT itself, and the NT context that are the main factors in coming to a decision about which use is most probable and fits the best. The categories of uses in this chapter are based on my own past study together with the findings of other scholars who work in this field. Sometimes scholars make many interesting observations about OT passages cited in the NT, but too often they do not comment on how the NT author is actually interpreting the OT text such as answering, Does he indicate fulfillment? Or does he draw an analogy? If so, how? The particular names that I assign to the various uses below are not sacrosanct, and other scholars may refer to the same categories by different nomenclature.[1] The important issue is to understand the concept involved with each use. The categories discussed

1. Thus the various contributors to G. K. Beale and D. A. Carson, eds., *Commentary on the New Testament Use of the Old Testament* (Grand Rapids: Baker Academic, 2007), do not all

will not be an exhaustive list since there is always the possibility of finding new uses. Furthermore, some uses may simply be difficult to categorize for a variety of reasons. We will also find that *sometimes more than one category may be applicable in a use of an OT text in the NT and that some uses may even be subcategories of other uses.* Some uses are also more prevalent than others, which will be pointed out. Finally, only representative examples will be discussed under each category since the purpose here is not to be exhaustive but to focus on the kinds of uses that illustrate the broad range of ways in which the NT interprets the OT.

To Indicate Direct Fulfillment of Old Testament Prophecy

Here a NT author wants to show how something that has happened in Jesus's life or in the lives of his followers (including the church) is a fulfillment of a direct verbal prophecy from an OT passage. Some of these uses may have introductory fulfillment formulas of various types (e.g., "that what was spoken through the prophet might be fulfilled" or "it is written"). Sometimes there is no introductory formula. There are several classic examples of this use. This category of usage is the most straightforward and, usually, the easiest to understand: an OT passage makes a specific prediction, and an event in the NT is seen as the fulfillment of the prediction.[2]

Matthew 2:5–6

When Herod inquired from the priests and scribes where it was prophesied that the Messiah would be born, "they said to him, 'In Bethlehem of Judea; for this is what has been written by the prophet: "And you, Bethlehem, land of Judah, are by no means least among the leaders of Judah; for out of you shall come forth a Ruler who will shepherd My people Israel."'" This is a quotation of Micah 5:2 (with a few changes). In the context of Matthew 2, this quotation functions to indicate the fulfillment of direct prophecy since the following verses show that Jesus indeed was born in Bethlehem.

Matthew 3:3

In introducing John the Baptist as the forerunner of Jesus, Matthew 3:3 says, "For this is the one referred to by Isaiah the prophet when he said, 'the voice of one crying in the wilderness, "make ready the way of the Lord, make His

---

use the same names for the same conceptual uses of the OT by NT writers, and sometimes they do not try to categorize by any name at all but rest content in explaining the use conceptually.

2. The Scripture examples adduced throughout this section and in the remainder of this chapter will be explained only briefly since there is not space for in-depth elaboration. The purpose is only to give basic illustrations of the various uses discussed.

paths straight!"'" Matthew portrays John the Baptist as fulfilling the prophecy in Isaiah 40:3 of the one who would prepare the way for the end-time coming of the Lord to restore his people from exile. This presents a high view of Jesus, since it identifies him with Yahweh in the Isaiah prophecy (cited almost identically in application to John the Baptist also in Mark 1:3; Luke 3:4; John 1:23).

Luke 4:17–21

Jesus goes to Nazareth, attends a synagogue service, and is handed the scroll of Isaiah the prophet. He turns to Isaiah 61:1–2, where it says,

> "The Spirit of the Lord is upon Me, because He anointed Me to preach the gospel to the poor. He has sent Me to proclaim release to the captives, and recovery of sight to the blind, to set free those who are oppressed, to proclaim the favorable year of the Lord." And He closed the book, gave it back to the attendant and sat down; and the eyes of all in the synagogue were fixed on him. And He began to say to them, "Today this Scripture has been fulfilled in your hearing."

Jesus sees himself as beginning to fulfill this explicit verbal prophecy from Isaiah.

The examples of direct fulfillment of OT verbal prophecy discussed here are good examples among others that may be found elsewhere in the NT (e.g., Matt. 4:12–16; 8:16–17; 12:17–21; Acts 1:16–26; 2:15–21; 8:31–35; Rom. 9:24–29).

To Indicate Indirect Fulfillment of Old Testament Typological Prophecy

We directly addressed the issue of typology in chapter 1, so there is no need here to go into detail about the definition, the debate, and the nature of typology, though there will be more elaboration about the theological basis of typology in chapter 5. Earlier we defined typology as the study of analogical correspondences among persons, events, institutions, and other things within the historical framework of God's special revelation that, from a retrospective view, are of a prophetic nature. According to this definition, we saw that the essential characteristics of a type were (1) analogical correspondence, (2) historicity, (3) a pointing-forwardness, (4) escalation, and (5) retrospection.[3]

3. Though in chap. 2 this last element of "retrospection" was qualified by observing how ongoing research is finding that in the context of some of these OT passages viewed as types by the NT, the OT narrative itself yields exegetical evidence of the foreshadowing nature of the passage, which then is better understood after the coming of Christ (on which see the examples of Hosea 11:1 in Matt. 2:15 below in this chapter, and Isa. 22:22 in Rev. 3:7 in chap. 7 below). We also saw that various links and similarities to the wider OT canonical context of an OT passage usually provide indications or hints that the passage has a forward-looking aspect. Nevertheless, from a retrospective viewpoint these OT passages receive clarification about their foreshadowing function.

Distinguishing Direct Fulfillment of Prophecy and Indirect Typological Fulfillment

The main difference between direct fulfillment of prophecy and indirect typological fulfillment is that the direct fulfills what was explicitly predicted by the words of a prophet, while the indirect fulfills what was implicitly foreshadowed by historical events, which have been narrated. Both ultimately prophesy about the future but do so in a different manner: one by words and the other by events. In this sense, one could identify indirect typological prophecy as "event prophecy." The NT sees that OT episodes point forward to events to come in the new covenant era.

The *ultimate* equation of direct verbal prophecy and indirect typological prophecy is illustrated by the observation that introductory fulfillment formulas are attached to both. The following chart makes this clear:

Varied fulfillment formulas with direct prophetic fulfillments	Varied fulfillment formulas with indirect typological fulfillments
E.g., Matt. 8:17 cites Jesus's miracle of healings as a fulfillment of Isa. 53:4: "*This was* to fulfill what was spoken through Isaiah the prophet: 'He Himself took our infirmities and carried away our diseases.'" For further examples, also see Matt. 4:14–16; 12:17–22; 21:2–6; Luke 3:3–6; 4:17–21; John 12:37–38; 19:36a, 37; Acts 2:14–21, 29–36.	E.g., Matt. 2:14–15: Joseph's taking Jesus and his mother into Egypt "was to fulfill what had been spoken by the Lord through the prophet: 'Out of Egypt I called My Son'" (Hosea 11:1). For further examples, also see Matt. 1:22;* 2:17; 13:35; 27:9; John 13:18; 15:25; 17:12; 19:24, 36; Acts 1:16–22.

* Yet, as we have seen in chap. 1, some take this to be a direct verbal prophecy fulfilled in Jesus's birth of a virgin while others view it fulfilled first in the child born to Isaiah (see Isa. 7:13–14 in comparison to 8:3–4, cf. 8:8, 10) and then fulfilled again in Jesus.

Some scholars try to argue that "fulfill" has a different meaning when used of OT direct verbal predictions (in the left column) than when "fulfill" is used of OT persons, events, and institutions (in the right column). But "fulfill" in both sets of uses appears naturally to refer to fulfillment of OT prophecy, whether that is a direct prophecy through a prophet's direct words or an indirect prophecy through a person, event, or institution that points forward to a greater person, event, or institution. The parallel nature of the meaning of "fulfill" is especially seen where the word is found to introduce both a direct prophecy and an event *in the very same passage*:[4]

> But though He had performed so many signs before them, yet they were not believing in Him. This was to fulfill the word of Isaiah the prophet which he spoke: "Lord, who has believed our report? And to whom has the arm of the

4. Some passages with a fulfillment formula appear to be broad or thick descriptions of several OT passages that are both direct verbal prophecies and indirect typological events: e.g., Matt. 2:23; 3:15; 5:17; 26:54–56; Mark 1:15; 14:49; Luke 24:27, 44.

> Lord been revealed?" [Isa. 53:1 is direct prophecy about those testifying to the messianic Servant's ministry.] For this reason they could not believe, for Isaiah said again, "He has blinded their eyes and He hardened their heart, so that they would not see with their eyes and perceive with their heart, and be converted and I heal them." [Isa. 6:10 describes the imminent event of Isaiah's ministry of judgment in Israel's past history.[5]] These things Isaiah said because he saw His glory, and he spoke of Him. (John 12:37–41)

The same phenomenon appears in John 19:36–37, where the piercing of Jesus without breaking his bones is seen to fulfill OT prophecy:

> For these things came to pass to fulfill the Scripture, "Not a bone of Him shall be broken." [Exod. 12:46 and Num. 9:12 give historical description of the Passover lamb.][6] And again another Scripture says, "They shall look on Him whom they pierced." [Zech. 12:10 is direct verbal prophecy about Israel's future response to the Messiah.]

Examples of Typology

Exodus 12:46/Numbers 9:12/Psalm 34:20 (21 MT) in John 19:36

We need to discuss only a few examples to illustrate the typological use of the OT. John 19:36, just noted above, is a good illustration. The historical description of the requirement that the bones of the Passover lamb not be broken points forward to the ultimate Passover lamb, Jesus Christ. The Roman soldiers' decision not to break Jesus's bones, as they did the two criminals flanking him, is viewed as not by chance but a fulfillment of what the Passover lamb's preparation prefigured (in Exodus 12/Numbers 9).

It is also possible that John 19:36 has alluded to Psalm 34:20 (21 MT): "He keeps all his bones; not one of them is broken," which refers to God's deliverance of the righteous from their afflictions (with David as the focus) (v. 19 [20 MT]). LarsOlov Eriksson prefers the likelihood that Psalm 34:20 (21 MT) is in mind in John 19:36, though he allows for the possibility that Exodus 12:46 is linked to Psalm 34:20 (21 MT) and may be secondarily included in John 19:36.[7] It would seem that the Psalm verse makes use of the Exodus/Numbers text and applies it to David as a righteous sufferer and that John 19:36 has all of these texts in mind, the Psalm text being part of the basis for typologically

5. Yet it is also quite possible to understand the use of Isa. 6:10 here to indicate ongoing fulfillment of direct verbal prophecy. For both options of typology and fulfillment of direct verbal prophecy, see G. K. Beale, *We Become What We Worship: A Biblical Theology of Idolatry* (Downers Grove, IL: IVP Academic, 2008), 163–66.

6. See also Ps. 34:20, which is discussed below.

7. L. Eriksson, *"Come, Children, Listen to Me!": Psalm 34 in the Hebrew Bible and in Early Christian Writings*, Coniectanea biblica, OT Series 32 (Stockholm: Almqvist & Wiksell International, 1991), 107, 121–23.

applying the Exodus/Numbers Passover lamb passages to Jesus (and note the repeated reference to the Passover in John [13 times, three of which are in 18:28, 39, and in 19:14]). The Psalm 34 passage about David is also applied typologically to Jesus.[8]

Psalm 41:9 (10 MT) in John 13:18

The use of Psalm 41:9 (10 MT) in John 13:18 is another classic example of typology. With respect to the betrayal of Jesus by Judas, John 13:17–18 reports Jesus as saying, "If you know these things, you are blessed if you do them. I do not speak of all of you. I know the ones I have chosen; but it is that the Scripture may be fulfilled, 'He who eats My bread has lifted up his heel against Me.'" Psalm 41:9 (10 MT) is a historical reflection by David of his trusted counselor Ahithophel's betraying ("lifting up his heel against") David. This is clearly not a direct verbal prophecy of the Messiah. Nevertheless, Jesus sees in the historical relationship of Ahithophel to David a pattern foreshadowing Judas's deceptive relationship to Jesus. Accordingly, Judas's betrayal "fulfills" that to which Psalm 41:9 (10 MT) points forward.

Hosea 11:1 in Matthew 2:15

Finally, Matthew understands that Joseph's taking Jesus into Egypt and back out again is a "fulfillment" of Israel's past journey into Egypt and their exodus back out again, which was narrated by Hosea 11:1 in its context: "So Joseph got up and took the Child and His mother while it was still night, and left for Egypt. He remained there until the death of Herod. This was to fulfill what had been spoken by the Lord through the prophet: 'Out of Egypt I called My Son'" (Matt. 2:14–15). To explain this use of Hosea more thoroughly would take us far beyond the bounds of our task here, but some explanation may prove helpful.[9] There will be more detailed elaboration of this particular example of usage elsewhere in this chapter, since this is such a notoriously thorny passage and because it illustrates well how I attempt to apply many of the principles about typology that have been discussed earlier. Some have thought that Matthew wrongly read Hosea's description of Israel's past exodus as a prophecy. But Matthew's interpretation fits into the same typological pattern as the others above.

The main point or goal of Hosea 11:1–11 itself is the accomplishment of Israel's future restoration from the nations, including "Egypt."[10] The overall meaning of chapter 11 is to indicate that God's deliverance of Israel from Egypt, which led to their ungrateful unbelief, is not the final word about

8. So also see A. J. Köstenberger, "John," in *Commentary on the NT Use of the OT*, 503–4.

9. For an expansion of the following section on Hosea 11:1 in Matt. 2:15, see G. K. Beale, "The Use of Hosea 11:1 in Matthew 2:15: One More Time." *JETS* [forthcoming].

10. Hosea 11:12, concerning Israel's deception and rebellion, is actually the beginning of the next literary segment, which is a negative narrative continuing throughout chap. 12.

God's deliverance of them. Though they will be judged, God will deliver them again, even from "Egypt." The chapter begins with the exodus out of Egypt and ends with another exodus out of Egypt, the former referring to the past event and the latter to a yet-future event. According to Hosea 11, the pattern of the first exodus at the beginning of Israel's history will be repeated again at the end of Israel's history, in the end time. It is unlikely that Hosea saw these two exoduses to be accidental or coincidental or unconnected similar events. Hosea appears to understand that Israel's first exodus (11:1) is to be recapitulated at the time of the nation's latter-day exodus.

This mention of a first exodus from Egypt outside of 11:1 occurs elsewhere in Hosea, and a future return from Egypt appears to be implied by repeated prophecies of Israel's returning to Egypt in the future; 1:10–11 and 11:11 are the only texts in Hosea explicitly affirming a future return from Egypt:

First exodus out of Egypt (Hosea)	**Future return to Egypt, implying a future return from Egypt (Hosea)**
2:15b And she will sing there [in the wilderness and promised land] as in the days of her youth, As in the day when she came up from the land of Egypt [comparing the first exodus with a future exodus].	**7:11** So Ephraim has become like a silly dove, without sense; They call to Egypt, they go to Assyria. **7:16b** Their princes will fall by the sword Because of the insolence of their tongue. This *will be* their derision in the land of Egypt. **8:13b** Now He will remember their iniquity, And punish *them* for their sins; They will return to Egypt.
12:13 But by a prophet the LORD brought Israel from Egypt, And by a prophet he was kept.	**9:3** They will not remain in the LORD's land, But Ephraim will return to Egypt, And in Assyria they will eat unclean *food*. **9:6** For behold, they will go because of destruction; Egypt will gather them up, Memphis will bury them. Weeds will take over their treasures of silver; Thorns *will be* in their tents. **1:11** And they [Israel] will go up from the land [of Egypt].[1] **11:5** He [Israel] assuredly will return to the land of Egypt.[2] [Note the implication of a future exodus from Egypt in 2:15 above.]

[1] On this, see the discussion below.
[2] Several commentaries and English translations render Hosea 11:5 as "He will not return to the land of Egypt." Several other commentaries and English translations, however, have "He will assuredly return to the land of Egypt"; others render v. 5 as a question, "Will he not return to the land of Egypt?" on which see Beale, "Hosea 11:1 in Matthew 2:15," where I argue for a translation with the sense of "He will return to Egypt."

If one would have asked Hosea whether he believed that God was sovereign over history and that God had designed the first exodus from Egypt to be a historical pattern that foreshadowed a second exodus from Egypt, would he not likely have answered yes? This at least appears to be the way Matthew understood Hosea, especially using the language of the first exodus from Hosea 11:1 in the light of the broader and particularly the immediate context, especially of Hosea 11,[11] where a "return to Egypt" is predicted (11:5), and whose main point and goal is the end-time exodus back out from Egypt (11:11). What better language to use for Hosea's prophecy of the second exodus and the beginning of its fulfillment in Jesus than the language already at hand describing the first exodus? This is a short step away from saying that the first exodus was seen by Hosea and, more clearly, by Matthew as a historical pattern pointing to the reoccurrence of the same pattern later in Israel's history. In this respect, Matthew's use of Hosea 11:1 may also be called "typological" in that he understood, in the light of the entire chapter 11 of Hosea, that the first exodus in Hosea 11:1 initiated a historical process of sin and judgment, to be culminated in another final exodus (11:10–11). Duane Garrett has also said in this regard: "We need look no further than Hosea 11 to understand that Hosea, too, believed that God followed patterns in working with his people. Here the slavery in Egypt is the pattern for a second period of enslavement in an alien land (v. 5), and the exodus from Egypt is the type for a new exodus (vv. 10–11). Thus the application of typological principles to Hosea 11:1 [by Matthew] is in keeping with the nature of prophecy itself and with Hosea's own method."[12]

Many commentators have observed that the placement of the quotation of Hosea 11:1 in Matthew 2:15 appears to be out of order since the quotation is appended directly only to the report of Joseph, Mary, and Jesus going *into* Egypt and *not coming out* of Egypt. Rather, they are said to come out of Egypt only later, in 2:21. In this connection, the repeated OT pattern of Israel or Israelites reentering Egypt and then coming back out of Egypt stands in the background of Matthew's reference to Hosea 11:1 and has bearing on the apparent odd placement of the quotation. The reference to Hosea 11:1, we have argued, is to be seen within the repeated references throughout the book to a past exodus *and* Israel's future *reentering and subsequent return out of* Egypt. In particular, this pattern is fully found within Hosea 11 itself: Hosea 11:5, only four verses after Hosea 11:1, says that "he [Israel] indeed will return to the land of Egypt," and this is followed by the main narratival point of the entire chapter that "his sons . . . will come trembling like birds from Egypt" (11:10–11). Thus chapter 11 of Hosea begins with Israel's past exodus from Egypt (11:1), is punctuated in the middle with reference to Israel's reentering Egypt, and concludes with a promise of their future return from Egypt (11:11).

11. And in light of the hopes of the first exodus and implied second exodus elsewhere in the book.

12. D. A. Garrett, *Hosea, Joel*, NAC (Nashville: Broadman & Holman, 1997), 222.

Some have seen it to be problematic that what was spoken of the nation in Hosea 11:1 is applied by Matthew to an individual messianic figure, not to the nation. Accordingly, some reckon that Matthew is distorting the original corporate meaning of Hosea 11:1.

However, the application of what was applied to the nation in 11:1 to the one person, Jesus, also may have been sparked by the prophecy at the end of 1:11: "They will go up from the land" is a reference to going up from the "land" of Egypt,[13] especially since it is an allusion to Exodus 1:10 and Isaiah 11:16.[14] After all, what sense would it make if this refers to the land of Israel since at the end time Israel is to be restored *back to its land*? To describe this as Israel's "*going up from its own land*" would be exceedingly odd. But if this is a reference to Israel's future return from Egypt, it fits admirably with the hope expressed in 11:10–11 (and other such implied references noted above), and it would specifically affirm that such a future exodus would be led by an individual leader: "And they will appoint for themselves one leader [literally, "one head" in Hebrew], and they will go up from the land" (1:11). Such a return led by an individual leader appears to be further described in 3:5 as a latter-day Davidic king: "Afterward the sons of Israel will return and seek the LORD their God and David their king, and they will come trembling to

13. In Hosea the Hebrew word for "land" (*'ereṣ*) refers to Israel (7x), Egypt (5x), earth (2x), Assyria (1x), and the wilderness of Israel's sojourn (1x). However, the idea of "going up from the land" occurs only in 1:11 (2:2 MT) and 2:15 (17 MT): the former text has "They will go up from the land [*wĕʿālû min-hāʾāreṣ*]," and the latter has "She [Israel] went up from the land [*ʿălōtāh mēʾereṣ*] of Egypt," the latter referring to Israel's first exodus. This identifies the two passages, suggesting that 1:11 is a reference to Israel's "going up from the land" of Egypt at the time of the future restoration.

14. What confirms that the expression in Hosea 1:11 refers to "coming up from the land" of Egypt is the observation that it is an allusion to either Exod. 1:10 or Isa. 11:16, which has *ʿālâ* + *min-hāʾāreṣ* in the expression "they [or "he" = Israel] went up from the land [of Egypt]" (though Judg. 11:13 and esp. 19:30 are nearly identical to Isa. 11:16; almost identical to Isa. 11:16 is Zech. 10:10, though it uses the verb "return" followed by "from the land," and both Egypt and Assyria are referred to as in Isa. 11:16). Fifteen other times in the OT the same Hebrew wording is used but refers to God's causing Israel to "go up from the land" of Egypt (Exod. 3:8; 32:4, 8; Lev. 11:45; 1 Kings 12:28; 2 Kings 17:7, 36; Ps. 81:10 [11 MT]; Jer. 2:6; 7:22; Amos 2:10; 3:1; 9:7; Mic. 6:4; cf. Deut. 20:1); five times the expression is used with reference to Moses's doing the same thing (Exod. 32:1, 7, 23; 33:1; Num. 16:13). It is possible that the expression in Hosea 1:11 (2:2 MT) is a collective allusion to all of these references, which would only enforce a reference to "going up from the land" of Egypt in the Hosea passage. See D. D. Bass, "Hosea's Use of Scripture: An Analysis of His Hermeneutics" (PhD diss., Southern Baptist Theological Seminary, 2009), 128–29, who has proposed that Exod. 1:10 is the allusion in Hosea 1:11 (2:2 MT). Uppermost in the prophet's mind may be Isa. 11:16 since it is the only other reference using this wording that refers to Israel's future restoration and uses it in conjunction with restoration from "Assyria," which Hosea 11:11 also does together with restoration from Egypt. (Note the similar combination of Egypt and Assyria in Hosea 7:11; 9:3; 12:1. Isaiah [written between ca. 739–690 BC] could be dependent on Hosea [written between ca. 755–725 BC] since their ministries overlapped by about fifteen years. If so, then a plausible inner-biblical trajectory would be Exod. 1:10 > Hosea 1:11 > Isa. 11:11.)

the Lord . . . in the last days." This image of "trembling" in Hosea 3:5 to describe the manner in which Israel approaches God when they are restored is parallel to the description of the manner of their restoration in 11:10–11, where also "they will come trembling from Egypt" (where the same Hebrew word for "trembling" is repeated twice in 11:10–11). This may point further to Hosea's biblical-theological understanding that when Israel would come out of Egypt in the future (according to 1:11 *and* 11:10–11), they would indeed be led by an individual king, which enhances further why Matthew could take the corporate national language of Hosea 11:1 and apply it to an individual king, Jesus. Could Matthew not have had such a biblical-theological understanding of Hosea?

There is one last rationale for understanding how Matthew can take what applied to the nation in Hosea 11:1 and apply it to the individual Messiah. Duane Garrett has analyzed the use of Genesis in Hosea and has found that repeatedly the prophet alludes to Genesis descriptions of the individual patriarchs and to other significant individuals in Israel's history. Sometimes these are good portrayals and sometimes bad. The prophet Hosea applies these descriptions to the nation of his day. For example, the iniquity of Israel in the present involves its following the same pattern of disobedience as that of Adam (6:7) or Jacob (12:2–5), and the promise made to the individual Jacob to "make your seed as the sand of the sea, which cannot be numbered for multitude" (Gen. 32:12 KJV; cf. also Gen. 15:5 and 22:17 addressed to Abraham) is now reapplied and addressed directly to the nation Israel: "Yet the number of the sons of Israel will be like the sand of the sea, which cannot be measured or numbered" (Hosea 1:10). Similarly, "the valley of Achor," where Achan and his family were taken to be executed for his sin (Josh. 7:24–26), is taken by Hosea and reversed to indicate that God would reverse Israel's judgment of defeat and exile: Israel would not be exterminated for its sin but would have a hope of redemption (Hosea 2:15). Instead of going from the one to the many, Matthew goes from the many (Israel) to the one (Jesus); yet he utilizes the same kind of "one-and-many" corporate hermeneutical approach to interpreting and applying earlier Scripture as did Hosea.[15]

I have elaborated on this typological use of Hosea 11:1 more than the other examples since it is an illustration of a type that is not purely retrospective from the NT vantage point. That is, this was not a perspective understood by Matthew *only after* the events of Jesus's coming. Rather, there are substantial indications *already in Hosea 11 itself and its immediate context* that Israel's past exodus out of Egypt was an event that would be recapitulated typologically in the eschatological future.

15. See D. A. Garrett, "The Ways of God: Reenactment and Reversal in Hosea" (his inaugural lecture as professor of Old Testament at Gordon-Conwell Theological Seminary, South Hamilton, MA, Fall 1998; on VHS cassette at the seminary; to be published). See also Bass, "Hosea's Use of Scripture," written under the supervision of Garrett.

Other Examples of Typology

In the discussion of typology in chapter 1, we looked at segments of the OT where there are repeated narrations of Yahweh's commissioning people to fill certain offices (e.g., judges, prophets, priests, kings, and other leaders), the repeated failure of the one commissioned, followed by judgment, and then the cycle starts again in the following narrative. Readers of these narratives would also have been aware of texts elsewhere in the OT ascribed as messianic, affirming a final universal rule by an ideal individual. We have argued, following Gerhard von Rad, that the repeated lack of fulfillment points to an eschatological figure who would finally fulfill these commissions.

This use of the OT in the NT occurs at various points (e.g., in chap. 1 we discussed the use of Isa. 22:22 in Rev. 3:7 and will expand on this passage in chap. 7). This use may also be termed "fulfillment of intended design." Certain offices have a design that is to be followed in order to successfully carry out the commission of the office. Genesis 1:28 and its use elsewhere in the OT and in the NT is another example of this kind of use:

> God blessed them; and God said to them, "Be fruitful and multiply, and fill the earth, and subdue it; and rule over the fish of the sea and over the birds of the sky and over every living thing that moves on the earth." (Gen. 1:28)

The design of the commission in Genesis 1:28 involves the following elements:

1. God blessed them.
2. Be fruitful and multiply.
3. Fill the earth.
4. Subdue it [the earth].
5. Rule over . . . all the earth. (so Gen. 1:26; reiterated in 1:28)

Adam fails in accomplishing this commission, and the commission is reiterated to Noah (Gen. 9:1, 6–7), Abraham (Gen. 12:2–3; 17:2, 6; 22:17–18), Isaac (26:3–4, 24), and Jacob (28:3–4, 13–14; 35:11–12; 48:3–4).[16] At times the patriarchal seed, Israel, is seen as beginning to fulfill the commission (Gen. 47:27; Exod. 1:7, 12, 20; Num. 23:10–11), but they become sinful and do not fully carry out the commission.

Therefore the promise that the nation would fulfill the commission of Genesis 1:28 at some point in the future is reiterated for the future (Lev. 26:9; Deut. 7:13; 15:4, 6; 28:11–12 LXX; 30:16; 2 Sam. 7:29 LXX). At various points throughout the succeeding history of Israel, the language of the Genesis 1:28 commission is reapplied to individual Israelites or the nation to indicate some

16. Though beginning with Abraham, God's promises to fulfill the commission are mixed with the commission itself.

apparent degree of beginning fulfillment (1 Chron. 4:10; 17:9–11, 27; Pss. 8:5–8 [6–9 MT, LXX]; 107:37–38; Isa. 51:2–3).

However, sinful events make it clear that the king and nation only partly accomplish the commission. These apparent beginning fulfillments fade and do not come to consummate fruition. Ultimately they also fail in trying to do what Adam and their forefathers had failed to do. Therefore, in response, there is reiteration of the promise that eschatological Israel and its end-time king will finally succeed in fully accomplishing the Adamic commission (Pss. 8:5–8 [6–9 MT, LXX]; 72:8, 17, 19; Isa. 51:2–3; 54:1–3; Jer. 3:16, 18; 23:3; Ezek. 36:9–12; Dan. 7:13–14; Hosea 1:10).[17]

The NT then picks up on this promise and sees it beginning fulfillment in Christ (1 Cor. 15:27 and Eph. 1:22, both alluding to Ps. 8:6 [7 MT, LXX])[18] and in those trusting in and being identified with Christ (Acts 6:7; 12:24; 19:20; Col. 1:6, 10).[19] The Messiah and his people finally fulfill the Genesis 1:28 commission, which neither Adam nor his progeny were able to fulfill. The repeated failure and lack in fulfilling the design of the original commission (esp. in light of the associated promises that at some point in the future it would definitely be fulfilled) pointed to the end time, when the latter-day progeny would fulfill it. Thus the above NT references to the commission indicate "fulfillment of intended design," which is an important category of typology.

To Indicate Affirmation That a Not-Yet-Fulfilled Old Testament Prophecy Will Assuredly Be Fulfilled in the Future

This is a third important use of the OT. Sometimes an OT prophecy is appealed to, not to indicate beginning fulfillment, but to affirm that it will assuredly be fulfilled at the very end of the age. Second Peter 3:11–14 is a good example of this kind of usage:

> Since all these things are to be destroyed in this way, what sort of people ought you to be in holy conduct and godliness, looking for and hastening the coming of the day of God, because of which the heavens will be destroyed by burning, and the elements will melt with intense heat! But according to His promise we are looking for new heavens and a new earth, in which righteousness dwells.
>
> Therefore, beloved, since you look for these things, be diligent to be found by Him in peace, spotless and blameless.

17. For further discussion of the above reiterations of Gen. 1:28 in the OT, see G. K. Beale, *A New Testament Biblical Theology: The Unfolding of the Old Testament in the New* (Grand Rapids: Baker Academic, 2011), 46–52.

18. The Ps. 8 verse directly alludes to Gen. 1:26, 28.

19. For discussion of the use of Gen. 1:28 in the Acts and Colossians passages, see G. K. Beale, "Colossians," in Beale and Carson, *Commentary on the New Testament Use*, 842–46.

The phrase "according to His promise we are looking for new heavens and a new earth" (v. 13) refers to the promises in Isaiah 65:17 and 66:22, which are virtually identical: "For behold, I create new heavens and a new earth" (65:17). Though Paul views these new-creation prophecies to have been inaugurated (see 2 Cor. 5:17; Gal. 6:15), Peter is looking to their yet future consummation. He encourages the readers to persevere in godly conduct now by assuring them that a new creation will come in which only those who are prepared now by being righteous will be able to enter.

Interestingly, the same two Isaiah prophecies of a "new heavens and a new earth" are referred to in Revelation 21:1 as being completely fulfilled in the future, in a very similar manner as in 2 Peter 3.

To Indicate an Analogical or Illustrative Use of the Old Testament

Another important use of the OT is the employment of it for analogical purposes. A NT writer will take something from the OT and compare it to something in the new covenant age in order to illustrate or draw an analogy (or perhaps a contrast) between the two. The purpose is to emphasize a gnomic, broad, or universal principle. It is crucial to consider the surrounding immediate OT context from which the analogy is taken in order more fully to understand the analogy in the NT.

Again, only a few examples will suffice to make the point.

Deuteronomy 25:4 in 1 Corinthians 9:9–10

First Corinthians 9:9–10 cites Deuteronomy 25:4 to support Paul's argument that servants of the gospel who "sow spiritual things" among people should benefit materially from those same people: "For it is written in the Law of Moses, 'You shall not muzzle the ox while he is threshing.' God is not concerned about oxen, is He? Or is He speaking altogether for our sake? Yes, for our sake it was written, because the plowman ought to plow in hope, and the thresher *to thresh* in hope of sharing *the crops*." The primary intention in Deuteronomy is care for animals. Paul's point, going from the lesser to the greater and comparing the two, says that if animals are to benefit from their own labor, how much more should humans.

For commentators like Moffatt[20] and Barrett,[21] however, Paul is allegorizing and spiritualizing like Philo, without properly considering the context in Deuteronomy. Verse 9b says, "God is not [*mē*] concerned about oxen, is He?"

20. J. Moffatt, *The First Epistle of Paul to the Corinthians* (London: Hodder & Stoughton, 1938), 117.

21. C. K. Barrett, *A Commentary on the First Epistle to the Corinthians* (New York: Harper & Row, 1968), 205–6.

(expecting a negative answer in Greek and English). Verse 10a then reinforces this statement by asking, "Is He [God] speaking *altogether* [or, '*entirely*'] for our sake?" The expected answer is "yes." According to Moffatt and Barrett, Paul takes this law about oxen in Deuteronomy as written not really for oxen but exclusively for our sake. And that is why they see this use of the OT as allegory. This command from Deuteronomy is not for oxen in Israel's day, but it is for our sake.

Yet while the Greek word *pantōs* can mean "completely" or "altogether," it can also just as easily mean "surely," "above all," or "doubtless," which fits admirably in this context. If such a latter rendering is viable, then Paul is saying that while this text of Deuteronomy has meaning for animals, how much more so does it have application to human laborers. And the question expecting a negative answer at the end of verse 9 should not be taken absolutely (as "God is in no way concerned for oxen, is he?") but understood in the sense that "God is not concerned only for oxen, is he? No." Paul has freely applied Deuteronomy 25:4 in an analogical sense.

Some OT commentators suspect that the Deuteronomy 25 text was already understood proverbially in its own context because it is the only verse that deals with animals in that chapter and the overall context is justice to other human beings. Every other verse in Deuteronomy 25 is about justice between humans. If this were the case, then it is possible that Paul is saying that Deuteronomy 25:4 was not originally written for the welfare of animals but for humans, and Paul would be right.[22] First Corinthians 9:10b and 11 may also have been proverbs circulating in Paul's own time.

Whichever is the case, Paul sees that the statement from Deuteronomy 25:4 in its context had reference to the moral principle of justice or equity, and he applies this to laborers in the gospel.[23] Paul most likely was doing something like early[24] and later Jewish interpreters[25] were doing in making various analogies of justice from Deuteronomy 25:4 and applying them to humans. Paul alludes to the general moral principle of justice that even animals should enjoy the benefits of their labor and thus analogically applies this to human laborers.

22. If this is what Paul is doing, then this use might better be categorized under the next use below, "symbolic use of the OT," a subcategory of the analogical use.

23. For a good explanation of the use of Deut. 25:4 in 1 Cor. 9:9–10 along these lines, see S. L. Johnson, *The Old Testament in the New* (Grand Rapids: Zondervan, 1980), 39–51.

24. See Philo, *On the Virtues* 125–60, in the midst of which he cites Deut. 25:4 (see *On the Virtues*, 145); and cf. Philo, *On the Special Laws* 1.260, which in the light of the preceding references in *On the Virtues* should not be taken to be allegorical; likewise see Josephus, *Antiquities* 4.233 in the light of the preceding and following contexts. See further discussion in R. E. Ciampa and B. S. Rosner, *The First Letter to the Corinthians*, PNTC (Grand Rapids: Eerdmans, 2010), 404–7.

25. Cf. *Targum Pseudo-Jonathan* Deut. 25:4; *b. Sanh*. 65b; *b. Giṭ*. 62a; *b. Yebam*. 4a; *b. Pesaḥ*. 41b; *b. Mak*. 13b; *t. B. Meṣiʿa*. 8:7—though some of these uses involve somewhat more complicated reasoning than Paul's basic analogy.

Paul reasons analogically from the lesser (a law about animals) to the greater (applying the principle of this law to humans).

The Old Testament Figure of Jezebel in Revelation 2:20

In Revelation 2:20 Jesus confronts a problem of sin in the church of Thyatira: "But I have this against you, that you tolerate the woman Jezebel, who calls herself a prophetess, and she teaches and leads My bond-servants astray so that they commit acts of immorality and eat things sacrificed to idols." As in Jesus's address to Pergamum (Rev. 2:12–17), the church of Thyatira is accused of permitting a group of false teachers to have free rein in influencing God's servants to compromise with idolatrous aspects of pagan society. Possibly the reference is to only one individual false teacher, who could be a woman. However, the reference to "the woman" and "her children" (2:23) evokes the phrase "to the elect lady and her children" in 2 John 1 (NRSV), which in the context of that epistle refers, respectively, to the community as a whole and the individual people who comprise that community.[26] This compromising teaching is explained through allusion to the compromising relationship Jezebel had with Israel in the OT, and it is virtually identical to the false teaching of the Balaam party and the Nicolaitans in Pergamum (see above on Rev. 2:14–15).

Jezebel incited King Ahab and Israel to compromise and "fornicate" by worshiping Baal (cf. 1 Kings 16:31; 21:25; LXX: 4 Kingdoms 8:18; 9:22). Similarly, the false teachers in the church were arguing that some degree of participation in idolatrous aspects of Thyatiran culture was permissible. And just as Jezebel was from the outside pagan culture and had come to have a respected place in the covenant community as the wife of Ahab, queen of Israel, so one may presume that this false teacher and the followers were apparently recently converted pagans, who professed Christian faith and who had come to have some prominence in the church but had not shed all of their pagan religious allegiances. And just as Jezebel was fostering, at the least, a syncretistic merging of worship of Israel's God with that of Baal, so it appears that the false teachers in Thyatira were encouraging the legitimacy of some syncretistic combination of worshiping Jesus and pagan idols.

The Comparison of Israel to the Church in Revelation 3:17–18

Revelation 3:17–18 portrays Christ saying to the church of Laodicea: "Because you say, 'I am rich, and have become wealthy, and have need of nothing,' and you do not know that you are wretched and miserable and poor and blind and naked, I advise you to buy from Me gold refined by fire so that you may become rich, and white garments so that you may clothe yourself, and that

26. S. Smalley, *1, 2, 3 John*, WBC 50 (Nashville: Thomas Nelson, 1984), 318–19.

the shame of your nakedness will not be revealed; and eye salve to anoint your eyes so that you may see."

Some boast about material welfare is in mind since whenever the words *rich* (*plousios*) and *I am rich* (*plouteō*) are used negatively in Revelation outside the letters, the reference is to unbelievers who have prospered materially from exploiting others while doing business within the ungodly world system (6:15; 13:16; 18:3, 15, 19). The same idea is present here.

That this is an economic-spiritual boast is also hinted at by the parallel of Hosea 12:8 with Revelation 3:17, which has been observed by many commentators: "And Ephraim said, 'Surely I have become rich, I have found wealth for myself; in all my labors they will find in me no iniquity, which would be sin'" (Hosea 12:9 MT). The distinctive wording and thought in common between Hosea and Revelation 3:17 (in italics) suggest that Hosea is more than a mere coincidental parallel, but that intentional allusion has been made to Hosea. The immediate context of Hosea points further to this. Hosea 12:7 (8 MT) refers to Israel as a "merchant" who prospers through oppression. In the wider context of the book, Israel attributes its material welfare to the benevolence of its idols (e.g., Hosea 2:5, 8; 12:8 [9 MT]; cf. Hosea 11 and 13). These Israelites, like some of the Christians in Asia Minor, may have thought that idolatrous syncretism was not inconsistent with their belief in Yahweh and that their material riches indicated their good relationship with Yahweh. But Yahweh's indictment of these Israelites is that they are in reality "worthless" (Hosea 12:11 [12 MT]).

Like Israel in Hosea's time, the Laodiceans are probably doing well economically because of some significant degree of willing cooperation with the idolatrous trade guilds and economic institutions of their culture. Already in the preceding letters, spiritual compromise because of economic factors has been identified as an unavoidable temptation for Christians living in the major Asia Minor cities (see the letters to Pergamum and Thyatira).[27] Not only are the words used for "rich" in Revelation 3:17 applied elsewhere in the book to unbelieving "merchants" who do business with idolatrous Babylon (so 18:3, 15, 19) but also overtly to those who make gains by involvement with idolatry (so 6:15, alluding to the idolaters of Isa. 2:10–19, 21; Rev. 13:16). The analogical use of Hosea 12:9 shows that the Laodicean Christians are repeating the sin of Israel of old.

Conclusion

Sometimes it is difficult to distinguish between analogy and typology since typology also includes analogy within itself. If the interpreter cannot clearly discern indications of typology, then likely only an analogy is in mind. Recall

27. On which see G. K. Beale, *The Book of Revelation*, NIGTC (Grand Rapids: Eerdmans, 1999), 245–69.

that there are the following indications of something in the NT being part of a typological foreshadowing: (1) an OT person, event, institution, and so forth, which is introduced by or concluded with an OT fulfillment formula (e.g., "this was to fulfill what was spoken"; "as it is written"); (2) other clues in the immediate context of the NT quotation or allusion indicating that it has some kind of fulfillment sense; (3) features in the immediate context of the OT quotation or allusion indicating that it has some kind of fulfillment sense from the vantage point of the OT author; (4) features in the focus OT passage that have literary or thematic links with other material or ideas elsewhere in the canonical context that suggests a foreshadowing sense in that focus passage. Without these three indications, one must conclude that the quotation or allusion is probably referring to an OT person, event, or institution is a mere analogy.

To Indicate the Symbolic Use of the Old Testament

This is similar to the analogical use and might even be considered a subset of it. Overt symbols in an OT passage are taken over and applied again to something in the NT. Something that was already symbolic for a historical reality in the OT is used again to be a symbol for some reality in the NT. So, on one level, a symbol from the OT is compared to something in the NT, and this is like an analogy. On the one hand, the difference between this use and the simple analogical use is that the symbol in the OT has already been compared or made analogous to some person or institution in the OT context itself. On the other hand, when a NT writer makes a fresh analogy with something in the OT, he is doing it for the first time. As in the case of analogy, however, it is important to study the preceding and following immediate OT context from which the symbol is taken in order better to apprehend the way the symbol is being used in the NT.

A good example of the symbolic use is found in Revelation 13:2: "And the beast which I saw was like a leopard, and his feet were like those of a bear, and his mouth like the mouth of a lion. And the dragon gave him his power and his throne and great authority." In Daniel 7:3–8 the images of the lion, bear, leopard, and "terrifying" beast, respectively, represent four successive world empires, which persecute the saints of the covenant community. In Revelation 13:2 these four images are all applied to the one beast. This probably includes a connotation of Rome as the fourth beast, which Daniel predicts will be more powerful and dreadful than the previous three beasts of Daniel 7:4–6 (see Rev. 13:1 and the specific allusions to Daniel's fourth kingdom).[28]

For Daniel, each beast represents a political entity that is antagonistic to the people of God. The beast in Revelation 13 must therefore represent political

28. The same Danielic imagery of the fourth beast's "ten horns" being "ten kings" (cf. Dan. 7:7 with 7:24) is applied to the "beast" in Rev. 13:1 as "having ten horns, . . . and on his horns were ten diadems" (diadems = kings), which shows that Daniel's fourth beast is indeed in mind in Rev. 13:1–2.

power that persecutes God's people. Yet there is a difference. John combines the different animals from Daniel that represent different kingdoms and combines them into one animal. Why does he combine all the animals into one? This is not an easy question to answer. Nevertheless, likely the piling up of Daniel's multiple beasts (= kingdoms) into one in Revelation 13:1–2 at least appears to highlight the extreme fierceness of this beast. This is intensifying what Daniel says about the beasts by combining them into one and may show how horrific they are, especially in their persecuting nature.

Could there be a further reason in making this change? Perhaps combining the multiple beasts also represents a combining of a number of extended temporal reigns into one to indicate the transtemporal nature of the beast (= the persecuting kingdom). Perhaps in Revelation 13 this is not merely one historical beast in one historical epoch (i.e., Rome), but John is also seeing this as a beast that transcends any one epoch, from the first to the final coming of Christ. Rome represents the fourth beast, yet the fourth beast's persecuting role extends until the second coming of Christ.

Interpreters may debate what ideas of Daniel's symbols carry over into Revelation 13, but at least the most univocal element of symbolic meaning between Daniel's and John's beasts is clear: they represent kingdoms that persecute God's people.

Such symbolic pictures, whether in the book of Revelation or elsewhere in the NT, show continuity between the OT and the NT uses.[29]

To Indicate an Abiding Authority Carried Over from the Old Testament

Here again there may be overlap with the analogical use of the OT since there is a comparison of an OT passage with something in the NT. However, what is uppermost in mind now is to highlight the authority of the OT statement and underscore that it is just as true and authoritative today as it was when it was first spoken in the OT passage. And, as was true with the analogical and symbolic uses, it is imperative to analyze the immediate OT context from which the authoritative statement is taken in order to more deeply appreciate the way the statement is being used in the NT. Sometimes the introductory formula "as it is written" indicates that an OT passage is being adduced as an abiding authority that continues into the present situation of the NT writer. However, such a formula is not necessary for such a use of the OT.

A typical example of this kind of usage occurs in Romans 3:2–4. There Paul says that the benefit of being a Jew is "great in every respect. First of all, that they were entrusted with the oracles of God. 'What then? If some [Jews] did not believe, their unbelief will not nullify the faithfulness of God, will it? May

29. For other examples, see the image of the "book" in Rev. 5:1–9 and the "dragon" in Rev. 12:3–4.

it never be! Rather, let God be found true, though every man be found a liar, as it is written, "That You may be justified in Your words, and prevail when You are judged."'" Part of "the oracles of God" included promises about Israel's end-time salvation (see below on Rom. 9:6). Paul asks, Will "their unbelief . . . nullify the faithfulness of God" in fulfilling those promises? Romans 9:6–11:32 answers this question negatively: No! God will remain faithful to his promise to Israel (though commentators differ in their understanding of how God will fulfill the promise of Israel's eschatological salvation).[30] In Romans 3:2–4 Paul anticipates his expanded discussion in Romans 9:6–11:32 by affirming that although the majority of Israel has not believed, this does not mean that God is or will be unfaithful to his OT promise to save Israel in the latter days. Paul emphatically says in this respect, "May it never be! Rather, let God be found true, though every man be found a liar, as it is written, 'That You may be justified in Your words, and prevail when you are judged.'"

The quotation comes from Psalm 51:4 (6 MT), where David confesses that he has sinned, which includes his own deception in the Bathsheba affair. David contrasts his undependable sinfulness with God's unswerving truthfulness, who is "justified" in his words and thus prevails when he is judged by anyone trying to doubt his absolute faithfulness. David says this was true of God in his day; Paul says the same is just as true in his own day. The majority of God's people (Jews, as in Rom. 3:1) are "unbelieving" and "liars," but God stands as unswervingly true and faithful to his word of promise to Israel (3:3–4). He will fulfill his promise about their salvation, as Romans 9–11 goes on to elaborate further. Psalm 51:4 is just as authoritative in Paul's day as in David's.

Likewise, Paul uses the formula "as it is written" in Romans 3:10 to introduce a number of OT quotations (3:10–18) from the Psalms and Isaiah about humanity's sin and depravity and thereby demonstrate that what was true about humanity's fallen condition in the OT epoch is still true in his own day. Other typical examples of this usage (introduced by a formula similar to "as it is written")[31] are 1 Corinthians 9:9 (discussed above under the heading "To Indicate an Analogical or Illustrative Use of the Old Testament")[32] and 1 Timothy 5:18.[33]

30. Some regard the OT promise as made to only a remnant of Israel and that the remnant of Jews who believe throughout the church age is the fulfillment (accordingly, Paul would be responding to Jews who had the wrong belief that God had promised that the majority of Israel would be saved in the end time); on the other hand, other commentators believe God promised that the majority of Israel would be saved in the eschaton, which would be fulfilled at the very end of the age, at the final coming of Christ.

31. Yet earlier in this chapter we have seen that the formula "it is written" can introduce prophetic fulfillment. Only context will reveal how the formula is being used.

32. As we observed at the beginning of this chapter, some of these uses can overlap, and sometimes the difference between them is a matter of emphasis.

33. In addition, see Acts 23:5; 2 Cor. 8:10–15; 9:8–12.

To Indicate a Proverbial Use of the Old Testament

This use is more difficult to explain than the others. Nevertheless, I will include it even though it involves more elaboration to do so. A "proverb" can be defined as a pithy saying or even a single word (cf. "byword") commonly used and recognized, the truth of which is ascertained by observation and is familiar to all. "The early bird gets the worm" is based on observing how birds that hunt earlier than others catch the best worms, which then is applied to many different human situations in which various kinds of industriousness are rewarded (esp. doing something well before someone else does it or using the full day to do a good amount of work).

In this respect, a biblical author may use an OT word or phrase that has already been often repeated, widely known, and applied to different situations in the OT and Judaism. It comes to be used so much that it has taken on a common proverbial meaning, even without knowledge of its first use. A word or phrase comes to be repeated so much and applied to so many different circumstances that it becomes proverbial and often unlinked from its original OT use, yet retains a common meaning that has its roots in that OT context.

For example, today one might say that "Afghanistan is another Vietnam." America's past involvement in Latin America and Iraq may have also been compared to Vietnam. The original meaning of "Vietnam" points to America's long involvement in a war that inevitably ended in defeat. This then comes to be applied to other similar crises in American foreign policy. People who may not remember the original meaning of Vietnam still understand that calling a crisis "another Vietnam" means a long, drawn-out struggle ending, at least potentially, in sure defeat. The reason they would have this understanding is because they have heard the proverbial mention of "Vietnam" applied so often to other comparable situations (though recollection of the original use would enhance the meaning of the common use). We could also refer to this as a stock-in-trade use since it is commonly used (just as a hardware store's stock-in-trade is nails, screws, and tools; the store repeatedly sells these same items and hence keeps them well stocked).

To say "that was their Waterloo" may apply to many situations of nations, sports teams, and other competitive situations over many years. Nevertheless, the varied application of "Waterloo" always has the idea of a decisive defeat (sometimes after a preceding string of victories), since the original meaning arose from Napoléon's decisive defeat at Waterloo at the hands of the British, a defeat that ended his career. Again, a person may not know about Napoléon, this battle, and his decisive defeat, but "meeting one's Waterloo" is used so much in the culture to designate decisive defeats that the typical person understands that association (though again, knowledge of the original historical context would enhance the meaning of the variously applied term). Other contemporary examples like these could be multiplied.[34]

In the OT, the phrase "Edom, Moab, and the sons of Ammon" often occurs. The first place is in 2 Samuel 8:12 (= 1 Chron. 18:11),[35] where these are nations that David has defeated in battle. The same enemies are listed again in Psalms 60:8–9; 83:6–8; 108:9; Jeremiah 9:26; 25:21; 27:3.[36] This threefold enemy formula is used in Isaiah 11:14 and Daniel 11:41, where it is prophesied that in the eschatological future these nations will again be opposed to God's people and will be defeated. It would appear that these eschatological uses do not refer to the literal nations of "Edom, Moab, and Ammon" but that these nations now represent all those who stand in antagonism to God's kingdom and people. That these last two uses are not literal seems to be indicated further by the fact that these nations ceased to exist in the second century BC. Accordingly, the allusion to this threefold enemy list in early Judaism likely also represents generally the enemies of God's people and not the specific ethnic Edomites, Moabites, and Ammonites (1 Macc. 5:3–6; *Jubilees* 37:6–10; 1QM [*War Scroll*] 1.1; 4Q554 [*New Jerusalem*[a]] 3.18; cf. also *Midrash Rabbah Numbers* 14.1[37]). Therefore this triadic enemy reference comes to be used in a proverbial manner to refer generally to the enemies of God, who will be defeated no matter how hard they try to overcome God's people. This is an example of a stock-in-trade or proverbial use in the OT itself and in Judaism.

The single word *mystery* (*mystērion*) in the NT likely fits into this category of usage as a kind of byword (though without negative connotations). "Mystery" (*mystērion*) occurs first in the Greek OT in Daniel 2 (eight times),[38] where it refers to the hidden meaning of King Nebuchadnezzar's dream about the latter days (e.g., see Dan. 2:28–29). There the statue seen in the dream is explained to represent earthly kingdoms, whose destruction means the defeat of earthly kingdoms and the establishment of God's kingdom in the last times. God revealed the meaning of this dream to Daniel, who told it to the king. This was likely a startling interpretation for Nebuchadnezzar.[39] He was

34. During allegations of corruption during President Ronald Reagan's administration in the 1980s, e.g., some might well have said, "Is this Reagan's Watergate?" referring to Nixon's original Watergate fiasco.

35. In Dan. 11:41 these three nations "escape" the wrath of the end-time opponent likely because of their allegiance to him (e.g., see J. G. Baldwin, *Daniel*, TOTC [Leicester: Inter-Varsity, 1978], 202–3; A. Lacocque, *The Book of Daniel*, trans. David Pellauer [Atlanta: John Knox, 1979], 233). Presumably, these nations suffer defeat when the ally, the eschatological opponent himself, is defeated (see Dan. 11:45).

36. Sometimes only "Edom" and "Moab" occur among these verses.

37. This midrashic text has only "Edom and Moab."

38. Where it is a translation of *rāz* in Dan. 2.

39. On the meaning of "mystery" in Dan. 2, see, among others, G. K. Beale, *The Use of Daniel in Jewish Apocalyptic Literature and in the Revelation of St. John* (Lanham, MD: University

probably surprised not only that the statue he saw in his dream represented gentile nations (including his own Babylonian kingdom) but also that these nations would be unexpectedly (from their viewpoint) defeated by Israel's God in the latter days.

In Qumran the word *mystery* (*rāz*) occurs well over a hundred times, and the vast majority have various kinds of eschatological associations. There is general consensus that Daniel's eschatological understanding of "mystery" has shaped Qumran's. Furthermore, just as the revelation of Daniel's end-time mystery was surprising, so Qumran sees that OT Scripture has an eschatological fulfillment that is surprising. There are other similar eschatological uses of "mystery" elsewhere in Judaism (e.g., the targums and *1 Enoch*), but Qumran develops this notion more than any other sector of Judaism.[40]

In addition, Qumran sometimes uses "mystery" to connote the beginning fulfillment of end-time prophecy because the Teacher of Righteousness and his followers believed that they had specially given insight into the meaning of the prophecies that the OT prophets themselves did not have. The new insight that they had was the precise manner in which the prophecies were being fulfilled, which entailed an unexpected element in the fulfillment. For example, the prophecies of Israel's salvation and deliverance from pagan oppression were being fulfilled not in the nation of Israel in general, but in the Qumran covenanters in particular, who represented the true remnant of Israel (e.g., cf. "the remnant of your people" twice in 1QM 14.8–9).

Another example of this occurs with reference to Habakkuk 2:3, which says the fulfillment of the Habakkuk prophecy will assuredly come, but there will be a period in which God's people must wait faithfully for it to happen. The Qumran commentator interprets this to mean that the eschatological climax of history is to occur within the generation of the Qumran covenanters; however, the "mystery" is that "the final time will last long, . . . for the mysteries of God are marvelous" (1QpHab 7.7–8; likewise 7.9–14, where "mystery" also appears). According to OT and Jewish expectations, the final tribulation and defeat of ungodly forces in one final battle at the end of history apparently was to occur quickly (e.g., cf. Dan. 2:31–45; 2 Esd. [*4 Ezra*] 11–13; and *2 Baruch* 36–42, which directly allude to Dan. 2 and 7). The Habakkuk commentator says that such a lengthening of an expected brief eschaton "exceeds everything spoken of by the Prophets" (1QpHab 7.7–8), which is his way of saying that the revelation of the elongation is part of the unexpected end-time aspect of fulfillment.[41]

Press of America, 1984), 12–22; and B. L. Gladd, *Revealing the* Mysterion*: The Use of Mystery in Daniel and Second Temple Judaism with Its Bearing on First Corinthians*, BZNW 160 (New York: de Gruyter, 2009), 17–50.

40. In this paragraph on Qumran, we have followed Gladd, *Revealing the* Mysterion, 51–107, who also cites others in agreement.

41. For other examples of these kinds of uses in Qumran, see Beale, *Use of Daniel*, 23–42.

The NT uses "mystery" (*mystērion*) twenty-seven times and almost always links it in some way either to an OT quotation or allusion. And, as is typical in Qumran, it refers to an end-time beginning fulfillment of something from the OT. In addition, as sometimes also in Qumran, these beginning fulfillments are somewhat unexpected. For example, "mystery" in Matthew 13:11 is sandwiched between Jesus's telling of the parable of the soil and the explanation of its interpretation and is part of a larger interlude of verses 10–17. This interlude introduces not only the interpretation of the soils parable but also a number of other parables about the kingdom in verses 24–52. The point of the interlude is to underscore the purpose of the parables.

Jesus's disciples ask him why he speaks in parables. His first response is "To you it has been granted to know the mysteries of the kingdom of heaven, but to them it has not been granted" (13:11). Verses 12–17 give reasons supporting this initial response, but we will focus only on the response because of the limited scope of the present discussion. The crucial word in the response is *mysteries*, which G. E. Ladd has briefly explained against the background of Daniel: he says that "mystery" in Daniel refers to a divine revelation about eschatological matters that is hidden from human understanding, but then is revealed by God himself to the prophet; Ladd sees "mystery" having the same general idea in Matthew and the rest of the NT.[42] The OT, and especially Daniel, prophesied that the kingdom would come visibly, crush all opposition, judge all godless gentiles, and establish Israel as a kingdom ruling over all the earth. The mystery is the revelation that "in the person and mission of Jesus, . . . the kingdom which is to come finally in apocalyptic power, as foreseen in Daniel, has in fact entered into the world in advance in a hidden form to work secretly within and among men."[43]

In addition to the Daniel 2 background for "mystery," the Isaiah 6 quotation in Matthew 13:14–15 further explains Jesus's initial response to the disciples,[44] as do the following parables in Matthew 13, which contain OT allusions. Ladd explains how these parables in Matthew 13:18–52 portray the hidden or unexpected fulfillment of the beginning form of the prophesied end-time OT kingdom (note the explicit notion of "hiddenness" in verses 33, 44). Instead of coming with external manifestations of power and forcibly imposing a kingdom on people, the kingdom rather concerns internal decisions of the

42. G. E. Ladd, *The Presence of the Future* (Grand Rapids: Eerdmans, 1974), 223–24; likewise A. E. Harvey, "The Use of Mystery Language in the Bible," *Journal of Theological Studies*, n.s. 31 (1980): 333.

43. Ladd, *Presence of the Future*, 225.

44. The limits of the present study prevent analysis of other uses of "mystery" in the NT though other examples like Matt. 13 are Eph. 3:3–5, 9; 2 Thess. 2:7—all of which possibly also have Daniel in mind. Others like these but without possible Danielic reference would be, e.g., Rom. 11:25; 16:25; 1 Cor. 2:7; Eph. 5:32; Col. 1:27; 2:2. For discussion of most of the uses of "mystery" in the NT, see G. K. Beale, *John's Use of the Old Testament in Revelation*, JSNTSup 166 (Sheffield: Sheffield Academic, 1998), 215–72.

heart to receive or not receive the message of the kingdom (the parable of the soils). Consequently, the growth of the kingdom cannot be gauged by eyesight (parable of the leaven).

Final judgment has not yet come, so the righteous and wicked are not yet separated from one another but continue to coexist until the very end of history (parable of the tares of the field). The completed form of the kingdom is not established immediately but begins very tiny and then, after a process of growth, fills the world (parable of the mustard seed). Though the kingdom appears to be hidden, it is to be desired like a treasure or priceless pearl.[45] Even if Ladd is wrong and there is no allusion to Daniel 2, as some commentators think, the same ideas of an unexpected end-time inaugurated fulfillment of the OT prophecies are still in mind, and Jesus's use of "mystery" would convey such a proverbial notion—no longer directly linked to Daniel but carrying the same ideas.

Both in Qumran and in the NT, "mystery" may be a direct reference to Daniel, but at other times it may merely carry the general notion of an end-time prophetic mystery that is beginning fulfillment, often in an unexpected manner.[46] This more general notion of a beginning unexpected fulfillment of an end-time mystery becomes the customary meaning, which is no longer necessarily linked to a Danielic background and can be understood apart from Daniel (though when its ultimate Danielic roots are recalled, the notion becomes more understandable).

Thus the use of "mystery" in Judaism and in the NT is a good example of a proverbial use of the OT. The original meaning of "mystery" in Daniel 2 is that of an eschatological interpretation of a hidden divine prophecy that is surprising. This then comes to be often applied to other similar eschatological events by Qumran and the NT, events seen as beginning unexpected fulfillments and revelation of OT prophecy, the meaning of which was formerly hidden. The use of "mystery" in Daniel 2 itself may not always be in mind in these uses, but in mind is the general proverbial idea of the revelation of a formerly hidden meaning of a divine prophecy about unexpected end-time events.

To Indicate a Rhetorical Use of the Old Testament

One understanding of this use is that OT language is expressed with a view only to being persuasive or impressive in rhetorical effect. Some understand that this style does not give information from the OT context but only embellishes what the NT writer has been saying.

Romans 10:6–8 is sometimes adduced as a classic example of this usage. In Romans 10:5–9 Paul includes a quotation of Deuteronomy 30:12–14:

45. Beale, *John's Use of the Old Testament*, 229–42.

46. The use of "mystery" in 1 Cor. 15:51 refers exclusively to the future, which nevertheless will still be fulfilled in some kind of unexpected manner.

> For Moses writes that the man who practices the righteousness which is based on law shall live by that righteousness. But the righteousness based on faith speaks as follows: "Do not say in your heart, 'Who will ascend into heaven?' (that is, to bring Christ down), or 'Who will descend into the abyss?' (that is, to bring Christ up from the dead)." But what does it say? "The word is near you, in your mouth and in your heart"—that is, the word of faith which we are preaching, that if you confess with your mouth Jesus as Lord, and believe in your heart that God raised Him from the dead, you will be saved.

Some contend that Paul is not at all concerned about the original contextual meaning of the Deuteronomy passage. He has taken wording from what Moses says about the law and applies it to the gospel about Christ, of which Deuteronomy appears to have nothing to say. His only purpose in doing so is to embellish the gospel with OT-sounding language in order to enhance its persuasiveness to the readers. It would be as if a modern Israeli politician were to sprinkle a political speech to an orthodox Jewish audience with OT allusions and quotations, but with no intention to carry over the meaning of each of those OT references. The politician would merely intersperse the speech with OT-sounding language, which has the rhetorical effect of implying to his audience that he has solidarity with them in the faith of Israel. The point of the rhetorical device is to bring about more receptivity among the hearers to the actual content of the speech, which has to do only with modern Israeli political issues and nothing about the meaning of the OT.

Earlier, in chapters 1 and 3, we have addressed the rhetorical use of the OT. We found there that NT writers certainly use the OT for persuasive purposes, to move their hearers to accept their message. But we also found that the contextual meaning of the OT passage enhances the rhetorical effect, whether that is to believe in a theological doctrine (e.g., the deity of Christ), to trust in Christ's redemptive work, or to apply ethical teachings to their lives (in each case the OT meaning would enhance the rhetorical power of the author's overall argument). Such a conclusion about this heightening is an exegetical decision, needing analysis on a case-by-case basis, for which there is not space to do here.[47] Therefore, there are two ways to understand the rhetorical use: the OT wording is used to persuade *without* OT contextual meaning being in mind, and the OT is used to persuade *with* the OT contextual meaning in mind, which makes the rhetorical punch even stronger. I believe that the latter is the case when the OT is being used rhetorically in the NT.

47. The reader is directed to Beale and Carson's *Commentary on the New Testament Use*, where such analysis is given at points throughout. For another example of this, see G. K. Beale, "The Old Testament Background of Paul's Reference to the 'Fruit of the Spirit' in Galatians 5:22," *Bulletin for Biblical Research* 15 (2005): 1–38, esp. 1, 28–29.

To Indicate the Use of an Old Testament Segment as a Blueprint or Prototype for a New Testament Segment

Sometimes a NT author takes over a large OT context as a model after which to creatively pattern a segment in his own writing. Such modeling can be apparent (1) through observing a thematic outline that is uniquely traceable to only one OT context or (2) by discerning a cluster of quotations or clear allusions (or a mix of quotations and allusions) from the same OT chapter or segment. Sometimes both are observable, thus enhancing the clarity of the OT blueprint.

Such OT prototypes in the NT typically have woven within them allusions or quotations from other parts of the same OT book and from elsewhere in the OT. Many of these other OT references outside the model being used are linked by the NT author through common themes, pictures, catchphrases, and keywords. The purpose of interweaving these other OT allusions is to amplify interpretatively the one OT segment providing the model. This is another example of "Scripture interpreting Scripture."

There will be more elaboration of this usage than others since it is not commonly discussed in studies on the NT use of the OT. There are several examples of these literary prototypes. I have argued in some depth that broad patterns from Daniel 7 have been followed in chapters 4–5, 13, and 17 of Revelation.[48] The same use of sections from Daniel as blueprints for segments in Jewish apocalyptic works is also observable.[49]

There is space for only a few examples here. Daniel 7 provides the blueprint for the vision of Revelation 4–5. An overview of the two chapters together reveals that they exhibit a unified structure, which corresponds more to the structure of Daniel 7 than with any other vision in the OT. If we begin with Daniel 7:9–27 and observe the elements and the order of their presentation that are in common with Revelation 4–5, a striking resemblance is discernible:

1. Introductory vision phraseology (Dan. 7:9 [cf. 7:2, 6–7]; Rev. 4:1).
2. The setting of a throne(s) in heaven (Dan. 7:9a; Rev. 4:2a [cf. 4:4a]).
3. God is sitting on a throne (Dan. 7:9b; Rev. 4:2b).
4. The description of God's appearance on the throne (Dan. 7:9c; Rev. 4:3a).
5. Fire before the throne (Dan. 7:9d–10a; Rev. 4:5).
6. Heavenly servants surround the throne (Dan. 7:10b; Rev. 4:4b, 6b–10; 5:8, 11, 14).

48. See Beale, *Use of Daniel*, 178–270, for explanations of these literary prototypes in Revelation. See also Beale, *Revelation*, 87, for some who have observed that broad segments of Ezekiel have been the dominant influence on sections of Revelation.

49. See, e.g., 1QM 1; *1 Enoch* 69:26–71:17; 90:9–14; *2 Baruch* 36–40; *4 Ezra* 11–13; on which see Beale, *Use of Daniel*, 42–153.

7. Book(s) before the throne (Dan. 7:10c; Rev. 5:1–10).
8. The "opening" of the book(s) (Dan. 7:10d; Rev. 5:2–5, 9).
9. A divine (messianic) figure approaches God's throne in order to receive authority to reign forever over a kingdom (Dan. 7:13–14a; Rev. 5:5b–7, 9a, 12–13).
10. This "kingdom" includes "all peoples, nations, and tongues" (Dan. 7:14a [MT]; Rev. 5:9b).
11. The seer's emotional distress on account of the vision (Dan. 7:15; Rev. 5:4).
12. The seer's reception of heavenly counsel concerning the vision from one among the heavenly throne servants (Dan. 7:16; Rev. 5:5a).
13. The saints are also given divine authority to reign over a kingdom (Dan. 7:18, 22, 27a; Rev. 5:10).
14. A concluding mention of God's eternal reign (Dan. 7:27b; Rev. 5:13–14).

Both visions also contain the image of a sea (Dan. 7:2–3; Rev. 4:6). From the comparison it can be seen that Revelation 4–5 repeats the same fourteen elements from Daniel 7:9–27 in the same basic order, but with small variations, which result from the creative expansion of images. For example, on the one hand, Revelation 5 places the messianic figure's approach to the throne after the mention of the seer's emotional distress and reception of angelic counsel, and before the actual opening of the books. On the other hand, Daniel 7:10 has the opening of books before the approach of the "Son of Man" (7:13), which is followed by the seer's distress and reception of counsel (7:15–16). Further, Revelation 4–5 contains more description of the heavenly throne servants than Daniel 7 and repeatedly portrays their presence around the throne, while they are mentioned only three times in Daniel 7:10.[50]

Within this Daniel 7 framework of Revelation 4–5 are woven numerous allusions from elsewhere in Daniel and from other OT books. An illustration of one segment of this vision will demonstrate the various specific OT allusions that occur within this Daniel 7 blueprint.

50. If, however, only the first section of the vision in Rev. 4:1–5:1 is considered, then it is evident that one other OT vision—Ezek. 1–2—is the source of an even larger number of allusions and has many of the same elements as in the above outline. It has consequently been held to be the dominant influence in Rev. 4–5. But Rev. 4–5 has more variations in order when compared with Ezek. 1–2, and five important elements are lacking when all of chaps. 4 and 5 are viewed together: (1) the opening of books; (2) the approach of a divine figure before God's throne in order to receive authority to reign forever over a kingdom; (3) which consists of all peoples of the earth; (4) the reign of the saints over a kingdom; (5) mention of God's eternal reign. Therefore, it is the structure of Dan. 7 that dominates the whole of the Rev. 4–5 vision. In Rev. 5:2–14 the structure of Ezek. 1–2 and allusions to it fade out.

The function of heavenly attendants in praising God for his work of creation (4:8b–11b)

Revelation 4:8b–11b	Virtually Certain Allusion	Probable Allusion	Possible Allusion or Echo
8b Day and night they do not cease to say, "Holy, holy, holy is		Isa. 6:3	
8c the Lord God, the Almighty,			(On this, see Beale, *Revelation*, 332–33.)
8d who was and who is and who is to come."			Exod. 3:14; Isa. 41:10; 43:10; 48:12
9a And when the living creatures	Ezek. 1; 10		Isa. 6 (and other OT theophany descriptions)
give glory and honor and thanks to Him who sits on the throne,			
9b to Him who lives forever and ever,	Dan. 4:34 Θ; 12:7 Θ; cf. LXX; cf. also 6:27 Θ		Isa. 24:23.
10a the twenty-four elders will fall down			Isa. 6 (and other OT theophany descriptions)
before Him who sits on the throne, and will worship Him			
10b who lives forever and ever, and will cast their crowns before the throne, saying,	Dan. 4:34 Θ; 12:7 Θ; cf. LXX; cf. also 6:27 Θ		
11a "Worthy are You, our Lord and our God, to receive glory and honor and power;			(On this, see Beale, *Revelation*, 336–37.)
11b for You created all things, and because of Your will they existed, and were created."		Dan. 4:35 Θ; 4:37 LXX	Isa. 40:12–28

Note: This chart is adapted from Beale, *Use of Daniel*, 193–94; Θ = Theodotion's recension of the LXX.

The point of Revelation's use of the Daniel 7 blueprint is to indicate that Daniel's prophecy of the kingdom of the Son of Man and of the saints has been inaugurated in Christ's death and resurrection. In addition to this idea, the judgment mentioned in Daniel 7 has also begun fulfillment in Christ, especially in the climactic defeat of the kingdom of evil forces.

A similar phenomenon occurs in Revelation 13:1–18, though this time there is no discernible outline from Daniel 7 that Revelation follows. Instead, the chapter is so saturated with allusions from Daniel 7 that it appears to dominate the thought of Revelation 13, within which other OT allusions occur together with those of Daniel 7. A survey of the allusions in Revelation 13:5–8 should serve to illustrate the point.

Revelation 13:5a–8b	Virtually Certain Allusion	Probable Allusion	Possible Allusion or Echo
[5a] And there was given to him a mouth speaking great things and blasphemies, and	Dan. 7:6 Θ, LXX; 7:8, 11, 12b, 14, 20, 25, 27		
[5b] authority to act for forty-two months was given to him.	Dan. 7:6 Θ, 12b, 14, 25, 27; 12:7, 11–12		Dan. 8:12, 24; 11:28, 30
[6a] And he opened his mouth in blasphemies against God to blaspheme his name and		Dan. 7:25 Θ; 11:36 LXX	Dan. 7:6 LXX, 8, 11, 20
[6b] His tabernacle, that is, those who dwell in heaven.		Dan. 8:10 (cf. LXX), 11, 13 (cf. LXX)	Dan. 11:31 (cf. LXX)
[7a] And it was also given to him to make war with the saints and to overcome them;	Dan. 7:21 MT, Θ; 7:8 LXX		
[7b–8a] and authority over every tribe and people and tongue and nation was given to him. All who dwell on the earth will worship him,		Dan. 7:14	Dan. 6:26–28 LXX; 3:7; 3:95–96 Θ, LXX; 4:1 Θ; 6:26 Θ
[8b] everyone whose name has not been written from the foundation of the world in the book of life		Dan. 12:1–2; Ps. 69:28 (69:29 MT; 68:29 LXX)	
of the Lamb who has been slain.			Passover, Lamb—Isa. 53:7

Note: This chart is adapted from Beale, *Use of Daniel*, 232–33. A similar saturation of Dan. 7 allusions in Rev. 13:1–4 can be observed in the same chart format in Beale, *Use of Daniel*, 229–30, and for a discussion of all of Rev. 13 in this respect see pp. 229–48.

The point of using Daniel 7 as a framework for all of Revelation 13 is to show that the portrait of the "beast" who persecutes God's people has been shaped mainly by the prophetic portrait of the beast in Daniel 7, who is prophesied to persecute the saints of Israel. This helps the reader to interpret the beast in Revelation 13 as a leader of state persecution, as in the prophecy of Daniel 7, which likely began fulfillment in the Roman Empire and would continue through other persecuting states until the final parousia.

In the Gospels, an example of an OT section being the model for a broad segment in the NT may be observed in the synoptic eschatological discourse of Jesus in Mark 13:1–27 (= Matt. 24:1–31 and Luke 21:5–28). Lars Hartman has demonstrated that this eschatological discourse is shot through with citations and allusions from Daniel 7–12. And within this Danielic framework, citations and allusions from other OT passages are woven in, interpretatively expanding the model of Daniel 7–12, which shapes the entire narrative.

Mark 13 [Matt. 24]	How link was established	OT
5 Be not led astray.		
6 Many will say, "I am";	The horn magnifies itself—the blasphemy of Babylon in Isa. 14:13	Dan. 7:8; 11:20; 8:10–11, 25; 11:36; 8:25
they will lead many astray.		
7 Wars and rumors of wars.	The blasphemy-war sequence in Dan. 7:20–21	Dan. 7:21; 9:26; 8:23–26; 11:25–45; 2:28–30, 45; 8:19
Be not alarmed; this must take place;		
the end is not yet.	"War," Dan. 11:25–45; "end," 11:27	Dan. 11:27
8 Nation against nation,	Associated themes ("war")	2 Chron. 15:6
kingdom against kingdom;	2 Chron. 15:6 and Isa. 19:2 joined by keywords in their contexts; associated themes	Isa. 19:2
earthquakes, famines.	More loosely associated with the theme of war	
9–11 The beginnings of the travail.		
12 Delivering up:		Dan. 7:25
a brother delivers his brother;	Connection with Isa. 19:2, just quoted; keywords in the context; associated themes	Isa. 19:2; Mic. 7:2–6
children, their parents.	Further on Mic. 7; same theme	Mic. 7:6
13 Hated by all.		Mic. 7:6
The one who endures	Mic. 7:7 may facilitate the return to Daniel	Mic. 7:7; Dan. 11:32
to the end		Dan. 11:35
will be saved		Dan. 12:1
14 The abomination of desolation;		Dan. 11:31; 12:11; 9:27
flee to the mountains.	Sodom as a type of the abomination; an implicit point of association: the destruction	Gen. 19:17
15 Nothing from the house;	Separate logion? (cf. Luke 17:31)	
16 one who is in the field must not turn back.		Gen. 19:17

Mark 13 [Matt. 24]	How link was established	OT
17 Alas for those with child	Separate logion? (cf. Luke 23:29)	
and those who give suck.		
18 May it not happen in winter [20 or on a Sabbath].	Keyword association from Gen. 19 ("go out from the place")	Exod. 16:29
19 Tribulation.	Cf. "flee"—"be delivered" in the same text (Dan. 12:1)	Dan. 12:1
20 The days are shortened.	Revocalization of Dan. 12:1, just quoted in the text	Dan. 12:1
21 "Here is the Christ."		
22 False prophets showing signs and wonders	Association from "god whom his fathers did not know" in Dan. 11:38 to similar phrase in Deut. 13:2*	Dan. 11:37–38; Deut. 13:2
to lead astray.	Still in Deut. 13	Deut. 13:2
24 The sun is darkened;	The day of Yahweh	Joel 2:10
the moon does not shine;	The Day of Yahweh; keyword and thematic association	Isa. 13:10
25 the stars fall, the powers are shaken.	The day of Yahweh; keyword and thematic association.	Isa. 34:4
[30 The sign of the Son of Man; the tribes mourn.]	Keyword and thematic association ("gather," "four")	Isa. 11:10–13
	Cf. Rev. 1:7	Zech. 12:12, 14
26 The Son of Man in clouds with great power and glory.		Dan. 7:13–14
[31 A trumpet call.]	Association via the context (the "gathering")	Isa. 27:13
27 The angels gather the elect.	The traditional motif of the gathering together is connected with the Danielic consummation (the eternal kingdom). The passages are joined by common themes and keywords.	Deut. 30:3–5; Zech. 2:10; Isa. 43:6

* Hartman's chart had Deut. 13:7 in this column and the next one, but it appears that the reference is to Deut. 13:2.

When one looks only at Mark by itself or Matthew or Luke by themselves, Daniel 7–12 does not look as prominent, but when all three are put together as one overall discourse, then the greater saturation by Daniel can be observed. Hartman argues that this evidence points to Jesus as the originator of the discourse, from which the synoptic writers drew selectively.[51]

51. On which see L. Hartman, *Prophecy Interpreted*, Coniectanea biblica: NT Series 1 (Lund: Gleerup, 1966), 145–77.

Prototypical uses of OT segments may also be detected in Paul's epistles. For example, Matthew Harmon has observed that Isaiah 49–55 may broadly be the main conceptual substructure within which Paul conceived what he was writing in the entire Epistle to the Galatians. He gives a summary of his thesis in the following chart, where in the right column the following code is used: c = citation; a = allusion; e = echo; tp = thematic parallel.[52]

1	Gal. 1:1	Apostleship	Isa. 52:7; 61:1 (tp)
2	Gal. 1:3	Peace	Isa. 40–66 (tp)
3	Gal. 1:4	Christ's death	Isa. 53:10 (a)[1]
4	Gal. 1:8–9	Gospel	Isa. 52:7; 60:1–3; 61:1 (tp)
5	Gal. 1:10	Slave of Christ	Isa. 42:1–8; 49:1–8; 52:13–53:12 (tp)
6	Gal. 1:15	Called from the womb	Isa. 49:1 (a)
7	Gal. 1:16	Reveal his Son	Isa. 49:3 (e); 49:6; 52:5, 7[2] (tp); 52:10; 53:1 (e)
8	Gal. 1:16	Preach the gospel to the gentiles	Isa. 42:6; 49:6, 8; 52:5, 7, 10; 53:1 (tp)
9	Gal. 1:17	Travel to Arabia	Isa. 42:11 (tp)
10	Gal. 1:23–24	Glorifying God "in me"	Isa. 49:3 (e)
11	Gal. 2:2	Running in vain	Isa. 49:4 (e)
12	Gal. 2:2, 8–9	Ministry to the gentiles	Isa. 42:6; 49:6–8; 52:5–7 (tp)
13	Gal. 2:16–21	Righteousness language	Isa. 40–66 (tp)
14	Gal. 2:20	Christ lives in me	Isa. 49:3 (e)
15	Gal. 2:20	Gave himself for me	Isa. 53 (a)
16	Gal. 3:2, 5	Hearing of faith	Isa. 53:1 (a)
17	Gal. 3:6–9	Look to Abraham	Isa. 51:1–8 (a)
18	Gal. 3:8	Gospel preached	Isa. 52:7–10 (tp)
19	Gal. 3:13	Christ as a curse for us	Isa. 53 (a)
20	Gal. 3:14, 16	Blessing, seed of Abraham, Spirit	Isa. 44:3–5 (a)
21	Gal. 3:16	Singular seed → plural seed	Isa. 41:8; 53:10; 54:3 (tp)
22	Gal. 3:15–18	Covenant, promise, seed, inheritance	Isa. 54:3–10 (e); 61:7–10 (tp)
23	Gal. 4:1–7	New exodus New creation Servant Abraham/seed	(1) Isa. 41:17–20; 43:16–21; 51:9–10 (2) Isa. 52:11–12; 52:13–53:12 (3) Isa. 41:8, 17–20; 51:1–8 Collective allusion or echo
24	Gal. 4:11	Labor in vain	Isa. 49:4 (e)
25	Gal. 4:19	Paul's birth pangs	Isa. 45:7–11 (a); 51:1–2 (e); 54:1 (tp)

52. M. S. Harmon, *She Must and Shall Go Free*, BZNW 168 (New York: de Gruyter, 2010), 261–65.

26	Gal. 4:27	Rejoice barren one	Isa. 54:1 (c)
27	Gal. 5:5	Waiting for righteousness in the Spirit	Isa. 32:15–17 (tp)
28	Gal. 5:13	Freedom	Isa. 40–55 (tp)
29	Gal. 5:13	Serve one another through love	Isa. 40–66 (tp)
30	Gal. 5:18	Led by the Spirit	Isa. 63:11–15 (tp)[3]
31	Gal. 5:22–23	Fruit of the Spirit	Isa. 32:15–20; 57:15–21 (a/e)[4]
32	Gal. 6:15	New creation	Isa. 40–66 (a)
33	Gal. 6:16	Peace and mercy on the Israel of God	Isa. 54:10 (a)

[1] Here the reference more likely is to Isa. 53:5 rather than 53:10, but Harmon has 53:10.
[2] The reference to Isa. 52:5, 7 here and below does not seem to fit.
[3] Yet I think this likely is an allusion; see Beale, "Background of 'Fruit of the Spirit,'" 12–14.
[4] I think this is likely an allusion; see ibid., 1–38.

If this is generally correct, then Paul throughout Galatians is concerned to relate what he says in Galatians to the "already and not yet" fulfillment of Isaiah's second-exodus restoration and new-creation prophecies. In this light the Christians in Galatia are to see themselves as located within a wider redemptive-historical context. They are not merely Christian gentiles (for the most part) who are trying to remain loyal to the truth while confronted by Judaizers, but in doing so they are end-time true Israelites, who are living in the dawning of the end-time restoration and new creation predicted by Isaiah 40–66, of which they are a part. This should lead to assurance that they really are God's true people and should motivate them to resist the false teachers who say otherwise.

Sometimes the OT matrix for a NT segment does not come from one OT chapter but from one dominating OT theme. An example of this kind of usage in Paul can be observed in Romans 9:25–11:35, where in the left column the following code is used:

√ = Captivity-restoration theme
C = Captivity-restoration theme in the context
ø = No presence of a restoration theme

	OT	Romans
√	Hosea 2:23 (25 MT)	9:25
√	Hosea 1:10 (2:1 MT; cf. LXX)	9:26
√	Isa. 10:22; Hosea 1:10 (2:1 MT)	9:27
√	Isa. 10:23 (cf. 28:22)	9:28
√	Isa. 1:9	9:29
ø	Isa. 8:14	9:32
C	Isa. 28:16	9:33
ø	Lev. 18:5	10:5

	OT	Romans
√	Deut. 30:12	10:6
√	Deut. 30:13	10:7
√	Deut. 30:14	10:8
C	Isa. 28:16	10:11
√	Joel 2:32 (3:5 MT; cf. LXX)	10:13
√	Isa. 52:7 (cf. Nah. 1:15 [2:1 MT])	10:15
√	Isa. 53:1 (cf. LXX)	10:16
ø	Ps. 19:4 (18:5 LXX; 19:5 MT)	10:18
C	Deut. 32:21 (cf. LXX)	10:19
C	Isa. 65:1 (cf. LXX)	10:20
C	Isa. 65:2 (cf. LXX)	10:21
ø	1 Sam. 12:22	11:2
√	Jer. 31:37	11:2
ø	1 Kings 19:10, 14 (remnant)	11:3
ø	1 Kings 19:18 (remnant)	11:4
ø	Deut. 29:3; Isa. 29:10; 6:9–10	11:8
ø	Ps. 69:22–23 (68:23–24 LXX; 69:23–24 MT)	11:9–10
√	Isa. 59:20–21; Ps. 14:7	11:26
√	Jer. 31:33–34	11:27
√	Isa. 27:9	11:27b
√	Isa. 40:13 (cf. LXX)	11:34
ø	Job 41:11 (41:3 MT)	11:35

In this segment of Romans, the dominating notion is the prophesied captivity-restoration theme. This theme is highlighted, for example, by citations from Hosea (2:23; 1:10 [MT: 2:25; 2:1]) in Romans 9:26–27, and Isaiah 10:22–23 plus 1:9 in Romans 9:27–29.[53] Paul has in mind that the prophesied restoration of Israel has begun but has not yet been fully consummated. He does not have in mind one OT segment (though Isaiah is important throughout)[54] but one theme, which he elaborates by adducing various restoration passages from throughout the OT. The OT references that do not come from OT restoration contexts are likely utilized to interpretatively expand the overall restoration theme.

A third kind of prototypical use of the OT may also be discerned. Some scholars have observed that certain segments of NT books are shaped primarily

53. These citations from Isaiah and Hosea appear to be influenced by the LXX, though there are some parallels with the MT. Constraints of space do not allow more analysis of textual issues here.

54. On this see J. R. Wagner, *Heralds of the Good News: Isaiah and Paul "In Concert" in the Letter to the Romans* (Leiden: Brill, 2002), who contends that Isaiah is a major OT influence together with other OT books within which Rom. 9–11 is to be understood.

by a broad narrative that derives from or spans several OT books. For example, Tom Wright and Silvia Keesmat contend that the narrative of the exodus, which is expressed broadly in the Pentateuch and other OT books, becomes a template that shapes sections in Paul's epistles. Keesmat argues, for instance, that the narrative of Israel's exodus out of Egypt provides the shape for Romans 8:18–39. The notion of God's adoption and deliverance of his people from captivity to sin, a new creation, the Spirit's leading them through trial and suffering and their crying out to God, and their subsequent inheritance—all are inspired by the corresponding themes from Israel's exodus.[55] Whatever else is discussed within this section of Romans 8, including any other OT allusions, is meant to be interpretative elaboration that expands the meaning of this exodus narrative framework.

To Indicate an Alternate Textual Use of the Old Testament

An author may choose one text form or translation of a phrase among others known to him to bring out more clearly what he sees as the intended meaning of the original OT passage.

This usage is not distinct from any of the above uses but overlaps with them. For example, a NT writer could cite an OT prophecy about the Messiah to indicate that the prophecy has begun fulfillment in Christ. The writer, however, may cite the Greek translation of the OT, which is quite different from the Hebrew. The reason for doing so may be to amplify the meaning of the original form of the OT prophecy in order to understand better how it is beginning to be fulfilled in Christ.[56] Revelation 17:14 says, "These will wage war against the Lamb, and the Lamb will overcome them, because He is Lord of lords and King of kings, and those who are with Him are the called and chosen and faithful." The beasts represent divine enemies in the very end of time, whom Christ defeats. The title for Christ, "Lord of lords and King of kings," comes from one of the Greek translations of Daniel (4:34 [37]) and does not occur in the canonical Aramaic of Daniel 4:34 (MT). In the Aramaic of Daniel 4:34, King Nebuchadnezzar praises God, after having been humbled and made like an animal and then restored to his senses again. There

55. S. C. Keesmaat, *Paul and His Story: (Re)Interpreting the Exodus Tradition*, JSNTSup 181 (Sheffield: Sheffield Academic Press, 1999), e.g., 228. For another example of this kind of approach, see F. Watson, *Paul and the Hermeneutics of Faith* (London/New York: T&T Clark, 2004); see the helpful summary of Watson's view by S. Moyise, *Paul and Scripture* (Grand Rapids: Baker Academic, 2010), 119–20.

56. This happens sometimes with OT citations in the Qumran Habakkuk scroll (*Pesher Habakkuk* [1QpHab]). There may be an awareness of different pointings in the Hebrew text, and an author chooses one option; cf. K. Stendahl, *The School of Matthew and Its Use of the Old Testament* (Philadelphia: Fortress, 1968), 183–206, for examples of this in the *Pesher Habakkuk*; also see E. E. Ellis, *Paul's Use of the Old Testament* (Grand Rapids: Baker, 1957), 139–49.

he "blessed the Most High, and praised and honored [Him]" (NRSV). The equivalent verse in one Greek version of Daniel (Θ = Theodotion)[57] renders the Aramaic fairly literally as the king "blessed the Most High, and praised him, . . . and gave him glory." But the Old Greek version of Daniel gives an interpretative paraphrase: "I acknowledge the Most High, and I praise, . . . I acknowledge, and I praise, because he is God of gods and Lord of lords and King of kings" (4:34 [37]). "God of gods and Lord of lords and King of kings" is an interpretative amplification of "the Most High" from the Aramaic text.

Revelation 17:14 refers to the Old Greek's "Lord of lords and King of kings" and applies it to Christ in order to highlight that he is to be identified with the God of Daniel 4. Just as God had humbled Nebuchadnezzar by making him a beast, so Christ will defeat and humble the divine opponents, who are portrayed as beasts. By referring to the textual form of the Old Greek, Revelation underscores the deity of Christ.[58]

Another example of the textual use of the OT occurs in Revelation 3:14, where Christ is said to be "the Amen, the faithful and true Witness." Isaiah 65:16 is the primary source for Christ's titles in Revelation 3:14, which is supported by several lines of evidence, of which only a few will be summarized here.[59] First, that "Amen" is an allusion to Isaiah 65:16 is evident from observing that Isaiah 65:16 (see the MT) and Revelation 3:14 are the only two passages in the entire Bible where "Amen" is a name.[60] Second, the twofold name in Revelation 3:14 of "faithful and true" is likely an expanded translation of Isaiah's "Amen." Such an amplification of Isaiah's "Amen" is shown where the Hebrew text refers twice to God as "the God of Amen [*'āmēn*]," which is translated in the following ways by different versions of the Greek OT:

Isaiah 65:16	Revelation 3:14
"the God of amen, . . . the God of Amen" (MT). At this point early Greek Bibles have "the God of amen [*amēn*]," others instead have "the true [*alēthinon*] God," and still others the "faithful [using a nominal participial form of *pisteuō*] God."*	Christ is "the Amen, the faithful and true Witness." *ho amēn, ho martys ho pistos kai alēthinos*

* The Septuagint has "the *true* God" (*ton theon ton alēthinon* [LXX]); the versions of Theodotion and Symmachus support the translation "the God of *Amen* [*amēn*]"; Aquila, Jerome, and MS 86 support the basic reading of "the God of *faithfulness*." Aquila reads *en tō theō pepistōmenōs*, which employs the adverbial form "faithfully" as part of the fuller phrase "by which the one blessing himself in the earth will be blessed *faithfully* by God."

57. So Dan. 4:31 [37], which is different versification but the equivalent to Dan. 4:34 of the MT and 4:34 [37] of the Old Greek.

58. See G. K. Beale, "The Origin of the Title 'King of Kings and Lord of Lords' in Rev. XVII.14." *New Testament Studies* 31 (1985), 618–20, for fuller discussion.

59. These lines of evidence are expanded upon in Beale, *Revelation*, 297–301.

60. In both the OT and NT, "Amen" usually is a response by people to a word from God or to a prayer, and sometimes it refers to Jesus's trustworthy statements.

In this light the title "the faithful and true Witness" in Revelation 3:14 is best taken as an interpretative translation of "Amen" from Isaiah 65:16. Thus the four Greek versions of Isaiah 65:16 together have virtually the same amplified renderings as that of Revelation 3:14. Nowhere else in Scripture are these three words, "Amen, faithful and true," found in combination, and even the pairing of "faithful and true"[61] is very rare. The risen Jesus here is interpreting the "Amen" of the Hebrew text by the textually expanded "faithful" and "true" from the Greek OT translations. Furthermore, what was true of God in Isaiah 65:16 is now seen to be true also of Jesus: he is the divine "Amen," the divine "faithful and true" Witness.[62]

To Indicate an Assimilated Use of the Old Testament

An author may express OT language merely because it has become part of the way he thinks and speaks. Such expressions may approximate certain OT phrases, though without any conscious intention to allude to a particular OT text. For example, the conclusion to the Lord's Prayer, "For Yours is the kingdom and the power and the glory forever" (Matt. 6:13)[63] is very close to the Greek version of Psalm 144:11: "They shall speak of the glory of Your kingdom, and talk of Your power" (cf. 145:11 MT, English; Dan. 2:37). But there are also passages that speak of the "kingdom, the power, . . . and the glory" of an earthly kingdom, features ultimately traceable back to God.[64] Possibly the allusion in Matthew 6:13 is to the Psalm passage, but it is just as likely that there is reference to the broad concept reiterated throughout the

61. A bit more loosely, Dan. 2:45 (Theodotion) also combines the two words ("*true* is the dream and *faithful* is its interpretation [*alēthinon to enypnion, kai pistē hē sygkrisis autou*]"), but there is no mention of new creation there (though see the possible secondary relevance of Dan. 2:45 in discussion of Rev. 22:6 in Beale, *Revelation*, 1122–25). See also the apocryphal 3 Macc. 2:11, where God is referred to as "indeed faithful and true" (*pistos ei kai alēthinos*), but in this reference there is nothing about creation or new creation (as there is in Rev. 3:14b): it is about God's faithfulness in eventually executing judgment. If creation were in mind, 3 Macc. 2:11 would still be making the same point about God's character. The Daniel and Maccabees texts themselves may well also be allusions to Isa. 65:16.

62. There are numerous other examples of NT writers citing interpretatively amplified translations of the Hebrew OT. Thus with respect to the use of Ps. 2:9 in Rev. 19:15, see also Johnson, *Old Testament in the New*, 14–20; with regard to the use of Exod. 3:14 in Rev. 1:4, see Beale, *Revelation*, 187–89. Space constraints prevent discussion of those cases where it appears that a NT writer has depended on an LXX text that seems to contradict or develop a meaning different from what is in the Hebrew text.

63. This is probably a later scribal addition motivated to adapt the Lord's Prayer "for liturgical use of the early church" (B. M. Metzger, *A Textual Commentary on the Greek New Testament*, 2nd ed. [New York: United Bible Societies, 1994], 14).

64. See the Old Greek of Dan. 2:37; on which cf. also Dan. 11:17 (OG), "the power of his whole kingdom"; 2 Chron. 22:9, "the power of the kingdom"; likewise 2 Chron. 20:6; Esther 10:1–2; Dan. 4:27, 34 (OG).

OT and early Judaism that the kingdom, power, and glory belong ultimately to God alone. This approach may at times be close to that of the proverbial use of the OT explained above. An expression or unique word may be used so much that it passes into the common language without reflection on its original usage. Many times I have heard people say, "This is the day that the LORD has made; let us rejoice and be glad in it." The expression comes from Psalm 118:24 (NRSV). When most people use the saying, they do not have in mind the original context but are usually applying it to various situations (e.g., if someone is having a bad day and complaining, another Christian may try to encourage the person by quoting this verse).[65]

There may be "instances, then, when the NT writers use biblical language simply because their minds are so steeped in Scripture that such verbal patterns provide the linguistic frameworks in which they think"[66] or express themselves. In such cases, there is no attempt to interpret the OT or to use it consciously with its original context in mind.

To Indicate an Ironic or Inverted Use of the Old Testament

Irony is the saying of one thing and meaning its opposite, for a variety of literary purposes. Not untypically, irony expresses ridicule or mocking. If one of my colleagues said to a class of students that "Greg Beale is a great tennis player," after they had seen me play a terrible game of tennis, the professor would intend to mock me and elicit laughter from the class. Such mocking and ridicule is often expressed through irony in biblical literature to highlight ironic judgment. Irony may also be used to encourage the faithful, who, while suffering persecution and defeat, are ironically overcoming the world as they persevere faithfully, indicating their ironic redemption. This literary use may also be called antithetical or inverted employment of the OT. Clear OT allusions are used but with the opposite meaning from the OT. Descriptions about God's incomparability from the OT are applied to the beast in order to mock his efforts to assume the role of God, since he will assuredly fail (e.g., Rev. 13:4, "Who is like the beast?" taken from Exod. 15:11, "Who is like you . . . , O LORD?"). Alternatively, descriptions of evil figures from the OT are applied to Jesus.[67] At first sight one might think that these are wrong uses of the OT, but upon further reflection, an intentionally inverted use can be perceived.

65. On this particular illustration, see further Beale and Carson, introduction to *Commentary on the New Testament Use*, xxiv–xxv.

66. Ibid., xxv.

67. Thus the depiction of the Lamb with seven horns in Rev. 5:6 appears to be taken from Dan. 7:7–8, 20–21, the only place in all of the OT where an animal is portrayed with seven horns (ten horns in v. 7 minus three horns in v. 8), but there the beast is the end-time opponent of God's people. When it is remembered that Rev. 4–5 is patterned on Dan. 7 (discussed earlier in this chapter), the validity of an allusion to the seven horns of Dan. 7 may be enhanced. (I first heard

Use of an OT passage to express restorative irony is well illustrated in Galatians 3:13–14: "Christ redeemed us from the curse of the Law, having become a curse of us—for it is written, 'cursed is everyone who hangs on a tree'—in order that in Christ Jesus the blessing of Abraham might come to the Gentiles."

The quoted passage in Galatians 3:13 is from Deuteronomy 21:23, where the curse of capital punishment is said to be executed on an evil Israelite criminal. Now, at the turn of the ages, this horrific punishment for the worst and most despicable of criminals was executed on the most honored Israelite: Jesus. Thus the Deuteronomy text is turned on its head and reversed to indicate a curse on the most innocent of Israelites. Christ underwent the curse of the cross, which led to a blessing of restoring sinners to God. The Deuteronomy passage is intentionally used in a reversed manner to indicate how the Messiah ironically was cursed to bring about a blessing on humanity.

There is likely an allusion in Acts 2 to the tongues of Genesis 10–11.[68] The confusion in understanding different tongues in Genesis 10–11 is a curse, leading to the dispersion of humanity, whereas the understanding of different tongues in Acts 2 is a blessing, leading to dispersion, which is to result in further blessing. The allusion in Acts 2 indicates that the very diversity of tongues leading to a curse in scattering humanity is the very thing that will ultimately be used to bring about a blessing of reunification of sinful humanity. Here again we have an indication that the means of a curse will be the very means by which a blessing of redemption will later occur.

Conclusion

The uses discussed in this chapter likely do not exhaust the ways that NT writers employ the OT. Nevertheless, the examples listed and elaborated upon here represent the most typical uses found in the NT, especially the employments that indicate direct fulfillment of prophecy, typology, analogy, an abiding authority, and a different textual form than the Hebrew. Throughout all of the above uses (except the assimilated use),[69] it is important to keep in mind the crucial role of the broad OT context.

about this Daniel 7 background for the "seven horns" years ago from R. T. France, who said he had heard this view from others.) Just as the evil beast in Dan. 7:7–8, 11, 19–27 is portrayed with the power of horns as conquering God's people, now Christ is portrayed with the very same horn imagery to indicate that in the way evil conquers, so must the defeat of evil be portrayed. On the one hand, this imagery metaphorically indicates a divine retributive irony that the way that one sins becomes the same way one is punished (e.g., see Pss. 7:15–16; 9:15–16). On the other hand, the beast with two horns like a lamb in Rev. 13:11 (patterned after Jesus as a Lamb with horns in 5:6) is likely meant as ironic mockery that this figure is trying to take a messianic role, which is doomed to failure from the start because he stands for all that the true Messiah does not.

68. Several commentators have observed the allusion; e.g., see the discussion in G. K. Beale, *The Temple and the Church's Mission* (Leicester: Inter-Varsity, 2004), 201–3.

69. In addition to some perspectives of the rhetorical use.

5

Hermeneutical and Theological Presuppositions of the New Testament Writers

Introduction

Chapter 3 presented a plan for studying the OT in the NT. One of the crucial steps in that approach is to analyze the NT writer's theological use of the OT. An aspect of this step is to reflect on whether any hermeneutical or theological presuppositions underlie any of the theological uses. This chapter will elaborate on this particular presuppositional aspect of the theological step. There are at least five presuppositions that can undergird a NT writer's use of the OT, though as alluded to in chapter 3, almost every one of them is debated to one degree or another. This chapter will briefly comment on the purported biblical origin for these presuppositions and the significance of the presuppositions for interpreting the OT in the NT. It is crucial for us to understand these presuppositions; without them it can sometimes be difficult to apprehend how a NT writer is interpreting the OT in line with its original meaning.

Presuppositions of NT Writers in Interpreting the OT

Before discussing these presuppositions, there is one grand assumption of all: Jesus and the apostles believed that the OT Scriptures were "sacred" and were the Word of God. Therefore all authoritative theological discussion had to be based on and proceed from this sacred body of literature.[1] For Jesus and his followers, what the OT said, God said; and what God said, the OT said.[2] Another assumption that follows on this and is almost as ultimate is that hearers and readers could not sufficiently understand Jesus's and the apostles' theological presuppositions and interpretations of the OT without the aid of God's Spirit.[3] These two more ultimate presuppositions are typically not discussed in connection with the following five presuppositions to be elaborated on, and so we have decided to include them here at the beginning of our discussion on presuppositions.

In chapter 3 we argued briefly that five presuppositions seem at times to underlie the NT writers' interpretation of the OT. Here these will be restated and their biblical basis briefly elaborated:

1. There is the apparent assumption of *corporate solidarity* or *representation*.[4]
2. In the light of corporate solidarity or representation, Christ as the Messiah is viewed as representing the *true Israel* of the OT *and* the true Israel—the church—in the NT.[5]
3. *History is unified* by a wise and sovereign plan so that the earlier parts are designed to correspond and point to the later parts (cf., e.g., Matt. 5:17; 11:13; 13:16–17).[6]

1. On which, e.g., see R. B. Hays and J. B. Green, "The Use of the Old Testament by New Testament Writers," in *Hearing the New Testament*, ed. J. B. Green (Grand Rapids: Eerdmans, 2010), 130.

2. On which see the discussion of B. B. Warfield, *The Inspiration and Authority of the Bible* (Phillipsburg, NJ: P&R, 1948), 299–407.

3. On which see, e.g., E. E. Ellis, *Old Testament in Early Christianity* (Grand Rapids: Baker, 1991), 116–21; e.g., see 1 Cor. 2:6–16 for a classic formulation of this by Paul.

4. For example, H. W. Robinson, *Corporate Personality in Ancient Israel* (Philadelphia: Fortress, 1964), as qualified by later critics, some of whose sources are included in his bibliography (e.g., see J. R. Porter, "Legal Aspects of Corporate Personality," *Vetus Testamentum* 15 [1965], 361–80, and see especially the introduction by Gene M. Tucker in Robinson's book on 7–13, which surveys the various criticisms of Robinson's view by various scholars). See also E. E. Ellis, *Prophecy and Hermeneutic in Early Christianity* (Grand Rapids: Eerdmans, 1978), 170–71, who discusses corporate solidarity or representation as an important presupposition in OT and NT studies.

5. Thus, e.g., Isa. 49:3–6 and the use of 49:6 in Luke 2:32; Acts 13:47; 26:23; note how Christ and the church fulfill what is prophesied of Israel in the OT; see also R. T. France, *Jesus and the Old Testament* (Grand Rapids: Baker, 1971), 50–60, 75; N. T. Wright, "The Paul of History and the Apostle of Faith," *Tyndale Bulletin* 29 (1978): 66–71, 87; H. K. LaRondelle, *The Israel of God in Prophecy* (Berrien Springs, MI: Andrews University Press, 1983); G. K. Beale, "The Old Testament Background of Reconciliation in 2 Corinthians 5–7 and Its Bearing on the Literary Problem of 2 Corinthians 6:14–7:1," *NTS* 35 (1989): 550–81; K. Snodgrass, "Use of the Old Testament in the New," in *The Right Doctrine from the Wrong Texts? Essays on the Use of the Old Testament in the New*, ed. G. K. Beale (Grand Rapids: Baker, 1994), 27.

6. C. H. Dodd, *According to the Scriptures* (London: Nisbet, 1952), 128, 133; and F. Foulkes, *The Acts of God: A Study of the Basis of Typology in the Old Testament*, Tyndale Monographs

4. The age of *eschatological fulfillment* has come in Christ.[7]
5. As a consequence of the preceding presupposition, it follows that the later parts of biblical history function as the broader context for interpreting earlier parts because they all have the same, ultimate divine author who inspires the various human authors. One deduction from this premise is that Christ is the goal toward which the OT pointed and is the end-time center of redemptive history, which is the *key to interpreting the earlier portions of the OT and its promises.*[8]

There is not space to argue substantially for the biblical support of these presuppositions, though we have provided brief support in the footnotes.[9] Other scholars working in this field have also recognized the viability of these assumptions.[10] However, not all scholars agree that the NT writers had all of these presuppositions. For example, some do not agree that Christ is viewed as representing the *true Israel* of the OT *and* the true Israel—the church—in the NT.[11] Some also would not accept the notion of inaugurated eschatology.[12] For the most part, however, since the 1980s scholars have generally accepted that the NT writers possessed these presuppositions.

It is within the framework of these five presuppositions that the whole OT was perceived as pointing to the new covenant eschatological age, both via direct prophecy and the indirect prophetic adumbration of Israel's history. This

(London: Tyndale, 1958); cf. the significance of the temporal merisms applied to God's—and Christ's—relation to history in Eccles. 3:1–11; Isa. 46:9–11; Rev. 1:8, 17; 21:6; 22:13; see likewise Rev. 1:4; 4:8; cf. Eph. 1:11.

7. See, e.g., Mark 1:15; Acts 2:17; 1 Cor. 10:11; Gal. 4:4; 1 Tim. 4:1; 2 Tim. 3:1; Heb. 1:2; 9:26; 1 Pet. 1:20; 2 Pet. 3:3; 1 John 2:18; Jude 18. Longenecker has a brief discussion of these first four presuppositions but does not relate them to the issue of contextual exegesis; cf. R. N. Longenecker, *Biblical Exegesis in the Apostolic Period* (Grand Rapids: Eerdmans, 1999), 76–79, 126–27, 134, 155; idem, "'Who Is the Prophet Talking About?' Some Reflections on the New Testament's Use of the Old," *Themelios* 13 (1987): 4–5.

8. On this, cf. 2 Cor. 1:20; Matt. 5:17; 13:11, 16–17; Luke 24:25–27, 32, 44–45; John 5:39; 20:9; Rom. 10:4.

9. On which see further Ellis, *Old Testament in Early Christianity*, 101–16.

10. Ibid.; Snodgrass, "Use of the Old Testament in the New," 36–41; Longenecker, *Biblical Exegesis*, 76–79, 126–27, 134, 155; D. L. Bock, "Scripture Citing Scripture," in *Interpreting the New Testament Text*, edited by D. L. Bock and B. M. Fanning (Wheaton: Crossway, 2006), 261–64, though Bock does not include presupposition 2 (Christ and the church as true Israel) nor presupposition 5 (canonical contextual interpretation as the key to interpreting the NT and Christ as the key to interpreting the OT).

11. For instance, scholars holding a dispensational view (and some holding a progressive dispensational view) and others believe that to identify Christ with Israel would be to hold a "replacement theology," thus denying any future nationalist hopes for the salvation of Israel as a nation—a position they resist. Yet one can hold to the notion of Christ as true Israel and still have room for a hope that the majority of ethnic Jews will be saved at some point in the future. Any such salvation would be in their identification with Christ as true Israel.

12. In mind here are primarily classic, traditional dispensationalists.

latter point is especially significant: OT history was understood as containing historical patterns that foreshadowed the period of the eschaton. Consequently, the nation Israel, its kings, prophets, priests, and its significant redemptive episodes compose the essential ingredients of this sacred history. This is what has been referred to earlier in the book as "typology," which we have earlier defined as the study of correspondences between earlier and later escalated events, persons, institutions, and so forth within the historical framework of biblical revelation, and which sometimes from a retrospective viewpoint are perceived to have a prophetic function. Typology is sometimes faulted for being not in line with original OT meanings because it sometimes refers to purely historical events as being prophetically "fulfilled" (cf. the introductory *plēroō* formula) when they appear not to be intended as prophecies from the OT author's perspective. But such an approach is understandable in view of its foundational assumption that history is an interrelated unity and that God has designed the earlier parts to correspond and point to the latter parts, especially to events that have happened in the age of *eschatological fulfillment* in Christ (see presuppositions 3–5). Consequently, the concept of prophetic fulfillment should not be limited to fulfillment of direct verbal prophecies from the OT but broadened to include also an indication of the "redemptive-historical relationship of the new, climactic revelation of God in Christ to the preparatory, incomplete revelation to and through Israel."[13]

The broad redemptive-historical perspective of these assumptions was the dominant framework within which Jesus and his followers thought, serving as an ever-present heuristic guide to the OT. The matrix of these five perspectives, especially the last four, is the lens through which the NT authors interpreted OT passages. Consideration of the immediate literary context of OT verses, which is what most interpreters affirm as an essential part of the historical-grammatical method, should therefore be supplemented by the canonical literary context, especially in the light of the last presupposition. In this respect, we need to consider that the NT may quote an earlier OT passage but understand it in the light of the way that passage has been interpretatively developed later in the OT canon. Sometimes an earlier text may undergo interpretative development by several subsequent OT texts, so that the canonical trajectory of that development may well need to be kept in mind in understanding how the NT understands the earlier text being cited.

When these five presuppositions are related closely to the NT's interpretative approach, they provide a satisfying explanation for C. H. Dodd's observations and conclusions in his book *According to the Scriptures*, especially accounting for why the NT does not focus on verses independent of their contexts. The

13. D. J. Moo, "The Problem of *Sensus Plenior*," in *Hermeneutics, Authority, and Canon*, ed. D. A. Carson and J. D. Woodbridge (Grand Rapids: Zondervan / Academie Books, 1986), 191, who cites others such as Moule, Banks, Metzger, Meier, and Carson in support.

NT writers' selection of OT texts was not random or capricious or out of line with the original OT meaning but determined by this wider, overriding perspective, which views redemptive history as unified by an omnipotent and wise design. Throughout this design are expressed the unchanging principles of faith in God, God's faithfulness in fulfilling promises, the rebellion of the unbelieving, God's judgment of them, and his glory. Therefore the NT authors had an emphatic concern for more overarching historical and canonical patterns or for significant persons (e.g., prophets, priests, and kings), institutions, and events that were essential constituents of such patterns. Such an emphasis was to a significant extent facilitated by the belief that Christ and the church now represent true Israel so that it was attractive to see various segments and patterns of Israel's history from the OT as recapitulated in Christ and the church in the NT. This then was a holistic perspective guiding the writers away from concentrating on exegetically or theologically insignificant minutiae in passages and directing them to quote individual references as signposts to the broader redemptive-historical theme(s) from the immediate and larger OT context of which they were a part. Is this not the most likely explanation for the earlier-observed phenomena in the NT of so few identical quotations but different citations from the same segments of the OT?

In addition, changed applications of the OT in general, whether or not typology is involved, do not necessitate the conclusion that these passages have been misinterpreted. For example, Matthew applies to Jesus what the OT intended for Israel (e.g., Matt. 2:4–22),[14] and Paul applies to the church what was intended for Israel (e.g., Rom. 9:24–26). Some believe that the NT's affirmation that a prophecy about Israel is fulfilled in the Messiah or in the church is clearly not in line with the original meaning of those prophecies. What should be challenged in these two kinds of apparently different applications (Matthew and Paul), however, is not their interpretation of the OT but the validity of the above-mentioned presuppositional framework through which they interpreted the OT, especially the assumption that Christ corporately represents true Israel and that all who identify with him by faith are considered part of true Israel. If the validity of these presuppositions is granted, then the viability of their interpretation of the OT in the two above categories of usage must also be viewed as plausible.

Therefore changes of application need not mean a *disregard* for OT context; this is not a logically necessary deduction. It seems likely that some confuse disregard for context with change of application. Assuming the viability of the presuppositions, although the new applications are technically different, they nevertheless stay within the conceptual bounds of the OT's contextual meaning, so that what results often is an extended reference to or application

14. See R. T. France's good discussion of this context in "The Formula-Quotations of Matthew 2 and the Problem of Communication," *New Testament Studies* 27 (1980–81): 233–51.

of a principle that is inherent to the OT text.[15] When a case-by-case study is made, our recognition of such presuppositions among the NT writers nevertheless helps us to see *how* their interpretations could have been contextual from their particular perspective and *why* they would have been sensitive to respecting contexts.[16] Yet there will always remain some enigmatic passages that are hard to understand under any perspectival reading.

Even when there is use of the OT with no apparent interest in prophetic fulfillment, there appears to be a redemptive-historical rationale at work behind the scenes. For example, when an OT reference is utilized only for the perceptible purpose of making an analogy, an idea in the OT context is usually in mind as the primary characteristic or principle applied to the NT situation. These comparisons almost always broadly retain an essential association with the OT context and convey principles of continuity between OT and NT even though they are handled with creative freedom. This is true even in the Apocalypse,[17] which is often unfortunately seen as creatively handling the OT in a hermeneutically uncontrolled manner.[18]

Nevertheless, it would be possible to hold these presuppositions and still interpret the OT noncontextually, as some scholars do.[19] Along these lines, some scholars, especially fueled by postmodern concerns, apparently believe that the NT writers' presuppositions distorted their interpretation of the OT since these were new presuppositions, foreign to the OT, that were created by the early Christian community in the light of the coming of Christ. Accordingly, reading these foreign presuppositions into the OT skewed the original meaning of the OT. What is often not acknowledged, however, is that every one of the above five presuppositions has its roots in the OT (on which see the footnotes earlier in this chapter for the sampling of biblical evidence undergirding these presuppositions, including the OT). Even the last presupposition about the Christ-oriented design of the OT is anticipated in the messianic strands of

15. For examples of these kinds of changes of application, see France, *Jesus and the Old Testament*; G. K. Beale, "The Use of the Old Testament in Revelation," in *It Is Written: Scripture Citing Scripture; Festschrift in Honour of Barnabas Lindars*, ed. D. A. Carson and H. Williamson (Cambridge: Cambridge University Press, 1988), 318–36; idem, "Background of Reconciliation."

16. Again, for numerous examples of inductive case studies where this can be argued, see the literature supporting a contextual approach cited throughout G. K. Beale, "Did Jesus and His Followers Preach the Right Doctrine from the Wrong Texts? An Examination of the Presuppositions of Jesus' and the Apostles' Exegetical Method," *Themelios* 14 (1989): 89–96.

17. For examples of this see Beale, "Old Testament in Revelation," 321–32; J. Cambier, "Les images de l'Ancien Testament dans l'Apocalypse de saint Jean," *La nouvelle revue théologique* (1955): 114–21; A. Vanhoye, "L'utilisation du livre d'Ezéchiel dans l'Apocalypse," *Biblica* 43 (1962): 462–67; idem, "L'utilizzazione del Deutero-Isaia nell'Apocalisse di Giovanni," *Euntes docete* 27 (1974): 322–39.

18. See, e.g., L. A. Vos, *The Synoptic Traditions in the Apocalypse* (Kampen: J. H. Kok, 1965), 21–37, 41.

19. On this, e.g., see Longenecker's works cited in nn. 7 and 10 above.

the OT beginning with Genesis 3:15 and developed, for example, in 49:9–10; Numbers 24:17–19; Psalms 2; 89; Isaiah 42; 49; 53; Zechariah 9:9–10; 12:10.

In addition, it is true that what makes the NT use of the OT different from other early Jewish uses of the OT is its unique presuppositions, though there was a significant overlap of presuppositions with some early Jewish movements (e.g., Qumran, which held in qualified ways to at least the first four presuppositions).[20] The reason for the similarity of presuppositions among some of these Jewish groups is that they too modeled their interpretative approach on that of the OT itself. Thus it is difficult to say that the NT community's presuppositions were radically new and the result of their own unique socially constructed mind-set, which had its origin within the first-century Christian context. Rather, these presuppositions go far back into the OT and span hundreds of years.

Thus the NT community's presuppositions are rooted in the OT. For instance, the NT authors assumed they were living in the age of the eschaton, partly on the basis that the OT prophesied that the messianic age was to be an "eschatological" period (e.g., Gen. 49:1, 9–10; Num. 24:14–19; Hosea 3:5). In addition, the OT also reflects the assumption that history is unified by a divine plan, so that earlier biblical history was designed to point typologically to later parts of biblical history.[21] It is striking, for example, that the well-known Suffering Servant prophecy of Isaiah 53 is itself a typological expectation of an anticipated second Moses, who was to do everything and more than the first Moses.[22] Therefore Matthew's understanding of Jesus as a typological fulfillment of the first Moses is in keeping with anticipations already embedded within the prophetic expectations of the OT itself and in Judaism.[23] Even the notion that Jesus corporately represents true Israel is likely

20. For example, Qumran held to corporate solidarity and that they were the true Israel but, of course, they did not believe Christ and the church were true Israel (first and second presuppositions above). They also held to inaugurated eschatology but not that the latter days had begun in Christ (fourth presupposition).

21. For discussion of the presence of typology as an interpretative method and hermeneutical presupposition in the OT, see Foulkes, *Acts of God*; G. von Rad, *Old Testament Theology* (New York: Harper & Row, 1965), 2:323–35, 365–74, 384–85; cf. 2:367: "Typological thinking [is] . . . one of the essential presuppositions of the origin of prophetic prediction"; L. Goppelt, *Typos* (Grand Rapids: Eerdmans, 1982), 38–41; M. Fishbane, *Biblical Interpretation in Ancient Israel* (Oxford: Clarendon, 1985), esp. 350–79; D. C. Allison, *The New Moses: A Matthean Typology* (Minneapolis: Fortress, 1993), 11–95, who includes typological uses in Judaism; so does S.-Y. Kim, *The Origin of Paul's Gospel* (Grand Rapids: Eerdmans, 1982), 187; G. P. Hugenberger, "The Servant of the Lord in the 'Servant Songs' of Isaiah," in *The Lord's Anointed*, ed. P. E. Satterthwaite, R. S. Hess, and G. J. Wenham (Grand Rapids: Baker, 1995), 105–39; D. A. Garrett, "The Ways of God: Reenactment and Reversal in Hosea" (his inaugural lecture as professor of Old Testament at Gordon-Conwell Theological Seminary, South Hamilton, MA, Fall 1998; on VHS cassette at the seminary; to be published); Garrett develops Hosea's typological use of Genesis.

22. So Hugenberger, "Servant of the Lord," 105–39.

23. So Allison, *The New Moses*; cf. Kim, *Origin of Paul's Gospel*, 187–92.

and partly due not only to the notion that Israel's past kings represented and summed up the nation in themselves in various ways but also that the same was true of Moses and was likewise expected to be true of the Servant whom Moses typologically anticipated.[24]

The OT rootedness of the NT's presuppositions makes it more difficult to say that the NT's interpretative assumptions distort the meaning of OT texts. In this respect, the authors of both Testaments are part of a broadly related interpretative community that shared the same general worldview and continued to develop earlier meanings with comparable hermeneutical perspectives as time went on.[25]

Conclusion

Some interpreters will disagree with my positive link between the NT's hermeneutical presuppositions and the basic contextual understanding of the various OT texts that NT writers interpret. Nevertheless, I believe that the presuppositions discussed in this chapter aid in understanding that the NT's interpretations of the OT fall in line to varying degrees with the contextual meaning of the OT texts themselves and with legitimate extensions and applications of the meaning of OT texts. This is also evident from recognizing that the NT writers were absorbed and soaked in the OT. In interpreting the OT with these presuppositions, the NT writers were following the model of the most grand redemptive-historical interpreter: Jesus Christ.

24. So Hugenberger, "Servant of the Lord," 111, 121, 131.

25. See N. T. Wright, *The New Testament and the People of God* (Minneapolis: Fortress, 1992) as well as his *Jesus and the Victory of God* (Minneapolis: Fortress, 1996), for an explanation of this shared worldview common to the OT, early Judaism, Jesus, and the early Christian community.

6

The Relevance of Jewish Backgrounds for the Study of the Old Testament in the New

A Survey of the Sources

This chapter elaborates a part of chapter 3 that sets forth a ninefold approach to interpreting the OT in the NT. The fourth part of that approach is to survey Judaism for the use of the particular OT text under focus. We saw there that the study of such texts involves three steps: (1) collect the references in Judaism and study the discussions of the specific OT passage being examined, (2) note any trends or patterns of similar or antithetical employments of the OT reference within the Jewish literature itself, (3) compare these Jewish uses to the manner in which the NT authors use the OT text. Are the uses similar, different, or antithetical? Do these Jewish references shed any interpretative light on the NT use?

The purpose here is not to repeat what was said above in that earlier section but to do two additional things. The first purpose is to provide an annotated bibliography of Jewish sources[1] designed to enable the researcher to discover whether Judaism refers to the same OT reference under focus in the NT and to examine how that reference is being interpreted by the various Jewish sources in their contexts. The second purpose of this chapter is to give an illustration showing the relevance of studying how Judaism uses the same OT passages from which the NT draws, especially to see how such usage may shed interpretative light on the NT employment.

1. I am grateful to my former teaching assistants Ben Gladd, Dan Brendsel, and Matt Dudreck for helping in the compilation of this bibliography.

An Annotated Bibliography of Jewish Sources: Discovering How Judaism Used Particular Old Testament Passages

The precise purpose of the following annotated bibliography is to aid researchers in discovering where and how Jewish writers understood and interpreted OT texts to which the NT also cites or alludes. The focus is on Jewish writers prior to, contemporaneous with, and relatively soon after the first century, though sources on latter Judaism will also be noted.

An Overview of the Three Basic Steps in Searching How Judaism Uses Specific Old Testament Passages

1. Consult background commentaries on key NT passages.
2. Consult major New Testament commentaries (e.g., ICC, WBC, NIGTC, BECNT, NICNT, Hermeneia, and various other major commentaries not in a series).
3. Consult primary sources in Jewish literature by utilizing topical and especially Scripture indexes of these sources in English translation.

See C. A. Evans, *Ancient Texts for New Testament Studies: A Guide to the Background Literature* (Peabody, MA: Hendrickson, 2005), 10–255, for an outstanding and more in-depth thumbnail guide of each of the eight areas of Judaism (below) in this annotated bibliography, to be elaborated on in the following pages. Evans mainly covers a summary of the primary works in each category, the main texts of these works, their approximate dates, a select bibliography of each, and various themes related to each. Likewise, similar to Evans's work, for a guidebook of the same areas see Emil Schürer, *The History of the Jewish People in the Age of Jesus Christ*, vols. 1, 2, 3.1, and 3.2, revised and edited by G. Vermes, F. Millar, and M. Black (Edinburgh: T&T Clark, 1973–87). Also, students should use the abbreviations for the Jewish literature cited in this chapter as found in *The SBL Handbook of Style* (Peabody, MA: Hendrickson, 1999).

The remainder of this section will elaborate on the three above steps in relation to the eight areas of Jewish literature. This will be followed by a brief survey of early Christian literature.

Step 1: Consult Background Commentaries on Key New Testament Passages.

The First Sources to Consult

In this search, the initial sources to look at are background commentaries on the NT. These are not "commentaries" on the NT in the usual sense of the word, since they do not comment verse by verse on the book being covered. Rather, these background commentaries discuss particular verses only when these verses are considered by the commentary writers to have a Jewish or Greco-Roman background. Such commentaries are simple to use: the reader merely looks up the chapter and verse of the NT book under focus to see if there is discussion of any background. If there is discussion, the important observations to make are the primary sources referred to in the discussion. The researcher should pay attention to how the commentators understand these sources and their relevance for the use of the OT in the NT passage at hand, but most of all, the primary sources in Judaism should be written down. Then the researcher looks up these references in the Jewish primary source documents in which they occur in order to determine what they mean in their original contexts. Do any of these Jewish references cite or allude to the OT?

If any of the Jewish sources refer to the same OT text as in the NT focus passage, how do they refer to the OT passage? How do they interpret and use the OT passage? How do these uses compare with the NT use? Do they provide insight on how the particular NT passage uses the same OT passage? Do they provide an interpretative perspective that gives us a clue to what the NT author may have in mind, if it is along the same lines as the Jewish references? This may be a perspective that we may never have thought of unless earlier we were exposed to the Jewish uses. These primary source documents will be elaborated on further directly below. Do these Jewish uses tend to employ the relevant OT passage in a diametrically opposite manner from the NT writer? Such antithetical uses may also shed light on how the NT is using the OT. Sometimes it is possible that the NT writer may even be intentionally contrasting his understanding of the OT with that of a Jewish understanding. If so, this may well show how the Christian writer understood some of the unique aspects of the early Jewish-Christian movement in contrast to other sectors of Judaism. If one finds a use of an OT passage in Judaism that is given a specific unusual interpretation and virtually the same unusual interpretation is found in the NT, it may mean one of two things: either the NT writer has been influenced to some degree by his acquaintance with the Jewish use or, if found in several Jewish sources, it could be a reflection of a common understanding of the OT current in the first century.

In addition, it is always possible that similar uses of the OT are due to Jewish and Christian writers making their own independent interpretations of the same text because separately they observed the same clues in the OT context itself. Another possibility is that both NT writers and early Jewish interpreters may well have patterned their interpretation of the OT after the model of the way later OT writers interpreted earlier OT passages. Consequently, the respective Jewish and Christian interpretations of the OT passage might end up being very similar but independent of one another.

Finally, it is also always possible that one may find Jewish references to OT texts that occur in the NT but which have no apparent bearing on a better understanding of the NT text.

The researcher should also follow the same above procedure of observation and evaluation of Jewish and NT references to identical OT passages in the following sections concerning primary sources in early (step 2) and late Judaism (step 3), which we will discuss after surveying the "background commentaries" (step 1) directly below. Recall from chapter 3 that references in early Judaism (second century BC–second century AD) are more relevant than those in later Judaism (third century AD–sixth century AD). It is more likely that a first-century NT writer could have been familiar with or influenced by early Jewish references and would not have had access to interpretative traditions that were created after the first century AD. Nevertheless, later Jewish references are still important since, like early references and even modern commentaries, they can function as commentaries, possibly providing interpretative insight to the meaning that a NT writer has given an OT text. Furthermore, later Jewish references may retain older interpretative traditions that go back to the first century, though not preserved in the earlier Jewish literature that we have, and therefore may still have relevance for NT interpretations of the OT.

The Most Important "Background" Commentaries for Step 1

Boring, M. E., K. Berger, and C. Colpe, eds. *Hellenistic Commentary to the New Testament*. Nashville: Abingdon, 1995.

Braun, H., ed. *Qumran und das Neue Testament*. 2 vols. Tübingen: Mohr Siebeck, 1966.

Chilton, B., D. Bock, D. M. Gurtner, J. Neusner, L. H. Schiffman, and D. Oden, eds. *A Comparative Handbook to the Gospel of Mark: Comparisons with the Pseudepigrapha, the Qumran Scrolls, and Rabbinic Literature*. The New Testament Gospels in Their Judaic Context 1. Boston: Brill, 2009.

Instone-Brewer, D. *Traditions of the Rabbis from the Era of the New Testament*. Vol. 1, *Prayer and Agriculture*. Grand Rapids: Eerdmans, 2004.

———. *Traditions of the Rabbis from the Era of the New Testament*. Vol. 2A, *Feasts and Sabbaths: Passover and Atonement*. Grand Rapids: Eerdmans, 2011.

Keener, C. S. *The IVP Bible Background Commentary: New Testament*. Downers Grove, IL: InterVarsity, 1993. Unfortunately, this commentary typically does not contain primary source references to either the Jewish or Greco-Roman sources on which so many of the discussions are based. Nevertheless, when there are discussions of background, it should alert the student to try to find the primary sources on which these discussions are based in order to evaluate them and to see if any of them represent Jewish interpretations of the OT.

Lachs, S. T., ed. *A Rabbinic Commentary on the New Testament: The Gospels of Matthew, Mark, and Luke*. Hoboken, NJ: Ktav, 1987.

Lightfoot, J., ed. *A Commentary on the New Testament from the Talmud and Hebraica: Matthew–Corinthians*. 1859. Repr., 4 vols. Grand Rapids: Baker, 1979. Lightfoot uses archaic references when citing the Talmuds, so the researcher may need to use some ingenuity to trace these references.

Strack, H., and P. Billerbeck, [Str-B] eds. *Kommentar zum Neuen Testament aus Talmud und Midrasch*. 5 vols. in 6. Munich: Beck, 1922–56, http://trove.nla.gov.au/work/797911. This can be a good source for finding references, though one needs to keep in mind some of its shortcomings.[2]

Strecker, G., and U. Schnelle, eds. *Neuer Wettstein*. 3 vols. New York: de Gruyter, 1996.

Wettstein, J., ed. *Novum Testamentum Graecum*. 1751–52. Repr., 4 vols. Graz: Akademische Druck- & Verlagsanstalt, 1962.

Some of the background commentaries (above) are written in German (Braun, Str-B, Strecker/Schnelle) or Latin (Wettstein). Those who do not know German or Latin can still benefit from these sources. One can merely scan the relevant section of the background commentary and write down the primary source references.[3] Then look up those primary source references in order to evaluate whether they are relevant background material for the use of the OT in the NT passage under focus.

Step 2: Consult Major New Testament Commentaries (e.g., ICC, WBC, NIGTC, BECNT, NICNT, Hermeneia, and various other major commentaries not in a series).

This step is so basic that not much explanation is needed. After looking up the NT passage in which the OT reference occurs, one should be alert to any passages in Judaism that are adduced as parallels. If there are some, then these Jewish references need to be looked up in the context of the Jewish source in which they occur to see how they are being used. Sometimes commentaries will list a few lines of primary sources in Judaism as parallel in some way with the NT passage of focus but will not discuss these references. The student should look at all of these references in their original Jewish literary context. Also, one may discover Jewish sources cited by a NT commentary as parallels

2. See, e.g., the evaluative comments by S. Sandmel, "Parallelomania," *Journal of Biblical Literature* 81 (1962): 8–11.

3. Yet one must try to achieve an initial familiarity with the German and Latin abbreviations of biblical books used in the above German and Latin background commentaries by consulting a German and Latin Bible (e.g., the Vulgate), and then the German and Latin abbreviations of these books will become self-evident. The German and Latin abbreviations of Jewish works in the above commentaries usually can be relatively easy to decipher, though the abbreviations in *Kommentar zum Neuen Testament aus Talmud und Midrasch* (Str-B) can sometimes be difficult. Therefore a key to many of these abbreviations is added at the end of this chapter.

to a NT passage where no OT allusion has heretofore been recognized. These sources might include reference to OT passages, which might be a tip-off that there is an OT allusion in the NT passage.

Step 3: Consult Primary Sources in Jewish Literature by Utilizing Topical and Especially Scripture Indexes of These Sources in English Translation.

The following are the major primary sources in Judaism[4] that should be consulted for possible background to various NT passages: (1) Septuagint (LXX), (2) the OT Apocrypha, (3) the Pseudepigrapha, (4) Qumran (DSS), (5) Philo, (6) Josephus, (7) targums, and (8) rabbinic literature (Mishnah, Tosefta, Talmuds, midrashim). The first six sources represent the literature of early Judaism, though some of the targums are also early, as is the Mishnah (the basis of the later Talmud). Though probably compiled in about the second century AD, the Mishnah represents traditions going back at least to the first century AD. The remainder of the rabbinic literature extends from the third century AD on to about the twelfth century AD. These sources can be found in many seminary or university libraries, and they are increasingly being put online. First, in English editions the student should look up the primary source references that have been gleaned from the above background and NT commentaries. Second, most of the English translations of the Jewish primary sources listed below have Scripture indexes. The researcher should check the OT reference of focus in the index. If it is listed, consult the passage or page in the English edition of the primary source to which the index directs you. You then can evaluate the reference according to the guidelines explained at the conclusion of step 1 above.

The following is an elaboration of the eight Jewish sources listed above.

The Septuagint (LXX)

The Septuagint is the Greek version of the OT, including the Apocrypha. Its translation began approximately in the mid-third century BC and extended on up to the early first century AD. It is very important to check how the Greek OT translates the Hebrew of the OT in the NT passage being studied. The LXX is the earliest translation of the Hebrew OT, and in those places where it paraphrases, it often represents an interpretation. In this respect, the LXX is the earliest commentary on the Hebrew OT. After checking, one may find that the Septuagint has not given a "literal" translation (as far as that is possible) and that the NT author has actually quoted from or alluded to the Septuagintal version and not the Hebrew. Then we must ask, why has the Septuagint been cited instead of the Hebrew? Several answers to this question are possible. Perhaps the Septuagint was merely the only translation of the OT of which

4. By "Judaism" is meant "postbiblical Judaism," which refers to those Jewish works written after the Hebrew and Aramaic OT.

the intended readers were aware or of which the writer was apparently primarily aware (as possibly, e.g., in the case of the book of Hebrews). Or it may be that the NT writer refers to the Greek version because the interpretation of the Hebrew that it gives is the point that he wants to make.

Particular Septuagintal Sources of Interest for Old-in-the-New Studies

The standard edition of the Septuagint for the research student is Alfred Rahlfs, ed., *Septuaginta*, Editio altera: revised and corrected by Robert Hanhart (Stuttgart: Deutche Bibelgesellschaft, 2006). This edition presents a semieclectic text that is mainly based on the three major uncials (Siniaticus [א], Alexandrinus [A], and Vaticanus [B]) together with incidental concern with other manuscripts and Septuagintal traditions (e.g., the rescensions (or translations) of Aquila [α], Theodotion [Θ], and Symmachus [σ]).

Researchers needing help with the English translation of the Greek OT should consult the Greek-English parallel by Lancelot C. L. Brenton. Originally published in 1870 by Samuel Bagster and Sons (London) under the title *The Septuagint Version of the Old Testament and Apocrypha: With an English Translation, and Various Readings and Critical Notes*, it was reprinted under the same title by Zondervan (Grand Rapids) in 1971, and then later under the title *The Septuagint with Apocrypha* by Hendrickson (Peabody, MA) in 1986. Brenton's edition is based on Codex Vaticanus. The most recent English translation of the Septuagint is Albert Pietersma and Benjamin G. Wright, eds., *A New English Translation of the Septuagint* (*NETS*) (New York: Oxford University Press, 2007), available for free download or use online, http://ccat.sas.upenn.edu/nets/edition/.

Special attention should be paid also to the following two sources:

Brooke, A. E., N. McLean, and H. Thackeray, eds. *The Old Testament in Greek: According to the Text of Codex Vaticanus, Supplemented from Other Uncial Manuscripts, with a Critical Apparatus Containing the Variants of the Chief Ancient Authorities for the Text of the Septuagint*. 3 vols. in 9. Cambridge: Cambridge University Press, 1940.

Septuaginta: Vetus Testamentum Graecum. Auctoritate Academiae Scientiarum Göttingensis editum. 16 vols. Göttingen: Vandenhoeck & Ruprecht, 1931–.

These last two sources are the best for laying out the textual variants for every verse in the OT and apocryphal books that they cover. They are necessary sources to consult, since the Rahlfs edition has only a very select textual apparatus at the bottom of each page. The *Septuaginta: Vetus Testamentum Graecum* has a more recent and updated textual apparatus than *The Old Testament in Greek: According to the Text of Codex Vaticanus*. The latter source has the apparatus for only Genesis through Ruth. The body of the text follows that of Codex Vaticanus, and the textual apparatus is presented at the bottom of each page. The body of each page of text in the *Septuaginta: Vetus Testamentum Graecum* presents what it considers the "eclectic" text of the Septuagint, and then the apparatus is presented at the bottom of each page. One of the hurdles that researchers must jump over is to learn the symbols (or sigla) that are used in these two textual apparatuses. The *Old Testament in Greek: According to the Text of Codex Vaticanus* has an explanation of each symbol at the beginning of each volume.[5] The *Septuaginta: Vetus Testamentum Graecum* also has an explanation of each symbol in each introductory volume, but the explanation is in German. For those who do not know German, there is a partial explanation of both the *Old Testament in Greek: According to the Text of Codex Vaticanus* and *Septuaginta: Vetus Testamentum Graecum* in K. Jobes and M. Silva, *Introduction to the Septuagint* (Grand Rapids: Baker Academic, 2000), 137–45. In addition, *Accordance Bible Software* (Altamonte Springs, FL: Oaktree Software, 1994–2011) also has a module that shows the variants in both the *Old Testament in Greek: According to the Text of Codex Vaticanus* (presently offering only Genesis through Ruth) and the *Septuaginta: Vetus Testamentum Graecum* (presently only Genesis through Deuteronomy)[6] and an explanation of many of the symbols (manuscript abbreviations and Latin phrases) in the textual apparatus. The *Logos Bible Software* (Bellingham, WA: Logos Research Systems, 1992–2011) also contains the entire apparatus of the *Septuaginta: Vetus Testamentum Graecum*.

These two textual apparatuses are important because each variant represents a different manuscript reading (or readings found in several or a group of manuscripts); if early enough, it might be a reading with which a NT author may well have been familiar and to which he may have alluded. Even later Septuagint manuscripts might contain readings that were present in earlier manuscripts. Also, the introductions to the Septuagint cited directly below have significant sections concerning the recensions of Theodotion, Aquila, and Symmachus, both with respect to dating and their relevance for pre-first-century and first-century readings. Yet one must always be aware that Christian scribes copying the Greek OT may have introduced readings from the NT into it.

General Sources Helpful for a Better Understanding of the Septuagint

Septuagintal studies have so proliferated over the past twenty-five years that the bibliography is massive. The sources listed below are only some of the most basic sources and tools to aid in Septuagint studies.

5. Vol. 1 of this work introduces most of the symbols used in that volume and the others; then later volumes introduce only sigla that represent manuscripts first used in that particular volume but do not repeat the majority of symbols found in the introduction to vol. 1.

6. Oaktree plans to keep adding more to these two apparatuses.

Hatch, E., and H. Redpath, eds. *Concordance to the Septuagint and the Other Greek Versions of the Old Testament: Including the Apocryphal Books*. 3 vols. Oxford: Clarendon, 1897 with a supplement volume published in 1906.

Jellicoe, S. *The Septuagint and Modern Study*. Oxford: Clarendon, 1968.

Jobes, K., and M. Silva. *An Introduction to the Septuagint*. Grand Rapids: Baker Academic, 2000.

Kalvesmaki, J. Septuagint Online: Resources for the Study of the Septuagint and Old Greek Translations of the Hebrew Scriptures, http://www.kalvesmaki.com/LXX/. Copyright 2011.

Lust, J., E. Eynkel, and K. Hauspie, eds. *A Greek-English Lexicon of the Septuagint*, rev. ed. Stuttgart: Deutsche Bibelgesellschaft, 2003.

Marcos, N. F. *The Septuagint in Context*. Boston: Brill, 2000.

Muraoka, T. *A Greek-English Lexicon of the Septuagint*. Louvain: Peeters, 2009.

Reider, J., ed. *An Index to Aquila*. Leiden: Brill, 1966.

Taylor, B. *The Analytical Lexicon to the Septuagint: A Complete Parsing Guide*. Grand Rapids: Zondervan, 1994.

Kalvesmaki, among other things, provides a thumbnail sketch of what is available in texts and translations of the Septuagint, offers his own brief bibliography of important works on the Septuagint, and lists several bibliographies of books, articles, and book reviews, including sources on the relation of the Septuagint to the NT. Additional relevant bibliography may be found in the introductions of Jellicoe, Jobes/Silva, and Marcos, also listed above.

The OT Apocrypha

"Apocrypha" means "hidden away, secret." The OT Apocrypha is comprised of about fifteen books (or perhaps fourteen since the Epistle of Jeremiah is sometimes incorporated into Baruch). Some consider these works to be hidden from the unwise but reserved for the mature and spiritually wise. Accordingly, Russian Orthodox, Greek Orthodox, Roman Catholic, and Coptic churches accept most of these books as authoritative or divinely inspired. Others believe these books are to be considered "hidden" because they contain so many false teachings, which should not be disseminated. Protestants do not accept these books as part of the canon.[7] It is true that there are some theologically aberrant notions in the Apocrypha, yet in many ways this collection of writings tries to develop parts of the OT in ways that may serve as helpful background to the NT.

7. This paragraph summarizes C. A. Evans, *Ancient Texts for New Testament Studies: A Guide to the Background Literature* (Peabody, MA: Hendrickson, 2005), 9.

The text of the OT Apocrypha is found in the Septuagint. The books in the Apocrypha were written from the second century BC up to and including the first century AD. Everything said about the Septuagint above therefore applies to the study of the Apocrypha. Among other English translations of the OT Apocrypha, in addition to the English translations of the Septuagint cited above, are these: B. M. Metzger and R. Murphy, eds., *The New Oxford Annotated Apocrypha* (New York: Oxford University Press, 1991); the *New Revised Version Bible* (New York: Oxford University Press, 1989); and H. F. D. Sparks, ed., *The Apocryphal Old Testament* (Oxford: Clarendon, 1984). A good introductory overview of the Apocrypha may be found in D. A. deSilva, *Introducing the Apocrypha* (Grand Rapids: Baker Academic, 2002).

How does the Apocrypha understand the same OT references also found in the NT? Does it shed any light on the NT usage?

The Pseudepigrapha

The Pseudepigrapha are writings that range from the second century BC to the fifth and sixth centuries AD and later. Typically these works are attributed to some of the great and famous figures of the OT, including writers of OT books. They are predominately Jewish writings, though some contain Christian interpolations, and a few are predominately Christian works expanded from an earlier, smaller core of Jewish compositions.[8] These works contain genres of apocalyptic, poetry, wisdom, rewritten OT history, midrash, and other kinds of literature. There is much in these works that develops passages and thinking of the OT. How do the various pseudepigraphic texts understand the identical OT references also found in the NT? Do they shed any light on their use in the NT?

Particular Pseudepigraphic Sources of Interest for Old-in-the-New Studies

Charlesworth, J. H., ed. *The Old Testament Pseudepigrapha*. 2 vols. Garden City, NY: Doubleday, 1983–85. This is the most important source for pseudepigraphic studies in examining the use of the OT in the NT. In the right and left margins and in the footnotes are lists of allusions to and parallels with the OT. These have all now been conveniently collected by Steve Delamarter in *A Scripture Index to Charlesworth's "The Old Testament Pseudepigrapha"* (New York: Sheffield Academic Press, 2002), which in one volume contains Scripture indexes to both volumes of Charlesworth's work. Also, the Online Critical

8. See J. R. Davila, "The Old Testament Pseudepigrapha as Background to the New Testament," *Expository Times* 117 (2005): 53–57, who proposes criteria for somewhat limiting what are normally considered to be pseudepigraphic works of Jewish origin, some of which he considers possibly to be of Christian provenance. See also R. Bauckham, *The Jewish World around the New Testament* (Grand Rapids: Baker Academic, 2010), 461–83, who reviews the issues surrounding the provenance of the Pseudepigrapha and evaluates and qualifies Davila's views.

Pseudepigrapha may be found at http://www.ocp.tyndale.ca. This source gives the texts of the pseudepigrapha in their earliest extant languages.

General Sources Helpful for a Better Understanding of the Pseudepigrapha

Charles, R. H., ed. *The Apocrypha and Pseudepigrapha of the Old Testament*. 2 vols. Oxford: Clarendon, 1913. This is dated but still helpful.

Charlesworth, J. H. *The Pseudepigrapha and Modern Research*. Missoula, MT: Scholars Press, 1976.

Collins, J. J., and D. C. Harlow, eds. *The Eerdmans Dictionary of Early Judaism*. Grand Rapids: Eerdmans, 2010. This source covers not only the Pseudepigrapha but also other aspects of early Judaism (e.g., LXX, Qumran, the Apocrypha).

Davila, J. R. Pseudepigrapha Bibliographies, http://www.marquette.edu/maqom/intertestbiblio.pdf.

Denis, A.-M. *Concordance grecque de pseudépigraphes d'Ancien Testament*. Louvain-la-Neuve: Université catholique de Louvain, Institute orientaliste; Leiden: Brill, 1987.

DiTommaso, L. *A Bibliography of Pseudepigrapha Research, 1850–1999*. Journal for the Study of the Pseudepigrapha: Supplement Series 39. Sheffield: Sheffield Academic Press, 2001.

This last bibliography is based on the one by Davila (above), but there is a sizable expansion of secondary literature references and a more usable reorganized table of contents.

Qumran (DSS)

The Dead Sea Scrolls were discovered in 1947–56. The writings date from the late second century BC up to about AD 69. Many of them were sectarian documents written for the Essene community itself. For example, among other things, there are writings to regulate its order, to reflect in various ways on its separation from the Jerusalem religious establishment, and to explain its identification as the true Israel of God, beginning to fulfill the eschatological prophecies of the OT. Many OT texts are included in the Qumran library. Like the Pseudepigrapha, these works contain genres of apocalyptic, poetry, wisdom, rewritten OT history, pseudepigrapha, targums, midrash, and other kinds of literature. There is also much in these works that develops passages and the thought of the OT. It is very important for the student to compare the Hebrew OT of Qumran with the Masoretic Hebrew text (MT) to see if a NT author has been influenced by the Hebrew version of Qumran perhaps known to him rather than the Masoretic version.[9] If so, is there an interpretative reason

9. More precisely, reference here is being made to the proto-Masoretic Hebrew version.

why a NT writer would have chosen the DSS version instead of the Masoretic Hebrew version? And the various writings of the Qumran community itself quote and allude to the OT. In this respect, the same questions asked with reference to the Apocrypha and the Pseudepigrapha should be asked of the Qumran quotations and allusions to the OT: How does Qumran understand the very same OT references also found in the NT? Does it shed any light on the NT usage?

Particular Qumran Sources of Interest for Old-in-the-New Studies

J. A. Fitzmyer, *The Dead Sea Scrolls* (Atlanta: Scholars Press, 1990), contains a list of DSS and a bibliography of where to find a published text and the English translation of that text. Fitzmyer gives references to the Qumran documents that are keyed to the translation of T. Gaster, *The Scriptures of the Dead Sea Sect* (London: Secker & Warburg, 1957). Fitzmyer's book also has a helpful index of OT texts and passages found in Qumran.

See likewise D. L. Washburn, *A Catalog of Biblical Passages in the Dead Sea Scrolls* (Atlanta: Society of Biblical Literature, 2002); and M. O. Wise, M. G. Abegg, and E. M. Cook, *The Dead Sea Scrolls: A New Translation* (San Francisco: HarperCollins, 1996), 506–13.

Very important for comparing the Hebrew version of the OT from the Qumran community with that of the Masoretic Hebrew text is M. Abegg Jr., P. Flint, and E. Ulrich, eds., *The Dead Sea Scrolls Bible* (San Francisco: HarperSanFrancisco, 1996). This is an English translation with textual variants in the scrolls listed at the bottom of each page. It may be used in an interlinear manner alongside the very similar collection of OT texts in Hebrew from Qumran in E. Ulrich, *The Biblical Qumran Scrolls* (Boston: Brill, 2010). Especially note the important series edited by D. Barthelemy and J. T. Milik, Discoveries in the Judaean Desert (Oxford: Oxford University Press, 1977–). This is the official principal edition in Hebrew (and some Aramaic) of the Qumran writings.

The following translations of the Dead Sea Scrolls are among the standard ones to consult:

Barthelemy, D., and J. T. Milik, eds. Discoveries in the Judaean Desert. Oxford: Oxford University Press, 1977–. This contains Hebrew with some English translations.

Dupont-Sommer, A. *The Essene Writings from Qumran*. York: Meridian, 1962. Its numbering is keyed to Lohse's *Die Texte aus Qumran*, which has Hebrew (with vowel points) and German on parallel pages (on which see directly below). This translation also has a Scripture index of quotations and allusions.

García Martínez, F. *The Dead Sea Scrolls Translated: The Qumran Texts in English*. Translated by W. G. E. Watson. 2nd ed. Leiden: Brill; Grand Rapids: Eerdmans, 1996.

García Martínez, F., and E. J. C. Tigchelaar, eds. *The Dead Sea Scrolls Study Edition*. 2 vols. Leiden: Brill; Grand Rapids: Eerdmans, 1997–98. This source has the Hebrew text on the left and the English translation on the facing page.

Lohse, E. *Die Texte aus Qumran*. Munich: Kösel, 1964.

Vermes, G. *The Complete Dead Sea Scrolls in English*. New York: Penguin, 1997.

Wise, M. O., M. G. Abegg Jr., and E. M. Cook. *The Dead Sea Scrolls: A New Translation*. San Francisco: HarperSanFrancisco, 1996.

General Sources Helpful for a Better Understanding of the Qumran Writings

Abegg, M. G. *The Dead Sea Scrolls Concordance*. Vol. 1, parts 1–2. With James E. Bowley and Edward M. Cook. Boston: Brill, 2003.

Charlesworth, J. H. *Graphic Concordance to the Dead Sea Scrolls*. Louisville: Westminster John Knox, 1991.

Flint, P., and J. C. VanderKam. *The Dead Sea Scrolls after Fifty Years*. Boston: Brill, 1998.

Kuhn, K. G. *Konkordanz zu den Qumrantexten*. Göttingen: Vandenhoeck & Ruprecht, 1960.

Schiffman, L., and J. C. VanderKam, eds. *Encyclopedia of the Dead Sea Scrolls*. 2 vols. Oxford: Oxford University Press, 2000.

Philo

Philo was a Jewish philosopher from Alexandria and a contemporary of Jesus and Paul. He wrote in the first half of the first century AD. His writings are voluminous. Philo refers extensively to the OT, often giving what he considers to be a literal interpretation, followed by an allegorical interpretation. Do his interpretations of OT quotations and allusions shed any light on the way NT writers interpret the OT?

The most exhaustive OT index for Philo is by Centre d'analyse et de documentation patristiques (Strasbourg), Centre de calcul (Strasbourg), and Centre national de la recherche scientifique (France) in the series Biblia patristica: Index des citations et allusions bibliques dans la littérature patristique 3 bis, *Supplément: Philon d'Alexandrie* (Paris: Centre national de la recherche scientifique, 1982).

BIBLindex is the online version of this and additional material, which is accessible for free once one registers for a username and password: http://www.biblindex.mom.fr/.

Important also to keep in mind are the two Scripture indexes to Philo found in the Loeb Classical Library edition of *Philo*, 1:xxviii–xxxvi and 10:189–268, although these are limited.

The standard critical editions of Philo are the following:

Cohn, L., and P. Wendland, eds. *Philonis Alexandrini Opera quae supersunt*. 7 vols. Berlin: G. Reimer, 1896–1930; repr. 1962.

Colson, F. H., G. H. Whitaker, and J. W. Earp (vol. 10 only), trans. *Philo*. 10 vols. Loeb Classical Library. Cambridge, MA: Harvard University Press, 1927–62.

Marcus, R., trans. *Philo: Supplement I, Questions and Answers on Genesis*. Loeb Classical Library. Cambridge, MA: Harvard University Press, 1953.

———, trans. *Philo: Supplement II, Questions and Answers on Exodus*. Loeb Classical Library. Cambridge, MA: Harvard University Press, 1953.

See also the English translation by C. D. Yonge, *The Works of Philo* (London: H. G. Bohn, 1854; repr., Peabody, MA: Hendrickson, 1993).

The best concordance is P. Borgen, K. Fuglseth, and R. Skarsten, eds., *The Philo Index: A Complete Greek Word Index to the Writings of Philo of Alexandria* (Leiden: Brill; Grand Rapids: Eerdmans, 2000). Actually, this is not a concordance, which puts words into their surrounding brief context, but it is an index that gives only references in Philo where the word may be found. One must look up the word in Philo's particular work to see its immediate syntactical context and its use there.

Josephus

Josephus was a Jewish historian who wrote in the last quarter of the first century AD. He traced the history of the OT, giving his own interpretative elaboration of the various events that he narrated. Josephus also wrote about the Second Temple period (traditionally called the "intertestamental" period) and events in Palestine during the era of Jesus and leading up to the fall of Jerusalem.

Important to keep in mind are the two Scripture indexes to Josephus: in volume 3 of his *Jewish War* in the Loeb Classical Library(pp. 686–87) and in the volume *Against Apion* (pp. 424–25), also in the Loeb Classical Library (for full bibliography of the Loeb Library edition see the next paragraph). These indexes are, however, brief. How does Josephus's understanding of particular OT passages, events, institutions, and offices relate to the NT's understanding?

A good Greek text of Josephus's works with an English translation on the facing page is H. St. J. Thackeray et al., eds., *Josephus*, 10 vols., Loeb Classical Library (Cambridge, MA: Harvard University Press, 1926–65).

The standard concordance for Josephus is K. H. Rengstorf, ed., *A Complete Concordance to Flavius Josephus*, 6 vols. (Leiden: Brill, 1973). A popular

English translation is that of W. Whiston, *Josephus: The Complete Works* (Nashville: Thomas Nelson, 1998). There is also an appendix on pp. 1104–10 that contains general OT parallels to the passages in Josephus's *Antiquities*, which discuss the OT.

The researcher needs to be aware that the various editions of Josephus's writings use different numbering systems.

Targums (or Targumim)

Targums are Aramaic translations of OT books that often include interpretative paraphrases of the OT. "Targum" comes from an Aramaic word that means "translate." Targums began to be written as early as the first century BC (or earlier?) and continued to be written up until about the fifth century AD. During the first century AD, an individual read the Hebrew text as a part of the synagogue worship, and another gave its Aramaic interpretation (there were four languages in which people were conversant in first-century Palestine: Hebrew, Aramaic, Greek, and Latin). Along with the Aramaic reading of an OT book, there would also be extemporaneous comments about the meaning or application of the text, many of which also became a part of the written targums. Thus an Aramaic Bible (targum) existed alongside the Hebrew text. Targums exist for every OT book except for some portions of Ezra–Nehemiah and Daniel, which were originally written in Aramaic.

Here the key task is relatively simple. The student merely looks up the translation of the OT passage in the targum and compares it with the same OT passage referred to in the NT (if it occurs there). Does the targumic rendering shed any light on the use in the NT?

The standard critical edition of the Aramaic Bible is A. Sperber, *The Bible in Aramaic Based on Old Manuscripts and Printed Texts*, 4 vols. (Leiden: Brill, 1959–73).

The standard English translation of the Targums is M. McNamara et al., eds., *The Aramaic Bible: The Targums*, 22 vols. (Collegeville, MN: Liturgical Press, 1987–). Volumes are still in production and forthcoming. Among other English translations are the following:

Clarke, E. G., with W. E. Aufrecht, J. C. Hurd, and F. Spitzer, eds. *Targum Pseudo-Jonathan of the Pentateuch: Text and Concordance*. New York: Ktav, 1984.

Etheridge, J. W., ed. *The Targums of Onkelos and Jonathan Ben Uzziel on the Pentateuch, with Fragments of the Jerusalem Targum from the Chaldee*. New York: Ktav, 1968.

Ginsburger, Moses, ed. *Pseudo-Jonathan*. New York: Georg Olms, 1971.

Levine, É., ed. *The Aramaic Version of Ruth*. Rome: Biblical Institute Press, 1973.

Macho, A. D., ed. *Targum Palestinense: Neophyti I, ms. de la biblioteca Vaticana*. 6 vols. Barcelona and Madrid: Consejo Superior de Investigaciones Científicas, 1968–79.

Smelik, W. R., ed. *The Targum of Judges*. Leiden: Brill, 1995.

Rabbinic Literature

The rabbinic literature is composed of the Talmudic literature (Mishnah, Tosefta, Jerusalem and Babylonian Talmuds, and the minor tractates of the Talmud), early midrashic writings, and late midrashic writings.[10]

Talmudic Literature

The Mishnah. The Hebrew word from which Mishnah comes means "to repeat," so that Mishnah means "repetition." Likely it was called this because the Mishnah contains earlier Jewish traditions that were valued and were to be remembered through oral repetition; eventually these traditions were put into written form. The Mishnah is organized topically into six major divisions, each of which have subdivisions. The Mishnah was published and edited between AD 200 and 220. It contains oral tradition of the Jewish sages and rabbis from the Tannaitic period (AD 50–200).

The standard Hebrew text of the Mishnah is that of P. Blackman, *Mishnah*, 7 vols. (Gateshead: Judaica Press, 1990), which also contains an English translation on facing pages. The standard English translations are H. Danby, *The Mishnah* (1933; repr., Oxford: Oxford University Press, 1983); and J. Neusner, *The Mishnah: A New Translation* (New Haven: Yale University Press, 1988). Danby's work is especially important since it has an OT Scripture index that indicates where the Mishnah refers to the OT. See also A. Samely, *Rabbinic Interpretation of Scripture in the Mishnah* (Oxford: Oxford University Press, 2002), which has a Scripture index to the Mishnah on pp. 459–62. Also of some help may be C. R. Gianotti, *The New Testament and the Mishnah: A Cross-Reference Index* (Grand Rapids: Baker, 1983).

The Tosefta. "Tosefta" means "addition" or "supplement" and comes from the Hebrew word for "to add." The Tosefta was compiled soon after the Mishnah (AD 220–30), builds on and expands the Mishnah (and is about twice the size), and like the Mishnah, its additional material derives from the Tannaitic period (AD 50–200). It follows the same format and structure as the Mishnah.

A standard Hebrew edition of the Tosefta is M. S. Zuckermandel, *Tosephta: Based on the Erfurt and Vienna Codices*, 2nd ed. (Jerusalem: Bamberger & Wahrmann, 1937). A good English translation is by J. Neusner, *The Tosefta*, 2 vols. (Peabody, MA: Hendrickson, 2002), which also has a Scripture index, indicating where OT references are found in the Tosefta.

10. This section follows generally and is an abbreviation of the more elaborate discussion of Evans, *Ancient Texts for New Testament Studies*, 216–55.

The Jerusalem Talmud. The Jerusalem Talmud is sometimes called the Palestinian Talmud or Talmud of the Land of Israel. The word *Talmud* literally means "study" or "learning," which is from a Hebrew word that means "to learn." The Jerusalem Talmud comprises the Mishnah, the Tosefta, and interpretative expansions known as "Gemara." This Talmud was completed around AD 400 to 425.

A Hebrew edition of this Talmud is *Talmud Yerushalmi*, 4 vols. (Jerusalem: Kedem, 1971).

A standard English translation of the Talmud is that of J. Neusner, *The Talmud of the Land of Israel*, 35 vols. (Chicago: University of Chicago Press, 1982–94). This set of volumes has a helpful Scripture index in the back of each volume.

The Babylonian Talmud. The Babylonian Talmud was completed in about AD 500 to 550. It is structured exactly like the Palestinian Talmud but has less of the Tosefta. Nevertheless this Talmud is longer than the Palestinian one since it has much more haggadic material (commentary of a homiletical nature).

A standard Hebrew edition of the Babylonian Talmud is that of I. Epstein, *The Babylonian Talmud*, 30 vols. (London: Soncino, 1960–90). A good standard English translation is by I. Epstein, *The Babylonian Talmud*, 35 vols. (London: Soncino, 1935–48). There is also an excellent *Index Volume* (1952) at the end of Epstein's edition that is thorough, containing a topical index and an excellent OT Scripture index, which is very useful for looking up how the Talmud uses the OT.

The Minor Tractates of the Talmud. These are fifteen tractates added to the end of the Babylonian Talmud, which contain pre-Tannaitic traditions (200 BC–AD 10), Tannaitic discussions (AD 10–220), and later Amoraic material (220–500).

A standard English translation can be found in A. Cohen, *The Minor Tractates of the Talmud*, 2nd ed., 2 vols. (London: Soncino, 1971). There is a useful Scripture index at the end of the second volume.

The Midrashic Literature

In contrast to the Talmudic literature, which is organized encyclopedically by topics, the midrashic writings are composed of commentaries on various OT books, so that they are arranged according to the chapters of the biblical book being commented on. These commentaries either try to explain the meaning of the OT text or elaborate on how to apply it to life. This literature is often composed of halakic material (explaining and applying the law) and haggadic material (of a homiletical and illustrative nature).

The key for the research of this material is to check the Scripture index in the back of every English translation of Jewish primary sources mentioned below. The student then turns to the right page, finds the relevant discussion of the OT passage of focus, and sees how the midrash is understanding or using the passage.

The Early (Tannaitic) Midrashic Literature (50 BC–AD 200 and Onward. The time when the Tannaitic midrashic literature was composed is not known; it does not date to the Tannaitic period though it contains material from that period. The following are the midrashic commentaries in this category, primarily English editions, most of which have Scripture indexes:

Hammer, R., trans. *Sifra on Deuteronomy.* New Haven: Yale University Press, 1986.[11]

Lauterbach, J. C., trans. *Mekhilta de-Rabbi Ishmael.* 3 vols. Philadelphia: Jewish Publication Society, 1933–35. Repr., 1976. A Hebrew edition: H. S. Horovitz and A. Rabin, *Mechilta d'Rabbi Ismael.* Frankfurt: J. Kauffmann, 1928–31. Repr., Jerusalem: Bamberger & Wahrmann, 1960.

Levertoff, P. P., trans. *Midrash Sifre on Numbers.* Translations of Early Texts: Series 3, Palestinian-Jewish and Cognate Texts (Rabbinic). London: SPCK, 1926.

Neusner, J., trans. *Sifra: An Analytical Translation.* 3 vols. Brown Judaic Studies 138–40. Atlanta: Scholars Press, 1988. This is a translation of the rabbinic commentary on Leviticus. There is no Scripture index, but the researcher merely has to turn to the appropriate section in the text of Leviticus and read the following commentary on it to see if other OT references are adduced in the commentary explanation.

The Later (Amoraic) Midrashic Literature (450–1100). The following are the midrashic commentaries in this category, primarily English editions, which have Scripture indexes:

Berman, S. A., trans. *Midrash Tanhuma-Yelammedenu: An English Translation of Genesis and Exodus from the Printed Version of Tanhuma-Yelammedenu with an Introduction, Notes, and Indexes.* Hoboken, NJ: Ktav, 1996.

Braude, W. G., trans. *The Midrash on Psalms.* 2 vols. New Haven: Yale University Press, 1959.

———, trans. *Pesikta Rabbati.* 2 vols. Yale Judaica Series 18. New Haven: Yale University Press, 1968.

Braude, W. G., and I. J. Kapstein, trans. *Pesikta de-Rab Kahana.* Philadelphia: Jewish Publication Society, 2002.

———, trans. *Tanna Debe Eliyyahu.* Philadelphia: Jewish Publication Society, 1981.

11. See ibid., 231–38, for a few other possibly relevant primary sources in the Tannaitic midrashic literature, as well as Hebrew editions of texts mentioned above in this section.

Freedman, H., and M. Simon, trans. *Midrash Rabbah*. 10 vols. London: Soncino, 1939. There is a separate topical and Scripture index volume to this set, which is thorough.

Friedlander, G., trans. *Pirke de Rabbi Eliezer*. 1916. Repr., New York: Sepher-Hermon, 1981.

Townsend, J. T., trans. *Midrash Tanhuma* [S. Buber recension]. Vol. 1, *Genesis*. Hoboken, NJ: Ktav, 1989.

———, trans. *Midrash Tanhuma*. Vol. 2, *Exodus and Leviticus*. Hoboken, NJ: Ktav, 1997.

———, trans. *Midrash Tanhuma*. Vol. 3, *Numbers and Deuteronomy*. Hoboken, NJ: Ktav, 2003.

Visotzky, B. L., trans. *The Midrash on Proverbs*. New Haven: Yale University Press, 1992.[12]

A Sampling of Other Books for a Better Understanding of the Rabbinic Literature

Ginzberg, L. *Legends of the Jews*. 7 vols. Philadelphia: Jewish Publication Society, 1909–38. Vol. 7 has an excellent topical reference index. This source, however, focuses more on the content of the Jewish works themselves rather than on the role of the OT in these works (as is apparent from observing that the OT Scripture index is relatively small).

Isaiah, A. B., and B. Sharfman. *The Pentateuch and Rashi's Commentary*. 5 vols. Brooklyn: S. S. & R. Pub., 1949.

Mielziner, M. *Introduction to the Talmud*. New York: Bloch, 1968.

Neusner, J., ed. *Dictionary of Ancient Rabbis*. Peabody, MA: Hendrickson, 2003.

———, ed. *Dictionary of Judaism in the Biblical Period: 450 B.C.E. to 600 C.E.* 1996. Repr., Peabody, MA: Hendrickson, 2002. This source is obviously also applicable to all of the Jewish literature discussed in this chapter.

———. *The Talmud of Babylonia: An Academic Commentary*. 36 vols. Atlanta: Scholars Press, 1994.

Patai, R., comp. *The Messiah Texts, Jewish Legends of 3,000 Years*. Detroit: Wayne State University Press, 1979.

Skolnik, F., and M. Berenbaum, eds. *Encyclopedia Judaica*. 2nd ed. 22 vols. New York: Macmillan Reference USA, 2006.

Strack, H., and G. Stemberger. *Introduction to the Talmud and the Midrash*. Translated by M. Bockmuehl. Edinburgh: T&T Clark, 1991.

12. See ibid., 238–45, for a few other possibly relevant primary sources in the Amoraic midrashic literature, as well as Hebrew editions of and dates of the texts mentioned above in this section.

Early Christian Literature

As with the sources in Jewish literature, so the following sources in the early Christian writings have Scripture indexes to the OT. This is important material since especially the earliest of these writings may preserve interpretative traditions that extend back into the first century AD. Even the somewhat later literature, however, can still serve as commentaries on the OT texts, which may provide interpretative perspectives that give insights into the meaning of various uses of the OT in the NT.

Particular Early and Later Christian Sources of Interest for Old-in-the-New Studies

Allenbach, J., et al, eds. Biblia patristica: Index des citations et allusions bibliques dans la littérature patristique. 7 vols. + supplement. Centre d'analyse et de documentation patristiques. Paris: Centre national de la recherche scientifique, 1975–2000.

These eight volumes (in French, but titles given here in English) cover the following: (1) Beginnings to Clement of Alexandria and Tertullian; (2) The Third Century (except Origen); (3) Origen; (4) Eusebius of Caesarea, Cyril of Jerusalem, Epiphanius of Salamis; (5) Basil of Caesarea, Gregory Nazianzen, Gregory of Nyssa, Amphiloque of Iconium; (6) Hilary of Poitiers, Ambrose of Milan, Ambrosiaster; (7) Didymus of Alexandria; (8) (Supplement) Philo.

Biblia patristica contains a very good Scripture index, both for OT and NT, as well as for patristic and apocryphal literature. Other important sources are the following:

Coxe, A. C., A. Robertson, and J. Donaldson, eds. *Ante-Nicene Fathers*. 10 vols. 1885–96. Repr., Peabody, MA: Hendrickson, 1999. Vol. 10 contains a Scripture index. Several of the fathers covered in these volumes represent some of the earliest Christian writings, thus vols. 1–3 up through the beginning of vol. 4 contain the Apostolic Fathers, Justin Martyr, Irenaeus, Hermas, Clement of Alexandria, and Tertullian, who extend from the early second century to the end of the third century AD. Online: http://www.ccel.org/fathers.html.

Hennecke, E., and W. Schneemelcher, eds. *New Testament Apocrypha*. 2 vols. Philadelphia: Westminster, 1963–65. Together with the Apostolic Fathers, the NT Apocrypha represents most of the remaining earliest Christian literature. It also contains a Scripture index.

Holmes, M. W., ed. *The Apostolic Fathers: Greek Texts and English Translations*. 3rd, rev. ed. Grand Rapids: Baker Academic, 2007. This is an important source since it has the Greek text of the Apostolic Fathers on the left and the facing page gives the English translation. There is a

Scripture index, as also in the *Ante-Nicene Fathers* (above). The Apostolic Fathers represent much of the earliest Christian literature.

Jurgens, W., ed. *The Faith of the Early Fathers*. 3 vols. Collegeville, MN: Liturgical Press, 1970–79. These three volumes from Jurgens are a valuable source of historical and theological texts from the Christian writings of the pre-Nicene, Nicene, post-Nicene, and Constantinopolitan eras through Jerome, and for Augustine of Hippo to the end of the patristic age. This work is a reader, but the back matter also includes helpful doctrinal, subject, and Scripture indexes.

Schaff, P., ed. *Nicene and Post-Nicene Fathers*. Series 1. 14 vols. 1886–90. Repr., Peabody, MA: Hendrickson, 1999. Each volume has a Scripture index. Online: http://www.ccel.org/fathers.html.

Schaff, P., and H. Wace, eds. *Nicene and Post-Nicene Fathers*. Series 2. 14 vols. 1890–1900. Repr., Peabody, MA: Hendrickson, 1999. Each printed volume has a Scripture index except 2 and 14. But all have indexes online: http://www.ccel.org/fathers.html.

General Sources Helpful for a Better Understanding of the Early Christian Literature

Other sources helpful for a better understanding of the early Christian literature are the following:

Altaner, B. *Patrology*. New York: Herder & Herder, 1960. Altaner introduces the various church fathers and their writings, as well as gives a bibliography of primary and secondary sources on each.

Evans, C. A. *Ancient Texts for New Testament Studies: A Guide to the Background Literature*, 256–77. Peabody, MA: Hendrickson, 2005. Evans provides a good thumbnail guide to the primary and secondary sources of early Christian literature.

Goodspeed, E. J. *Index patristicus*. Naperville, IL: Allenson, 1907. Goodspeed also lists everywhere any particular Greek word occurs in the Apostolic Fathers but does not give the immediate syntactical context of the word.

Kraft, H. *Clavis patrum apostolicorum*. Munich: Kösel, 1963. This is a lexicon yet also a concordance: it lists all the references of a word in its syntactical context in the Apostolic Fathers where the word occurs.

Quasten, J. *Patrology*. Vols. 1–4, which are best broken down into the following separate bibliographical references:

———. *The Ante-Nicene Literature after Irenaeus*. Vol. 2 of *Patrology*. Westminster, MD: Newman, 1953.

———. *The Beginnings of Patristic Literature*. Vol. 1 of *Patrology*. Westminster, MD: Newman, 1951.

———. *The Golden Age of Greek Patristic Literature: From the Council of Nicaea to the Council of Chalcedon*. Vol. 3 of *Patrology*. Westminster, MD: Newman, 1960.

———. *The Golden Age of Latin Patristic Literature: From the Council of Nicaea to the Council of Chalcedon*. Edited by A. di Berardino. Vol. 4 of *Patrology*. Westminster, MD: Christian Classics, 1986.

Quasten's volumes function virtually identically to Altaner's work (above).

An Illustration of the Relevance of Jewish Background for the Use of the Old Testament in the New

Numerous examples of Jewish exegesis of the OT have value to some degree for understanding the NT use of the same texts. As mentioned in chapter 3, many examples may be found in the *Commentary on the New Testament Use of the Old Testament*,[13] since, particularly in the discussion of OT quotations, there is typically a section dealing with how Judaism understood the quotation and what relevance this might or might not have for the NT use.[14] Though there are so many possible examples that could be cited, I will merely provide one here as illustrative, though it is not found in the *Commentary on the New Testament Use of the Old Testament*.

Acts 2 portrays the coming of the Spirit at Pentecost: "There appeared to them tongues as of fire, distributing themselves, and they rested on each one of them" (Acts 2:3). Could there be an OT or Jewish background to this image of "tongues as of fire"? And if such a background could be found, would it illuminate what the "tongues as of fire" means in the Acts 2 passage?

"Tongues of Fire" at Pentecost as a Theophany of a Latter-Day Sinai Sanctuary

The appearance of "tongues as of fire" in Acts 2 appears to be an expression of the coming Spirit that reflects a theophany, which is associated with the heavenly temple. A number of considerations point to this. First, the mention

13. G. K. Beale and D. A. Carson, eds., *Commentary on the New Testament Use of the Old Testament* (Grand Rapids: Baker Academic, 2007).

14. As noted in chap. 4, reference may also be made to other works on the use of the OT in the NT, on which see the representative bibliography at the end of this handbook. Likewise, the more technical commentaries on NT books will sometimes include discussion of relevant Jewish background to the OT references found in the book. Thus, e.g., see throughout G. K. Beale, *The Book of Revelation*, NIGTC (Grand Rapids: Eerdmans, 1999). See also the case study of James 4:13–5:6 in Bauckham, *Jewish World*, 214–20.

that "there came from heaven a noise like a violent rushing wind" and that there appeared "tongues as of fire" calls to mind the typical theophanies of the OT. God appeared in these theophanies with a thunderous noise and in the form of fire. The first great theophany of the OT was at Sinai, where God appeared in the midst of loud "voices and lightning flashes," "fire," "torches," and "a thick cloud" (Exod. 19:16–20; 20:18). This was the model theophany for most later similar divine appearances in the OT, and to some degree God's coming at Sinai stands in the background of the Spirit's coming at Pentecost.[15] Pentecost celebrated not only the firstfruits of harvest but also, beginning in the second century BC, commemoration of God's giving of the law to Moses at Sinai, which points further to the presence of that background in Acts 2.[16]

In this regard, Philo's first-century description of God's appearance at Sinai may not be a haphazard parallel: God's revelation came "from heaven" like a "flame" (*pyr* and *phlox*), which became "a dialect" (*dialectos*) and caused "amazement" (*Decal.* 46, a parallel noted by several commentators; see some identical wording in Acts 2:3, 6–7). Philo's rendering is not that far removed from the account in the book of Exodus, where "voices" is closely linked to "torches" of fire: "all the people saw the voices and the torches" (Exod. 20:18 AT; "torches" of fire also describe a heavenly temple scene in Ezek. 1:13). Later Judaism also preserves references saying that God's voice in giving the law at Sinai was like fire.[17]

This description of Sinai, and the way it was developed in early Judaism, is similar to that at Pentecost, where people saw "tongues of fire being distributed" (Acts 2:3 AT). While it may be true that Luke's account of Pentecost contains no direct reference to the Sinai theophany,[18] there are links and even more "indirect allusions" than we have shown here to indicate that Luke was aware of the background of Sinai in his depiction of Pentecost.[19] The scene of "tongues of fire" in Acts 2 may well be best understood through the common stock of Jewish interpretative tradition that tried to clarify the close association of the voices and fiery "torches" in Exodus 20:18 by explaining it as God's voice being like fire. Elsewhere I have argued that Mount Sinai was a sanctuary; if our analysis so far is correct, then the theophany at Pentecost may also be understood as the irrupting of a newly emerging temple in the midst of the old Jerusalem temple that was passing away.

15. So J. J. Niehaus, *God at Sinai* (Grand Rapids: Zondervan, 1995), passim, and in particular, 371; his work traces the biblical-theological development of the Sinai theophany throughout the OT and NT.

16. On which, e.g., see A. T. Lincoln, *Ephesians*, WBC (Dallas: Word, 1990), 243–44, who also points out that Exod. 19–20 and Num. 17–18 were read during Pentecost in the synagogue liturgy.

17. On which see G. K. Beale, "The Descent of the Eschatological Temple in the Form of the Spirit at Pentecost: Part I," *Tyndale Bulletin* 55 (2005): 77–78.

18. Though Acts 2:3 may be an exception.

19. So J. A. Fitzmyer, *The Acts of the Apostles*, AB 31 (New York: Doubleday, 1998), 234.

"Tongues of Fire" in the Old Testament as a Theophany from a Heavenly Sanctuary

Sinai is not the only background that portrays the image of speech in the midst of fire. The actual phrase "tongues as of fire" occurs in two OT passages. Isaiah 30:27–30 refers to God's "descending" (v. 30) from his temple ("a remote place" [v. 27], "the mountain of the LORD" [v. 29]) and appearing in "dense . . . smoke. . . . His *tongue is like a consuming fire* [v. 27]. . . . The LORD [comes] . . . in the flame of a consuming fire" and "will cause His voice of authority to be heard [v. 30]." This itself alludes to the prototypical Sinai theophany. Likewise a "tongue of fire" occurs as an emblem of judgment in Isaiah 5:24–25 with allusion to the Sinai theophany.[20] The "tongue like a consuming fire" in Isaiah 30:27 connotes God's judgment and could be different from the same image in Acts 2, since at first glance it appears to be a sign only of blessing. That the same flaming image even in Acts, however, may also allude both to blessing and judgment is apparent from the Sinai backdrop, where the fiery theophany is associated with both blessing (the giving of the law) and judgment (for those entering too close to the theophany or rebelling: cf. Exod. 19:12–24; 32:25–29). Elsewhere I have argued that the background of the Joel 2 quotation in Acts 2:16–21 confirms a dual blessing-cursing theme.[21] Consequently, Isaiah's linking of "tongues of fire" to God's theophanic presence in what appears to be a temple location points even further to the same link in Acts 2.

"Tongues of Fire" in Judaism as a Theophany from a Heavenly Sanctuary

Some early Jewish writings could show awareness of or be inspired by the OT image of "tongues of fire" being associated with a divine theophany in a heavenly or earthly temple. The phrase "tongues of fire" also occurs in these Jewish passages. Perhaps *1 Enoch* 14:8–25 offers a parallel to the fiery "tongues" in the Isaiah passages and in Acts 2:3.[22] There Enoch ascends in a vision to the heavenly temple. He comes to the wall of the outer court, which is "surrounded by tongues of fire," and he "entered into the tongues of fire" (14:9–10). Enoch then enters through the holy place and is able to peer into the holy of holies, which is "built with tongues of fire" (14:15). Likewise in 71:5, Enoch sees a temple-like "structure built of crystals; and between those crystals tongues of living fire." Thus the "tongues of fire" form part of the

20. Niehaus, *God at Sinai*, 307–8.

21. See Beale, "Descent of the Eschatological Temple: Part I," 93–99.

22. For the Qumran version of this portion of *1 Enoch*, see 4Q204 6.19–29, where also the phrase "tongues of fire" appears to occur similarly—though in reconstruction of lacunae; see *The Dead Sea Scrolls: Study Edition*, ed. F. García Martínez and E. J. C. Tigchelaar, 2 vols. (Leiden: Brill, 2000).

heavenly temple and contribute to the overall effect of the burning theophany in the holy of holies, where "the flaming fire was round about him, and a great fire stood before him" (14:22).

What could such a heavenly scene have to do with the earthly scene of Pentecost depicted in Acts 2? On the one hand, it is possible that the wording "tongues of fire" in *1 Enoch* is merely a coincidental parallel to Acts 2. On the other hand, the contextual usage of the wording in *1 Enoch* may have some overlap with the use of the same phrase in Acts 2. The *Enoch* passage may be a creative development of the above Exodus and Isaiah texts, the latter of which appears to be a development of imagery from the Sinai theophany. In the light of this *1 Enoch* text, could it be that the descent of the Holy Spirit at Pentecost "from heaven" in the form of "tongues of fire" is to be conceived as the descent of God's tabernacling presence from his heavenly temple?[23] Since the heavenly temple is partly pictured by "tongues of fire," it might be appropriate for the descent of that temple to be pictured with the same thing. Thus it may be perceivable that, just as the heavenly temple was constructed of "tongues of fire," the new temple on earth (God's people vivified by the Spirit) that had descended from heaven was beginning to be built with the same fiery image. This suggestion may gain more force when seen in the light of the other observations throughout this section that point from different angles to Pentecost as a phenomenon expressing the divine theophanic presence *in the temple*.[24]

In addition, the Dead Sea Scrolls say the Urim and Thummim stones shone gloriously with "tongues of fire" (1Q29). The Urim and Thummim were two stones placed in a pouch in the high priest's breastplate (Exod. 28:30; Lev. 8:8). He was to carry them "when he enters the holy place . . . before the LORD . . . continually" (Exod. 28:29–30). These stones were likely one of the means by which God's prophetic revelation came. They apparently would be cast by the priest or drawn out of the pouch ceremonially, and the way they came out revealed a "yes" or "no" answer to the question at hand.[25] According to Qumran (1Q29; 4Q376), the Urim and Thummim shone with "tongues of

23. The Greek *glōssais pyros* (by/with tongues of fire) from *1 Enoch* 14:9 and 15 (as well as the almost identical 14:10) is virtually the same as *glōssai hōsei pyros* (tongues as of fire) in Acts 2:3.

24. See Beale, "Descent of the Eschatological Temple: Part I," 73–102, where expansion of the argument of this whole section on the OT and Jewish background of Acts 2 is found together with other discussion supporting the idea that the coming of the Spirit is to be understood as the beginning establishment of the end-time temple among God's people (Jewish Christians at first and later gentile Christians). See, in addition, G. K. Beale, "The Descent of the Eschatological Temple in the Form of the Spirit at Pentecost: Part II," *Tyndale Bulletin* 56 (2005): 63–90, discussing Acts 2's other OT citations, which point to the same temple framework of understanding.

25. See J. A. Motyer, "Urim and Thummim," in *The New Bible Dictionary*, ed. J. D. Douglas (Grand Rapids: Eerdmans, 1970), 1306, for a concise explanation of the function of the Urim and Thummim in the OT. See 1 Sam. 28:6, e.g., for the prophetic use of these

fire" in the temple when God gave the prophetic answer to the high priest's question about whether a prophet is true or false.[26]

Therefore once more we have the "tongues of fire" as a phenomenon occurring within the "holy of holies" or, more likely, the "holy place" of the temple as an expression of God's revelatory presence.[27] Although it is the earthly and not the heavenly temple that is the focus, it should be recalled that the holy of holies was considered to be the bottommost part of God's heavenly temple-throne room, where he rested his feet on the ottoman of the ark of the covenant. Even more striking in this Qumran document is that the "tongues" is an occurrence not merely of God's revelatory presence but also of his prophetic communication. This is certainly what happens at Pentecost: not only are the "tongues as of fire" a manifestation of God's presence in the Spirit, but that presence also causes the people to "prophesy" (as Acts 2:17–18 makes clear). And the location from which God's Spirit descends at Pentecost appears not only to be generally "from heaven" but also from the heavenly holy of holies or temple. This is particularly true when similar imagery is recognized in descriptions of the Sinai theophany, in Isaiah 30 (and possibly Isa. 5)—and also in the images of "tongues of fire" in *1 Enoch* 14 and 71 and at Qumran, which may be developments from the OT Sinai theophany and Isaiah 30.

Conclusion about the Old Testament and Jewish Background for the "Tongues of Fire" in Acts 2

From various vantage points, it appears that all of these OT and Jewish passages together collectively contribute to a picture that resembles something like God's heavenly temple descending upon his people and making them a part of it. Luke does not mean the "tongues of fire" in Acts 2 to be an image dependent on any of the Jewish uses of the phrase but likely is intended to recall God's fiery voice at the Sinai sanctuary and his Sinai-like theophany from the heavenly temple described by Isaiah. The Jewish references to the "tongues of fire," however, probably represent a common stock understanding in early Judaism that "tongues of fire" is inextricably linked with God's appearance in the temple. Such a common use of the phrase may have been sparked by the biblical references to the fiery voices at Sinai and the tongues of fire in Isaiah. The Jewish references then serve as a commentary that gives

---

lots: "When Saul inquired of the LORD, the LORD did not answer him, either by dreams or by Urim or by prophets."

26. The Qumran text envisions the high priest as discovering the prophetic revelation of the Urim and Thummim in the temple and then revealing the prophetic answer to the congregation of Israel in the courtyard.

27. The square pouch on the high priest's breastpiece containing the Urim and Thummim symbolized the holy of holies.

further insight into the "tongues of fire" by confirming and clarifying the original biblical image.

Therefore, in the light of the OT background and the clarifying Jewish references, the "tongues of fire" contribute to a larger picture in Acts 2 of the divine theophanic Spirit building God's people into a latter-day temple.

Appendix: Abbreviations for Nontalmudic Jewish Works

This is a key to abbreviations of some general German terms, some biblical book titles, and nontalmudic Jewish works in the *Kommentar zum Neuen Testament aus Talmud und Midrasch*, edited by Hermann L. Strack and Paul Billerbeck (Str-B), http://trove.nla.gov.au/work/797911.[28]

Aboth RN	Aboth de Rabbi Nathan = Avot d'Rabbi Natan (minor tractates of Talmud)
Abs.	Absatz, paragraph; Abschnitt, section
Aggad Schir ha-Schirim	Aggadat Shir ha-Shirim = *Legend of Song of Songs* (midrash)
Aggadath Ber	Aggadat Bereshit = *Legend of Genesis* (midrash)
Anm.	Anmerkung, note
Ant./Antiq.	Josephus's *Antiquities*
Apg	Apostlegeschichte, Acts of the Apostles (NT)
Apok Abr	*Apocalypse of Abraham* (in the Pseudepigrapha)
Apok Bar	*Syraic Apocalypse of Baruch = 2 Baruch* (Pseudepigrapha)
Apok Bar (gr)	*Greek Apocalypse of Baruch = 3 Baruch* (Pseudepigrapha)
Apok Elias	*Apocalypse of Elijah* (Pseudepigrapha)
Apok Mos	*Apocalypse of Moses* = Greek recension of *Life of Adam and Eve* (Pseudepigrapha)
Ass Mos	*Assumption of Moses* (see *Testament of Moses* in the Pseudepigrapha)
b.	bei, at
b.	ben, son of
babyl. Rez.	Babylon recension

28. This list of keys to the abbreviations in *Kommentar zum Neuen Testament aus Talmud und Midrasch* (Str-B) has been adapted from N. E. Anderson, *Tools for Bibliographical and Backgrounds Research of the New Testament* (South Hamilton, MA: Gordon-Conwell Theological Seminary, 1987 [out of print; online sources may have used copies]), 285–88.

Bd.	Band, volume
Bell. Jud.	Josephus's *Jewish War*
Beth ha-Midr	*Bet ha-Midrasch*, collection of midrashim compiled by Adolph Jellinek (Leipzig: Friedrich Nies, 1853–77)
bT	Talmud Bavli = Babylonian Talmud
c. Apion	Josephus's *Contra Apion* = *Against Apion*
das.	daselbst, in the same place, same as above = ibid.
Dèrekh Ereç Z	*Derek Ereṣ Zuṭa* (minor tractates of Talmud)
d.h.	das heist, that is = i.e.
d.i.	das ist, that is = i.e.; namely = viz.
DtR	*Midrash Rabbah on Deuteronomy*
Einl.	Einleitung, introduction
Esra	Ezra; 4 Esra = *4 Ezra* = 2 Esdras
Exk.	excursus
ExR	*Midrash Rabbah on Exodus*
f.	and following (page)
ff.	and following pages
GenR	*Midrash Rabbah on Genesis*
Gr Baruch	*Greek Apocalypse of Baruch* = *3 Baruch* (Pseudepigrapha)
Hen	Ethiopic Apocalypse of Enoch = *1 Enoch* (Pseudepigrapha)
Hi	Hiob, Job (Hebrew Bible)
HL	Hohelied, Song of Songs/Solomon (Hebrew Bible)
i.	in the
J.	Jahr, year
Jahrh.	Jahrhundert, century
Jak	Jakobus, James (NT)
Jalqut	*Yalkut shimoni* (midrashic collection, 13th century)
Jerusch 1	*Targum Pseudo-Jonathan* = *Targum Yerushalmi 1*
Jerusch 2	*Fragment Targum* (VNL recension?)
Jes	Jesaja, Isaiah (Hebrew Bible)
Joseph.	Josephus
Jubil	*Jubilees* (Pseudepigrapha)
Kap.	Kapitel, chapter
Kg	Kings (Hebrew Bible)
KL	Klagelieder, Lamentations (Hebrew Bible)
Kol	Colossians
Kor	Corinthians

LvR	*Midrash Rabbah on Leviticus*
LXX	Septuagint (Greek version of Old Testament)
M	Mishnah
Makk	Maccabees (in the Apocrypha)
Mekh	*Mekilta de Rabbi Ishmael* (midrash on Exodus)
Mekh Ex	*Mekilta de Rabbi Ishmael* (midrash on Exodus)
Midr	midrash
Midr Esth	*Midrash Rabbah on Esther*
Midr HL	*Midrash Rabbah on the Song of Songs*
Midr KL	*Midrash Rabbah on Lamentations*
Midr Ps	*Midrash on Psalms* = *Midrash Shoher Tov* = *Midrash Tehillim*
Midr Qoh	*Midrash Rabbah on Ecclesiastes*
Midr S	*Midrash Samuel*
Midr Sach 14,5	*Pesikta Rabbati on Zechariah* 14:5 (see Str-B 3:554 on Gal. 3:19)
Midr Spr	*Midrash on Proverbs*
Midr v. d. 10 Exilen	*Midrash Eser Galuyyot* = *Midrash on the Ten Expulsions*
Midr Zeph 3,8	*Pesikta Rabbati on Zephaniah* 3:8 (see Str-B 3:782 on Jude 6)
n. Chr.	nach Christo, after Christ = AD
Nr.	Nummer, number
NuR	*Midrash Rabbah on Numbers*
Offb	Offenbarung, Revelation (NT)
Onq	*Targum Onqelos*
Orac Sib	*Sibylline Oracles* = *Oracula Sibyllina* (Pseudepigrapha)
p	Talmud Yerushalmi = Jerusalem Talmud = Palestinian Talmud
pal. Rez.	Palestinian recension
Pesiq	*Pesikta de-Rab Kahana* (midrash)
Pesiq R	*Pesikta Rabbati* (midrash)
Pirqe R El	*Pirke de Rabbi Eleazar* (midrash)
Ps Sal	*Psalms of Solomon* (Pseudepigrapha)
Psal Sal	*Psalms of Solomon* (Pseudepigrapha)
pT	Talmud Yerushalmi = Jerusalem Talmud = Palestinian Talmud
Qoh	Qohelet, Ecclesiastes (Hebrew Bible)
R	(in GenR, ExR, LevR, NuR, DtR) *Midrash Rabbah*
R.	Rabbi
Ri	Richter, Judges (Hebrew Bible)

s.	siehe, see
S.	Seite, page
S Dt	*Sifre/Sipre on Deuteronomy* (midrash)
S Lv	*Sifra/Sipra on Leviticus* (midrash)
S Nu	*Sifre/Sipre on Numbers* (midrash)
Sach	Sacharja, Zachariah (Hebrew Bible)
Seder Elij	*Seder Eliyahu* = *Eliyyahu Rabbah* = *Work of Elijah* (in *Tanna debe [dĕbê] Eliyahu*, midrash)
Seder Elij Rabbah	*Seder Eliyahu Rabbah* = *Eliyyahu Rabbah* = *Work of Elijah* (in *Tanna debe [dĕbê] Eliyahu*, midrash)
Seder Elij Zuta	*Eliyyahu Zuṭa* (in *Tanna debe [dĕbê] Eliyahu*, midrash)
Sir	Sirach = Ecclesiasticus = Wisdom of Ben Sira (Apocrypha)
sl Hen	*Slavonic Apocalypse of Enoch* = *2 Enoch* (Pseudepigrapha)
Spr	Sprüche, Proverbs (Hebrew Bible)
T	Tosefta
Tanch	*Midrash Tanhuma*
Tanch	*Midrash Tanhuma* (Buber edition)
Targ	targum
Tos	Tosefta
u.	und, and
usw.	und so weiter, and so forth, et cetera, etc.
v. Chr.	vor Christi, before Christ = BC
vgl	vergleiche, compare, see, consult = cf.
Weish	Weisheit, Wisdom of Solomon (Apocrypha)
zB	zum Beispiel, for instance/example = e.g.

7

A Case Study Illustrating the Methodology of This Book

Introduction

In chapter 4, I surveyed and discussed twelve different ways the NT uses the OT. There is not space in this handbook to dedicate a whole chapter to each of these uses, though brief examples of each were given in chapter 4. The point of this chapter is to provide an example of how to apply the ninefold methodology elaborated on in chapter 3 and partly elsewhere in this book to a typical use of the OT in the NT. The ninefold approach explained in chapter 3 consists of the following: (1) identify the OT reference; (2) analyze the broad NT context where the OT reference occurs; (3) analyze the OT context; (4) survey the use of the OT reference in Judaism; (5) compare the OT text form (MT, LXX, DSS, targum, and early Jewish citations) with the text of the NT reference; (6) analyze the NT's textual use of the OT (which text the author depends on and why, or, if making his own rendering, why); (7) analyze the interpretative (hermeneutical) use of the OT; (8) analyze the theological use of the OT; (9) analyze the rhetorical use of the OT.

I am taking the use of Isaiah 22:22 in Revelation 3:7 for the case study, though numerous other examples could have been chosen. Nevertheless, this particular case study will sufficiently illustrate each of the above nine steps of our approach.

Identifying the Old Testament Reference

If the OT reference is a formal or informal quotation, then the reference is easy to identify. If, however, the reference is an allusion, then the validity of the allusion has to be validated by several criteria, on which I elaborated in chapter 2. In the present case, it is a question about whether the OT reference is an informal quotation of Isaiah 22:22 or an abundantly clear allusion to it. The line between an informal citation and a very clear allusion is gray. In light of the parallels of several keywords and the order of these words (see the chart below), I think it likely that this is an informal citation. Whichever category one assigns to this OT reference, I am unaware of any major commentators who do not acknowledge that Revelation 3:7 makes a clear reference to Isaiah 22:22. For our purposes preliminary comparisons at this point can be made in English to show that the reference is to Isaiah 22:22:

Isaiah 22:22	Revelation 3:7
I will set the key of the house of David on his shoulder; when he opens no one will shut, when he shuts no one will open.	he . . . who has the key of David, who opens and no one will shut, and who shuts and no one opens . . .

Analyzing the Broad New Testament Context Where the Old Testament Reference Occurs

Revelation 3:7 is found in the second major section of Revelation, which is composed of Christ's seven messages to the seven churches in Asia Minor. The context of each message is shaped by the existing conditions and problems of each church. Each message is structured into seven parts: (1) address, (2) description of Christ, (3) commendation of the church, (4) a complaint, (5) an exhortation, (6) a threat, and (7) a promise (though the letters to Smyrna and Philadelphia lack complaint or threat sections because those churches are considered faithful).

The flow of thought in this letter generally conforms to the pattern of the other six letters except that the negative elements are omitted: (1) Christ presents himself with the attributes "holy" and "true" together with the descriptions from Isaiah 22:22 (which are particularly suitable to the situation of this church, and faith in this "holy" and "true" Christ provides the basis for overcoming the specific testing that they face [vv. 8–11]); (2) the church's situation and the particular problem they face are reviewed (introduced by "I know" [v. 8]); (3) on the basis of the situation and the problem, Christ issues an encouragement to persevere in the face of conflict (vv. 9–11); (4) then both the prior situation and problem, together with the corresponding encouragement to persevere, form the basis for the response of "overcoming" (v. 12a); (5) and "overcoming" becomes the basis for receiving Christ's promise of inheriting eternal life in the midst of his and his Father's presence, which uniquely corresponds to Christ's attributes in verse 7b; (6) then the concluding hearing formula (v. 13, "He who has an ear, let him hear . . .") is given to indicate either the basis or means for obtaining the promised inheritance. Therefore the thought flow of the letter climaxes with the promise of inheriting eternal life with Christ, which is the main point of this and each of the letters. The body of this letter, as of the others, provides the basis or condition on which the promise rests.

The main idea of the letter to Philadelphia may be stated as follows: Christ commends Philadelphia for its persevering witness, in which he will empower them further; he exhorts them to continue to persevere so that they may "overcome" and consequently inherit consummate end-time eternal life in fellowship and identification with Christ, which has been inaugurated in the present.

The informal quotation is found in the very first section of the letter (v. 7), where Christ presents himself with the attributes "holy" and "true" together with the descriptions from Isaiah 22:22. Thus, in the broader scheme of the letter, the Isaiah reference forms the beginning part of the overall basis (vv. 7b–12a) for overcoming and then receiving the inheritance promised by Christ.

Analyzing the Old Testament Context of Isaiah 22:22

The Broad Context

The first thirty-five chapters of Isaiah are prophecies of condemnation. The broad idea of Isaiah 1–39 is that of holy Yahweh punishing unholy humanity for the purposes of executing judgment, purging a faithful remnant from Israel and the nations, and restoring the Davidic kingdom—all of which will demonstrate God's glory. The context leading up to chapter 22 focuses on (1) God's coming judgment upon Judah (chaps. 1–6), (2) subsequent deliverance for an Israelite remnant (7–12), and (3) prophecies condemning the nations surrounding Israel (13–23).

In Isaiah 22, Israel is also condemned, thus demonstrating that Israel is to be judged just like the unbelieving and sinful pagan nations. Consequently, Israel comes to be identified with the nations (on which see also the notion that Israel has become like Sodom and Gomorrah in Isa. 1:9–10; 3:9; Jer. 23:14; Lam. 4:6; Ezek. 16:46–56; Hosea 11:8–9; Amos 4:11).

The Immediate Context

Isaiah 22:1–14 describes the wrong conduct of the people of Jerusalem during a siege and their defeat by the invading armies (probably by the king of Assyria in the days of Manasseh's rule during the middle of the seventh century BC, rather than by Nebuchadnezzar during the latter part of the sixth century BC). Hence this is a prediction of judgment upon Jerusalem, carried out by means of the Assyrian army, whose ultimate commander is Yahweh of hosts (v. 5).

Isaiah 22:15–19 predicts the divine removal of Shebna from his official position as second in authority to the king. Now the threat of judgment focuses no longer on the entire people but on an individual, since he is a representative of the people in his sin, likely even leading them into sin.

After narrating the displacement of Shebna, verses 20–25 recount his replacement. The Lord appoints Eliakim to be his servant, replacing Shebna (v. 20). The phrase "My servant" is wording found elsewhere in Isaiah (seventeen times). It is issued later in Isaiah to indicate Yahweh's divine appointment of his messianic servant to fulfill a specific purpose (cf. Isa. 42:6; 48:12; 49:1). The word *servant* itself in the singular is used twenty-four times by Isaiah, the vast majority bearing the idea of one who is uniquely appointed by Yahweh to serve him by fulfilling a specific purpose (e.g., Isaiah the prophet in Isa. 20:3; David in 37:35; the nation Israel in 41:8–9; 42:19; 43:10; and individual messianic servant passages in 42:1; 49:3, 6; 52:13; and 53:11). The idea of divine appointment for service is clear in Eliakim's name, which means "God will set up."

The Lord's purpose in calling Eliakim is reported in verses 21–22. Eliakim is to assume Shebna's rule, but now in the people's best interests. The replacement of Shebna by Eliakim is spoken of as investiture: "I will clothe him with your tunic and tie your sash securely about him" (v. 21a). This is a picture of a ceremony where Eliakim is directed into Shebna's office by the Lord's placing the symbols ("tunic" and "sash") of that office into his hands (v. 21a). That this office is not only political but may also include priestly responsibilities is suggested by the fact that "sash" ("girdle") always refers to a priestly garment, and "tunic" is also often related to priestly apparel (cf. the uses in the Pentateuch). The essential significance of the investiture ceremony is stated in political terms in verse 21b: "I will entrust him with your rule" (v. 21c). Eliakim is to be entrusted with the political "rule" that Shebna has formerly exercised. The nature of this "rule" is described in the remainder of verse 21 and in verse 22: "He will become a father to the inhabitants of Jerusalem and to the house of Judah" (v. 21c). Eliakim is to rule like a father does over his children, in the best interests of the people, a trait lacking with Shebna.

Verse 22 elaborates further on the nature of Eliakim's ruling office: "I will set the key of the house of David on his shoulder; when he opens no one shuts, when he shuts no one will open." Eliakim is to exercise absolute administrative control over the affairs of the royal household. The "key" is a picture denoting "power of control" over the affairs of "the house of David." This is not merely control of only Hezekiah's royal household at the time, but also that of the house of David. The "house of David" is a reference to the kingly office characterized by an eternal royal reign and kingdom promised to David (2 Sam. 7:13, 16; Pss. 89:4, 20–29; 132:11–12),[1] which his descendants are to inherit and carry on (cf. Rev. 21:7, which pictures future fulfillment of the inheritance mentioned in 2 Sam. 7:13–14). "Shoulder" represents the responsibility of Eliakim. The same metaphor is applied to the Messiah's kingship in Isaiah

1. The last two Psalm texts refer only to a throne and not a "house."

9:6–7 (cf. also there "rule/government," "his shoulder," "father," "throne," and "David"). Isaiah 22:21–22 is likely developing the thought of the Isaiah 9 passage and applying it to Eliakim, as if he might be the beginning fulfillment of this messianic prophecy.

The words "opening" and "closing" at the end of verse 22 are metaphors expressing the "power of royal administrative control."[2] This is a control specifically, for example, over who is admitted into the presence of the king to ask favors and who is admitted into the actual administrative service of the king. Therefore Eliakim's power is at least equal to the power of the king (Hezekiah) at the time. This kingly power is evident from recalling God's intention that Eliakim be granted the following things:

1. He is to be a *father* to all the inhabitants of Jerusalem.
2. He is to exercise the *rule* of Jerusalem.
3. He is to have control over the royal office that will continue forever, what the Lord promised David (Isa. 9:6–8).
4. He is to have power equal to that of the king (it is evident from history that King Hezekiah was sometimes dominated by his political assistants).

A final aspect of Eliakim's rule is stated in verse 23a. Yahweh will make his political office secure and successful: "I will drive him like a peg in a firm place" (v. 23a). The results of Eliakim's political security and success are prophesied in verses 23b–24: "He will become a throne of glory to his father's house. So they will hang on him all the glory of his father's house, offspring and issue, all the least of vessels, from bowls to all the jars." The Lord's securing of Eliakim's political success brings glory upon all of his relatives. "Glory" is a figure substituting the effect for the cause in that it represents the effects of the ruling efforts of Eliakim: his rule will result in he and his relatives being glorified and respected and benefiting in various material ways. Isaiah emphasizes that it is only because of Eliakim's successful and secure political position that his relatives receive glory (v. 24). There is an apparent pun between "glory" at the end of verse 23 and its repetition at the beginning of verse 24. The word *kābōd* can mean "weighty" in some contexts; in other contexts it conveys the idea of honor or respect. The idea of "honor," "glory," or "respect" is expressed in verse 23; the notion of "weight" is conveyed in verse 24. That is, the "honor" or "glory" resulting from his rule (v. 23b) is expressed as Eliakim is pictured like a firm peg on which hang heavy utensils (his father's relatives). Just as several utensils of great weight are held up on a wall by only one peg, so also

2. When the Hebrew words *pātaḥ* (open) and *sāgar* (shut) occur together elsewhere, the point is to underscore absolute control over a city (Isa. 60:11; Jer. 13:19), a kingdom (Isa. 45:1), or the temple precincts (Neh. 13:19; Ezek. 44:2; 46:1).

those many members of Eliakim's father's house will receive honor and favor due only to his political position and their familial relationship to him.

The phrase "all the least of vessels" in verse 24 indicates that even the least important of Eliakim's relatives will receive honor. Thus even the most insignificant of Eliakim's relatives will receive honor only because of his position and ability to carry out the functions of his office (perhaps involving nepotism). As Franz Delitzsch says, "The whole of this large but hitherto ignoble family of relations would fasten upon Eliakim and climb through him to honor."[3]

After predicting Eliakim's rise to a firm and successful position of rule, Yahweh predicts his eventual and sure fall from that position: "'In that day,' declares the Lord of hosts, 'the peg driven in a firm place will give way; it will even break off and fall, and the load hanging on it will be cut off, for the Lord has spoken'" (v. 25). Consequently, the office established by God for Eliakim would not continue to be possessed by him or his relatives because of the Lord's word. The verse begins and ends with the affirmation that Eliakim's fall is based on the decretive word of God, which is explicitly expressed at the end of the verse ("*because* [*kî*] the Lord has spoken" [AT]). Apparently the reason why God will bring about the demise of Eliakim is that, though he is described with specific features from the prophecy of the coming messianic king's eternal rule (Isa. 9:6–7), he is not the one to fulfill this prophecy. God's people must await another figure in subsequent history to fulfill this prophecy.

Conclusion: Summary of the Significance of Isaiah 22:22 in Its Immediate Context

Yahweh will appoint his servant Eliakim to replace the evil Shebna and rule in the best interests of Jerusalem. Eliakim will bring glory to his relatives but eventually will fall from office.

Surveying the Use of Isaiah 22:22 in Judaism

There are no significant uses of Isaiah 22:22 in Judaism except for the interpretative paraphrases in the Greek OT and the targum,[4] which will be addressed below in the textual comparisons.[5]

3. F. Delitzsch, *Biblical Commentary on the Prophecies of Isaiah* (Edinburgh: T&T Clark, 1881), 1:403.

4. An obscure use occurs in the *Midrash Sifre/Sipre on Deuteronomy*, piska 321, with reference to a "craftsman" who skillfully teaches others the Torah and who "opens and closes (the discussion) to fulfill that which is written" in Isa. 22:22; so virtually identical is *Seder Olam* [*Order of Eternity/the World*] 25. Both these uses come from later Judaism and likely do not represent earlier traditions.

5. Hebrew and Greek fonts are used in these charts below instead of English transliteration to clarify the textual comparisons.

Comparing Old Testament and New Testament Texts

Isaiah 22:22 (MT)	Isaiah 22:22 (LXX)	Revelation 3:7c
וְנָתַתִּי מַפְתֵּחַ בֵּית־דָּוִד עַל־שִׁכְמוֹ וּפָתַח וְאֵין סֹגֵר וְסָגַר וְאֵין פֹּתֵחַ 1QIsa[a] reads identically.	καὶ δώσω τὴν δόξαν Δαυιδ *αὐτῷ, καὶ ἄρξει, καὶ οὐκ ἔσται ὁ ἀντιλέγων.**	*ὁ ἔχων* τὴν κλεῖν Δαυίδ, ὁ ἀνοίγων καὶ οὐδεὶς κλείσει καὶ κλείων καὶ οὐδεὶς ἀνοίγει.

Note: Italics indicate unique wording in the LXX and Revelation in comparison with the Hebrew.

* Some LXX manuscripts and traditions conform to the MT, perhaps sometimes as the result of Christian scribal influence, on which see J. Ziegler, ed., Isaias, 3rd ed., vol. 14 of *Septuaginta: Vetus Testamentum Graecum*, Auctoritate Academiae Scientiarum Göttingensis editum (Göttingen: Vandenhoeck & Ruprecht, 1983), 199–200. Among the LXX traditions, of course, are the second-century Jewish versions of Aquila, Theodotion, and Symmachus (the latter two especially, which sometimes reflect first-century readings), which also give variant literal renderings of the Hebrew (or proto-MT) of Isa. 22:22. It is possible that these versions may have influenced both the later Greek manuscript variants and Rev. 3:7, which also reflect a more literal rendering. But note that in contrast to the three Jewish Greek versions above, the NT (as well as the eclectic LXX) omits the Hebrew's reference to "house" before "David" and "upon his shoulder" following "David," and Rev. 3:7 also apparently substitutes "the one having" for "I will give," which appears in the MT, LXX, Jewish versions, and other literal renderings. Furthermore, Rev. 3:7 is also different in the way it literally renders the rest of Isa. 22:22. All of these factors show that Rev. 3:7 is significantly different from the Jewish versions and LXX manuscript variants, and this points to John (Jesus) making his own literal translation.

Isaiah 22:22 (MT)	Isaiah 22:22 (LXX)	Revelation 3:7c
I have given the key of the house of David upon his shoulder; when he opens, then no one shuts, and when he shuts, then no one opens. [AT]	I will give the *glory* of David *to him, and he will rule, and there will be no one contradicting him*. [AT]	*The one having* the key of David, the one opening and no one will shut, and the one shutting and no one opens. [AT]

Note: Italics indicate unique wording in the LXX and Revelation in comparison with the Hebrew.

Analyzing the Author's Textual Use of the Old Testament

It is clear that Revelation 3:7 is in line with the Hebrew of Isaiah 22:22 and not the OT Greek. Therefore Revelation 3:7 draws from the Hebrew text, even though there are some minor differences between the Hebrew and Revelation 3:7. For example, instead of saying that God "has given the key of the house of David upon his shoulder," Revelation says Christ "has the key of David" (also omitting "house" and "shoulder" of the Hebrew text).

Even though John does not quote from the Greek OT or from the targum[6] (on which see below), it is worthwhile to observe how these versions interpret the Hebrew text, which is part of early Jewish interpretative tradition. For example, the LXX tries to give the meaning of the figurative pictures of the Hebrew text: "the key of the house of David" is rendered "the glory of David,"

6. Or a tradition represented by the targum.

and the repeated "opening and closing" phrases are summarized as "he will rule, and there will not be one who contradicts him [opposes his rule]." The targum also interprets the figurative pictures of the Hebrew text: "And he will place the key *of the sanctuary and the authority* of the house of David in his hand; and he will open and none shall shut; and he will shut and none shall open." The targum understands that Eliakim will exercise not only the kingly authority of "the house of David" but also the priestly authority over the temple. This interpretation appears to have been sparked by the preceding mention that Eliakim would be "clothed with a robe" and a "cincture" (or "belt" or "girdle"), typical clothing of priests in the OT, as we observed above. This priestly interpretation continues throughout the remainder of verses 23–25 of the targum, as we will later see.

These interpretative expansions in the LXX and Targum may have some relevance to the way the Isaiah 22:22 citation is developed in the conclusion to the letter to Philadelphia, which we will look at later in this chapter.

Analyzing the Interpretative (Hermeneutical) Use of the Old Testament: Revelation 3:7 in Its Context

Revelation 3:7 as a Typological Use of the Old Testament in the New

John applies Isaiah 22:22 to Christ. This is, at the least, an analogical use of the OT in the NT: what was described of Eliakim is now by analogy described of Christ. But there is reason to think that this is more than a mere analogy. John views Isaiah 22:22 as a prophecy of Christ, not through direct verbal means, but through the prophetic events narrated about Eliakim, which came to pass within the OT period. Since it is not a direct verbal prediction, it is typological in that it is a historical prefigurement or foreshadowing of what is to take place on a grander scale with regard to the future Messiah (see further elaboration on "typology" at the beginning of chap. 4 above, including examples of other typological uses). It may be that Isaiah's intent concerns only the historical context, but the divine intent includes this and also the prefigurement of the Messiah's future relation to the "house of David." We will see, however, that Isaiah the prophet himself is likely aware to some degree that the imminent history that he is narrating about Eliakim points beyond Eliakim to another who will come to do what Eliakim fails to do.

The main typological correspondence between Eliakim and Christ is that Christ, as Eliakim, is to have absolute control and power over the Davidic throne as king. Whereas Eliakim's authority is primarily political and exercised over a physical kingdom (though there are hints of his possible priestly role), the immediate context of Revelation 3:7 underscores that Christ's kingdom has begun in a spiritual manner. That is, his sovereignty is said to be exercised with respect to who would be received or not received into his spiritual palace or kingdom. This is highlighted by noticing that each of Christ's self-descriptions at the beginning of each of the letters is an allusive development of some reference to him in chapter 1. This second part of the self-description in 3:7 is based on 1:18b, where Jesus claims to "have the keys of death and of Hades." In this respect, the Isaiah 22:22 citation further interprets what it means that Jesus now "[has] the keys of death and Hades." That this imagery is based on 1:18b is apparent from two observations. First, virtually the exact expressions occur in both texts: compare "the one having the key" in 3:7 and "I have the keys" in 1:18b. Second, as noted above, all of the other introductory self-descriptions develop phrases from chap. 1 (even the immediately preceding phrase of 3:7b, "the true," develops "the faithful" in 1:5, as apparent from 3:14 where Christ calls himself the "*faithful* and *true* Witness," which also develops 1:5).

These keys are called the "keys of death and of Hades" in Revelation 1:18b; now in 3:7b the quotation from Isaiah 22:22 is substituted: "the one having the key of David, who opens and no one shuts, and who shuts and no one opens" (the difference in singular "key" and plural "keys" is likely not significant). The substitution is meant to amplify the idea of the original phrase in 1:18b by underscoring the sovereignty that Christ holds over the sphere "of death and Hades." This sovereignty is explained to be the promised Davidic kingship, which Christ has inherited and which he exercises.

The point of the citation from Isaiah is that Jesus holds the power over salvation and judgment. In Revelation 1:18 the stress is on his sovereignty over death and judgment, while in 3:7 the emphasis is on his authority over those entering the kingdom. John compares the historical situation of Eliakim in relation to Israel with that of Christ in relation to the church in order to help the readers better understand the position that Christ now holds as head of the true Israel and how this affects them. Furthermore, Eliakim's political control extended over Jerusalem, Judah, and the house of David, but Christ's inaugurated spiritual sovereignty was designed to extend over all peoples (including the gentiles in the Philadelphian church and elsewhere). In the light of the broader context of the entire book of Revelation, Christ's kingship begins to be exercised over a spiritual realm, but at the consummation of his messianic kingdom, he will rule both spiritually and over the physical realm of the new heavens and earth (e.g., see Rev. 11:15; 22:3). Thus Eliakim's rule prefigures Christ's greater rule.

The directly following context of Isaiah 22:22 reveals further possible typological correspondences between Eliakim and Christ, which could also be resonating in John's (Jesus's) mind:

1. As Eliakim's office may have included some sort of priestly concerns, so also such concerns are included on a grander scale with Christ's royal office.[7]

7. We saw above that the targumic paraphrase of Isa. 22:22, "I will place the key of the *sanctuary* and the authority of the house of David in his hand," understands Eliakim's office to have a

2. As Eliakim was to be a father to the people, so is Christ on a greater scale (note the reference to "Eternal Father" in the Isa. 9:6 messianic prophecy, which is likely echoed in referring to Eliakim as a "father" in Isa. 22:21).
3. As Eliakim's power was equal to the king's, so Christ's power is equal to God's.
4. Just as Eliakim's office was made secure and successful by the Lord, so Christ's office is made such, not only by God the Father but also by Christ himself; Eliakim did not have the intrinsic qualities and power to do so, but Christ, possessing the divine attributes of "holy" and "true" (3:7), does.[8]
5. Just as Eliakim's ability in performing the political functions of his office would bring temporary glory to his physical relatives, so Christ's ability to function in his office (death, resurrection, and subsequent reign) will result in his spiritual seed's sharing in his eternal glory (cf. Rev. 4:9–11; 5:12–13 with Rev. 21:11, 23–26).
6. Whereas Eliakim's office of kingly power was not to last forever, Christ's reign is to be eternal.

Although it is difficult to know whether all six contextual ideas from Isaiah were in the writer's mind to some degree, together the parallels show why this OT passage would have been so attractive to apply to Christ. In conclusion, Isaiah 22:22 is a typological-prophetic picture of Christ as the absolute

priestly nature (and v. 24 of the targum also views Eliakim's relatives as priests who rely on him for their glory); likewise, the later *Midrash Rabbah Exodus* 37:1 understands Eliakim in Isa. 22:23 as a "high priest." And it is not coincidence that in Rev. 3:12 Christ also is seen as having power over who enters God's temple, thus pointing further to priestly associations: "He who overcomes, I will make him a pillar in the temple of My God." Note also the probable priestly description of Christ in Rev. 1:13, on which see G. K. Beale, *The Book of Revelation*, NIGTC (Grand Rapids: Eerdmans, 1999), 208–9. In Rev. 3:12, the permanent establishment of the overcomer as a pillar in the temple may also continue the imagery of Isa. 22:22–24, where Eliakim's relatives achieve glory by hanging on him as on a *peg* firmly attached to a wall. Some Greek OT witnesses even refer to Eliakim as being set up as a "pillar" in Isa. 22:23 (Vaticanus, Origen, and Q read *stēloō*, "I will set up as a pillar" or "I will inscribe on a pillar," thus following H. Kraft, *Die Offenbarung des Johannes*, HNT 16a [Tübingen: Mohr Siebeck, 1974], 82; cf. J. Fekkes, *Isaiah and Prophetic Traditions in the Book of Revelation: Visionary Antecedents and Their Development*, JSNTSup 92 [Sheffield: JSOT Press, 1994], 130–33, though skeptical about LXX influence). In contrast to Eliakim's dependents, who eventually lost their glory and position in the palace when he was finally removed (cf. Isa. 22:23–25), the followers of Jesus will never be removed from their position in the temple-palace because Jesus, the "true" Messiah, will never lose his regal position in the presence of his Father (hence "pillar" is metaphorical for permanence).

8. The phrase "the holy, the true" describes a divine attribute elsewhere in Revelation (so 6:10) so that the use of it here suggests Jesus's deity. In fact, *hagios* (holy) is used of Yahweh almost exclusively in Isaiah as part of the title "the Holy One of Israel" (about twenty times). This Isaiah background is probably present here in anticipation of the directly following Isa. 22:22 citation and of the Isaianic allusions in Rev. 3:9, where Jesus assumes the role of Yahweh and his followers represent the true Israel (on which see further Beale, *Revelation*, 287–89).

sovereign and king of the messianic kingdom, being the final completion of what was only partially pictured through the historical figure and office of Eliakim.

Validation That Isaiah 22:22 Is an Indirect Typological Prophecy

In chapter 5 (above), it was argued that one of the presuppositions underlying the NT's use of the OT is that the same patterns of past historical events will occur again on a grander scale because of God's absolute sovereignty over history and his design that history will have an essential unity. It was also observed that this presupposition is an essential foundation for typology. That the Eliakim passage illustrates this is evident from the following considerations, which indicate that John's use of Isaiah 22:22 is not merely analogically applied but is also an indirect typological pointer (conveyed through Isaiah's historical narration rather than as a direct verbal, messianic prophecy). This sort of analysis must take place anytime one tries to categorize an OT use as typological rather than merely as analogical, and it is one reason why I have chosen this particular passage as an illustrative Old-in-the-New use for this chapter.

First, whenever David is mentioned in connection with Christ in the NT, there are usually discernible prophetic, messianic overtones (e.g., cf. Matt. 1:1; 22:42–45; Mark 11:10; 12:35–37; Luke 1:32; 20:41–44; John 7:42; Acts 2:30–36; 13:34; 15:16; Rom. 1:1–4; 2 Tim 2:8; cf. other places where David's sufferings are a type of Christ's: Ps. 22:18 in John 19:24; Ps. 69:21 in John 19:28). The only other occurrences of "house of David" in the NT have the same prophetic nuance (Luke 1:27, 69; so also "tabernacle of David" in Acts 15:16), as do the only remaining references to David in Revelation, both of which are allusions to Isaianic messianic prophecies (Rev. 5:5; 22:16 [cf. Isa. 11:1, 10]).

Second, the reference to Eliakim as "My servant" in Isaiah 22:20 would have been easily associated with Isaiah's messianic Servant prophecies of chaps. 42–53, since the phrase occurs there five times in this respect.[9]

Third, in Isaiah 22 the description of placing "the key of the house of David [= administrative responsibility for the kingdom of Judah] on his [Eliakim's] shoulder," the mention of his being a "father" to those in "Jerusalem and to the house of Judah," and the reference to him as "becoming a throne of glory"—all would have facilitated such a prophetic understanding of Isaiah 22:22 since this language is so strikingly parallel to the prophecy of the future Israelite ruler of Isaiah 9:6–7 ("The government will rest on *his shoulders*, . . .

9. The same phrase in the singular occurs nine times in Isa. 41–45 with reference to the unfaithful nation of Israel, with which the faithful messianic Servant is contrasted yet also is summing up and representing; outside of these occurrences, the Servant Songs, and Isa. 22:20, the phrase "My servant" occurs only twice elsewhere in Isaiah—in reference to the prophet himself (20:3) and to David (37:35).

and his name will be called . . . Eternal *Father*," who sits "on the *throne of David*"). As mentioned earlier, it is likely that Isaiah 22:22 intentionally applies the language of the coming messianic king to Eliakim to show him as a figure who might potentially fulfill the Isaiah 9 prophecy. As we saw, God did not deem that Eliakim be that figure, and so his decretive word causes Eliakim to fall and not to achieve what Isaiah 9 predicts. In contrast, God promises that at some point in the future he will finally accomplish the fulfillment in one who will realize the prophetic description: "The zeal of the LORD of hosts will accomplish this" (Isa. 9:7).

If the connection drawn between Isaiah 9:6–7 and 22:22 is correct, then it is probable that Isaiah himself would to some degree have been aware of the link and seen Eliakim not only as one who failed to fulfill the earlier prophecy but also as one whose failure pointed to the eventual success of another who would fulfill it. Accordingly, Revelation 3:7 sees that the Isaiah 9 pattern—partially and temporarily reflected in Eliakim and understood by Isaiah to point still forward to another—is finally fulfilled in Jesus.

Fourth, that Isaiah 22:22 is viewed with a prophetic, typological sense is further evident by observing the intentional allusions to prophetic Servant passages (Isa. 43:4; 45:14; 49:23) in the immediately following context of Revelation 3:9. These allusions, however, are now applied to the church instead of the theocratic nation of Israel (as in Isaiah), although the rationale for the application lies in an understanding of the church's corporate identification with Jesus as God's servant and true Israel[10] (e.g., Isa. 49:3–6 and the use of 49:6 in Luke 2:32; Acts 13:47; 26:23).

Fifth, Gerhard von Rad has also argued for a typological understanding of this OT text in Revelation 3:7, though on a somewhat different but plausible basis than so far argued in this chapter. In this connection, he says, the

> range of Old Testament saving utterances is that which tells of the calls of charismatic persons and of people summoned to great offices. . . . In the case of certain descriptions of the call and the failure of charismatic leaders (Gideon, Samson, and Saul), we are dealing with literary compositions which already show a *typological* trend, in that the narrators are only concerned with the phenomenon of the *rise* and *speedy failure* of the man thus called. Here, too, in each case there is a fulfillment, the proof of the charisma and victory. Suddenly, however, these men are removed, Jahweh can no longer consider them, and the story ends with the reader feeling that, since *Jahweh has so far been unable to find a really suitable instrument, the commission remains unfulfilled. Can we not say of each of these stories that Jahweh's designs far transcend their historical contexts?* What happened to the ascriptions of a universal rule

10. On which see Beale, *Revelation*, 386–89. Recall how Christ and the church fulfill what is prophesied of Israel in the OT, which is part of the reason for the presupposition discussed in chap. 5 concerning Jesus and the church as representing true end-time Israel.

> made by Jahweh to the kings of Judah? It is impossible that the post-exilic readers and transmitters of these Messianic texts saw them only as venerable monuments of a glorious but vanished past. . . . These men [Saul, David, etc.] all passed away; but the tasks, the titles and the divine promises connected with them, were handed on. *The Shebna-Eliakim pericope is a fine example of such transmission. . . . The almost Messianic full powers of the unworthy Shebna pass over, solemnly renewed, to Eliakim. Yet he too will fail. Thus, the office of "the key of David" remained unprovided for until finally it could be laid down at the feet of Christ.* (italics added)[11]

Thus, when various segments of the OT contain repeated clusterings of narrations about Yahweh's commissioning people to fill certain offices (e.g., judges, prophets, priests, kings), the repeated failure of the ones commissioned, followed by judgment, and followed by the same cycle of failure again and again—all this is the narrator's way of pointing the reader to think of one who would come and finally fulfill the commission. That at least some readers would have picked up on this narrative device is plausible since readers would also have been aware of ascriptions elsewhere in the OT of messianic texts, affirming a final universal rule by an ideal individual who would fulfill these commissions. It is plausible that Revelation 3:7 picked up the same narrative clue from the context of Isaiah 22:22 (esp. in light of the earlier parallel about the coming Messiah in Isa. 9:6–7) and thus applied it to Jesus the Messiah.

Sixth, the use of Isaiah 22:22 in Revelation 3:7 meets the essential requirements of a type: *correspondence*, *historicity*, *escalation*, *predictiveness*, and a *retrospective* interpretative stance (the latter of which clarifies Isaiah's own typological understanding in Isa. 22:22).

The Use of Isaiah 22:22 Elsewhere in the New Testament or in Early Christianity

This OT passage does not occur elsewhere in the NT,[12] nor does it occur significantly in the church fathers.[13]

11. G. von Rad, *Old Testament Theology* (New York: Harper & Row, 1965), 2:372–73. We adduced part of this quotation in chaps. 1 and 4, but since von Rad applies its significance specifically to the use of Isa. 22 in Rev. 3, it is appropriate to quote part of it again.

12. The NA[27] lists Isa. 22:22 as an allusion in Matt. 16:19; D. A. Carson, *Matthew, Chapters 13 through 28*, EBC (Grand Rapids: Zondervan, 1995), 370, sees Isa. 22:15, 22 as a possible allusion, though he does not comment further on its significance. The present discussion will not consider Matt. 16:19, since it is not clear whether it alludes to Isa. 22:22.

13. Origen's *Commentary on the Gospel of John* 5.4 cites Isa. 22:22 to indicate that the Lord is the ultimate revealer and interpreter of the Bible in a way similar to how we saw later Judaism referring to it. Gregory Thaumaturgus's *Oration and Panegyric Addressed to Origen* 15 cites either Isa. 22:22 or Rev. 3:7 to support the notion that a person can apprehend and rightly interpret Scripture only by the revealing work of the Spirit.

Theological Implications

Christology

1. John views Christ as identified with Yahweh. Just as Eliakim was equal in status to Israel's king, so Christ is equal in status to God, the eschatological king. The reference to Jesus as "holy" and "true" (the former of which we saw was a repeated attribute of God in Isaiah)[14] directly precedes the Isaiah 22:22 citation and thus enhances Jesus's identification with God.

2. Christ is also the ruler of eschatological Israel.

Soteriology

Christ's salvific authority pertains primarily to his sovereignty over who enters into the kingdom. Christ "opens" the door to some, while he "shuts" the door to others; salvation and exclusion from the kingdom are based in Christ's determinate will, not in human will or actions. Nevertheless, in the context of Revelation 1–3, people are also accountable for whether they respond in faith to the crucified and resurrected Christ (see 1:5–6, 17–18 for this portrayal of Christ).[15]

Eternal Security

To whomever Christ opens the door into the kingdom, that one shall remain there forever. This notion is indicated in 3:12 by the phrase "I will make him a pillar in the temple of My God, and he will not go out from it anymore."

Ecclesiology

In this passage Christ is depicted as the head of the local church body, the Davidic king of the true end-time Israel, guiding their activities and opportunities.[16]

Evangelism

Christ's sovereignty in providing the Philadephian Christians with an "open door" of salvation is also an "open door" for them to be effective in conveying the message of salvation to unbelievers. Such an understanding on the part of these Christians likely was a motivation for them to share the message of the gospel with others.

14. On which see note 8 about this phrase on p. 142. Likewise "holy" and "true" are divine attributes in Rev. 6:10.

15. Thus, there is a tension between divine sovereignty and accountability, on which see Beale, *Revelation*, 518.

16. Elaboration of this point is needed here, but I must be content in directing the reader to my discussion of Rev. 3:8–9, 12 in Beale, *Revelation*, 285–89, 293–96.

Rhetorical Use (Pastoral Application)

Rhetoric is the way an author uses his message to move the readers to affirm certain theological or ethical goals. Christ's sovereign position as eschatological king and priest as a greater Eliakim and the believers' identification with him are intended to assure the Philadelphian Christians that they really do participate as ruling conquerors in end-time salvation and the temple. They need this encouragement because they "have a little power" in comparison to the threatening society around them (Rev. 3:8). This assurance is meant to motivate them to continue to persevere boldly in the face of opposition in identifying with Christ and proclaiming the gospel (v. 8a), since they are assured that their witness will be effective (see v. 9). Furthermore, ethnic Israel, which claims to be the divine agent wielding the power of salvation and judgment, has excluded Christians from their "synagogue," even though ethnic Israel no longer maintains this position because of their rejection of Christ. However, because of their identification with Christ in the true temple (v. 12), Christ's followers can be assured that the doors to the true synagogue (temple) are open to them, whereas the doors to the true temple remain closed to those who reject Christ. Nevertheless, Christ will use their witness to "open the door" of the true temple to the very Jews who are rejecting Christ and them (3:8–9). Knowing that Christ will give them an "open door" to effectively convey the gospel to unbelievers should motivate them all the more to do so, even to the Jews who oppose them. When people have the power to fulfill God's difficult commands, they have all the more motivation to fulfill those commands.

As in the case of the other six letters, Christ presents himself in this letter (Rev. 3:7) with attributes particularly suitable to the problematic situation of the church. Faith in Christ who possesses these attributes provides the basis and motivation for overcoming the challenges facing them and inheriting the end-time promises of identification with Christ and all that this entails.

Conclusion

Many other examples could have been chosen as a case study on the use of the OT in the NT. Nevertheless, the one chosen for this chapter is an attempt to present a fairly typical case, particularly with respect to how important the OT context is for interpreting an OT reference in a NT passage. I will list sources in which to find a mere sampling of other passages in the following excursus that could also serve as classic case studies.

Excursus: A Sampling of Other Case Studies on the Use of the Old Testament in the New

As I mentioned in the introduction of this *Handbook*, the approach elaborated on throughout the book is an attempt to explain the interpretative method behind the many studies of the OT in the NT in our *Commentary on the New Testament Use of the Old Testament*.[17] Many examples from the commentary could be adduced here. For good examples of the approach explained in chapter 3 and of the various uses explained in chapter 4 of the handbook, one may merely consult the initial chapters by Craig L. Blomberg (on Matthew), Rikk E. Watts (on Mark), and David W. Pao and Eckhard J. Schnabel (on Luke), paying special attention to the discussion of actual quotations (and not allusions). These discussions provide more examples of how the approach displayed in this book has been worked out by other scholars in other books of the NT. In addition to the commentary, another source for good examples of the approach in this handbook is S. L. Johnson, *The Old Testament in the New* (Grand Rapids: Zondervan, 1980). Other sources could be mentioned here, a number of which can be found in the bibliography that follows.

17. G. K. Beale and D. A. Carson, eds., *Commentary on the New Testament Use of the Old Testament* (Grand Rapids: Baker Academic, 2007).

Select Bibliography on the New Testament Use of the Old

It would be difficult to provide a thorough bibliography on the OT in the NT since books and articles in this field have proliferated, especially in the last twenty years. This bibliography is not intended to be thorough: some significant works may not be included. I have tried to list (with occasional annotations) several works in the field, including the most significant. For supplements to this bibliography (e.g., more special technical studies), see the respective bibliographies at the end of each essay on each NT book in Beale and Carson, *Commentary on the New Testament Use of the Old Testament*, as well as the sources below, especially those marked with an asterisk.[1]

Tools for Comparing Various Old Testament Versions with Old Testament Quotations and Allusions in the New Testament

Aland, B., K. Aland, J. Karavidopoulos, C. M. Martini, and B. M. Metzger, eds. *The Greek New Testament*. 4th ed. Stuttgart: Deutsche Bibelgesellschaft/United Bible Societies, 1993. The UBS[4] cites a quotation, and the first and last principal word of the citation are given at the bottom. Similarly, at the bottom it also cites the principal words of which allusions are viewed to consist.

1. To a significant extent this bibliography reproduces that in G. K. Beale, ed., *The Right Doctrine from the Wrong Texts? Essays on the Use of the Old Testament in the New Testament* (Grand Rapids: Baker, 1994), though it has been selectively updated. Some of the sources in the book-by-book selections toward the end of the bibliography have been derived from, among other sources, the online bibliographies of Roy Ciampa at Gordon-Conwell Theological Seminary (http://www.viceregency.com) and the Paul and Scripture Seminar of the Society of Biblical Literature (which ceased functioning in 2010, though its bibliography on Paul is online: http://paulandscripturebibliography.blogspot.com/).

———, eds. *Novum Testamentum Graece*. 27th ed. Stuttgart: Deutsche Bibelgesellschaft/United Bible Societies, 1993. The margins list the quotations from OT passages as well as many allusions. There is also a summary of all marginal OT references in an appendix.

Archer, G., and G. Chinichigno. *Old Testament Quotations in the New Testament: A Complete Survey*. Chicago: Moody, 1983.

Beale, G. K., and D. A. Carson, eds. *Commentary on the New Testament Use of the Old Testament*. Grand Rapids: Baker Academic, 2007.

Bratcher, R. G. *Old Testament Quotations in the New Testament*. London: United Bible Societies, 1961. Repr., 1984.

Dittmar, W. *Vetus Testamentum in Novo: Die alttestamentlichen Parallelen des Neuen Testament im Wortlaut der Urtexte und der Septuaginta*. 2 vols. Göttingen: Vandenhoeck & Ruprecht, 1899. Vol. 1 on the Gospels through Acts is online at Google Books.

Evans, C. A. *Ancient Texts for New Testament Studies: A Guide to the Background Literature*. Peabody, MA: Hendrickson, 2005. See 342–409.

Fairbairn, P. *Hermeneutical Manual*. Edinburgh: T&T Clark, 1876. See 354–460. Online at Google Books.

Gough, H. *The New Testament Quotations Collated with the Scriptures of the Old Testament*. London: Walton & Maberly, 1855. Online at Google Books.

Hübner, H. *Vetus Testamentum in Novo*. Vol. 1.2, *Johannesvangelium*. Vol. 2, *Corpus Paulinum*. Göttingen: Vandenhoeck & Ruprecht, 1997–.

Hühn, E. *Die alttestamentlichen Citate und Reminiscenzen im Neuen Testamente*. Tübingen: Mohr Siebeck, 1900.

McLean, B. *Citations and Allusions to Jewish Scripture in Early Christian and Jewish Writings through 180 C.E.* Lewiston, NY: Edwin Mellen, 1992.

Toy, C. H. *Quotations in the New Testament*. New York: Scribner's, 1884. Online at Google Books.

Turpie, D. M. *The Old Testament in the New*. London: Williams & Norgate, 1868. Online at Google Books.

Books and Essays on Various Aspects of the Use of the Old Testament in the New

*Baker, D. W. *Two Testaments, One Bible: A Study of Some Modern Solutions to the Theological Problem of the Relationship between the Old and New Testaments*. Downers Grove, IL: InterVarsity, 1976. 3rd, rev. ed., 2010.

Barrett, C. K. "The Interpretation of the Old Testament in the New." In *The Cambridge History of the Bible*, vol. 1, *From the Beginnings to Jerome*, edited by P. R. Ackroyd and C. F. Evans, 377–411. Cambridge: Cambridge University Press, 1970.

*Beale, G. K., ed. *The Right Doctrine from the Wrong Texts? Essays on the Use of the Old Testament in the New*. Grand Rapids: Baker, 1994.

*Beale, G. K., and D. A. Carson, eds. *Commentary on the New Testament Use of the Old Testament*. Grand Rapids: Baker Academic, 2007.

Berding, K., and Jonathan Lunde, eds. *Three Views on the New Testament Use of the Old Testament*. Grand Rapids: Zondervan, 2008.

Betz, O., and G. F. Hawthorne, eds. *Tradition and Interpretation in the New Testament: Essays in Honor of E. Earl Ellis for His Sixtieth Birthday*. Grand Rapids: Eerdmans, 1987.

Black, M. "The Christological Use of the Old Testament in the New Testament." *New Testament Studies* 18 (1971–72): 1–14.

———. "The Theological Appropriation of the Old Testament by the New Testament." *Scottish Journal of Theology* 39 (1986): 1–17.

Bock, D. L. "Evangelicals and the Use of the Old Testament in the New." *Bibliotheca sacra* 142 (1985): 209–23, 306–19.

Bruce, F. F. *New Testament Development of Old Testament Themes*. Grand Rapids: Eerdmans, 1968.

*Carson, D. A., and H. G. M. Williamson, eds. *It Is Written: Scripture Citing Scripture; Essays in Honour of Barnabas Lindars*. Cambridge: Cambridge University Press, 1988. See especially the introductory essays by I. H. Marshall and M. Wilcox, as well as essays on the use of the OT in the respective NT books by G. Stanton, M. Hooker, C. K. Barrett, D. A. Carson, D. M. Smith, A. T. Hanson, R. Bauckham, and G. K. Beale; consult bibliographies at the end of each article.

Clowney, E. *Preaching and Biblical Theology*. Grand Rapids: Eerdmans, 1961. This work discusses typology.

Daniélou, J. *From Shadows to Reality: Studies in the Typology of the Fathers*. London: Burns & Oates, 1960.

———. "The New Testament and the Theology of History." *Studia evangelica* 1 (1959): 25–34.

*Davidson, R. M. *Typology in Scripture*. Andrews University Seminary Doctoral Dissertation Series 2. Berrien Springs, MI: Andrews University Press, 1981.

Dodd, C. H. *According to the Scriptures: The Sub-Structure of New Testament Theology*. London: Nisbet, 1952.

Drane, J. W. "Typology." *Evangelical Quarterly* 50 (1978): 195–210.

Edgar, S. L. "New Testament and Rabbinic Messianic Interpretation." *New Testament Studies* 5 (1958): 47–54.

Efird, J. M., ed. *The Use of the Old Testament in the New and Other Essays: Studies in Honor of William Franklin Stinespring*. Durham, NC: Duke University Press, 1972.

Ellis, E. E. "Biblical Interpretation in the New Testament Church." In *Mikra*, edited by M. J. Mulder, 691–725. Minneapolis: Fortress, 1990.

———. "How the New Testament Uses the Old." In *New Testament Interpretation: Essays on Principles and Methods*, edited by I. H. Marshall, 199–219. Grand Rapids: Eerdmans, 1977.

———. "Midrash, Targum and New Testament Quotations." In *Neotestamentica et Semitica: Studies in Honour of Matthew Black*, edited by E. E. Ellis and M. Wilcox, 119–219. Edinburgh: T&T Clark, 1969.

*———. *The Old Testament in Early Christianity*. Grand Rapids: Baker, 1992. Consult the helpful bibliography on 63–74.

———. *Prophecy and Hermeneutic in Early Christianity*. Grand Rapids: Eerdmans, 1978.

Eriksson, L. *"Come, Children, Listen to Me!": Psalm 34 in the Hebrew Bible and in Early Christian Writings*. Coniectanea Biblica, OT Series 32. Uppsala: Almqvist & Wiksell International, 1991.

Eslinger, L. "Inner-Biblical Exegesis and Inner-Biblical Allusion: The Question of Category." *Vetus Testamentum* 42 (1992): 47–58.

Evans, C. A., ed. *From Prophecy to Testament: The Function of the Old Testament in the New*. Peabody, MA: Hendrickson, 2004.

Evans, C. A., and W. Stinespring, eds. *Early Jewish and Christian Exegesis: Studies in Memory of William Hugh Brownlee*. Atlanta: Scholars Press, 1987.

Fairbairn, P. *The Typology of Scripture*. 2 vols. New York: Funk & Wagnalls, 1900. Repr., 2 vols. in 1, Grand Rapids: Kregel, 1989.

Farrer, A. "Typology (Ancient Hypotheses Reconsidered)." *Expository Times* 67 (1956): 228–31.

Feinberg, J. S., ed. *Continuity and Discontinuity: Perspectives on the Relationship between the Old and New Testaments; Essays in Honor of S. Lewis Johnson, Jr.* Westchester, IL: Crossway, 1988.

Fitzmyer, J. A. "The Use of Explicit Old Testament Quotations in Qumran Literature and in the New Testament." *New Testament Studies* 7 (1960–61): 297–333.

Foulkes, F. "The Acts of God: A Study of the Basis of Typology in the Old Testament." In *The Right Doctrine from the Wrong Texts? Essays on the Use of the Old Testament in the New*, edited by G. K. Beale, 342–71. Grand Rapids: Baker, 1994.

France, R. T. "'In All the Scriptures'—A Study of Jesus' Typology." *Theological Students Fellowship Bulletin* 56 (1970): 13–16.

Gage, W. A. *The Gospel of Genesis: Studies in Protology and Eschatology*. Winona Lake, IN: Carpenter Books, 1984.

Gaston, L. "The Theology of the Temple." In *Oikonomia: Heilsgeschichte als Thema der Theologie*, edited by F. Christ, 32–41. Hamburg-Bergstedt: Herbert Reich, 1967.

Gertner, M. "Midrashim in the New Testament." *Journal of Semitic Studies* 7 (1962): 267–92.

Goppelt, L. *Typos: The Typological Interpretation of the Old Testament in the New*. Grand Rapids: Eerdmans, 1982.

Greidanus, S. *Preaching Christ from the Old Testament*. Grand Rapids: Eerdmans, 1999.

Hagner, D. A. "The Old Testament in the New Testament." In *Interpreting the Word of God: Festschrift in Honor of Steven Barabas*, edited by S. J. Schultz and M. A. Inch, 78–104, plus notes on 275–76. Chicago: Moody, 1976.

Hanson, A. T. *Jesus Christ in the Old Testament*. London: SPCK, 1965.

———. *The Living Utterances of God: The New Testament Exegesis of the Old*. London: Darton, Longman & Todd, 1983.

*———. *The New Testament Interpretation of Scripture*. London: SPCK, 1980.

Harris, R. J. *Testimonies*. 2 vols. Cambridge: Cambridge University Press, 1916–20.

Hartmann, L. *Prophecy Interpreted*. Coniectanea biblica: New Testament Series 1. Lund: Gleerup, 1966.

Hay, D. M. *Glory at the Right Hand: Psalm 110 in Early Christianity*. Society of Biblical Literature Series 18. Nashville: Abingdon, 1973.

Hays, R. B., S. Alkier, and L. A. Huizenga, eds. *Reading the Bible Intertextually*. Waco: Baylor University Press, 2009.

Hengstenberg, E. W. *Christology of the Old Testament*. 4 vols. Edinburgh: T&T Clark, 1856–58. Repr., Grand Rapids: Kregel, 1956.

Hummel, H. D. "The Old Testament Basis of Typological Interpretation." *Biblical Research* 9 (1964): 38–50.

Instone-Brewer, D. *Techniques and Assumptions in Jewish Exegesis before 70 CE*. Texte und Studien zum antiken Judentum 30. Tübingen: Mohr Siebeck, 1992.

Johnson, S. L. *The Old Testament in the New*. Grand Rapids: Zondervan, 1980. This work demonstrates a good method for interpreting the OT in the NT.

Jonge, H. J. de, and J. Tromp. *The Book of Ezekiel and Its Influence*. Burlington, VT: Ashgate, 1988.

Juel, D. *Messianic Exegesis*. Philadelphia: Fortress, 1988. This focuses on the Gospels, though a few other NT texts are discussed.

Kaiser, W. C., Jr. *The Uses of the Old Testament in the New*. Chicago: Moody, 1985.

Lampe, G. W. H. "Hermeneutics and Typology." *London Quarterly and Holborn Review* 35 (1964): 17–25.

———. "The Reasonableness of Typology." In *Essays on Typology*, edited by G. W. H. Lampe and K. J. Woollcombe, 9–38. Studies in Biblical Theology 22. Naperville, IL: Alec R. Allenson, 1957.

———. "Typological Exegesis." *Theology* 56 (June 1953): 201–8.

LaRondelle, H. K. *The Israel of God in Prophecy*. Berrien Springs, MI: Andrews University Press, 1983.

LaSor, W. S. "The *Sensus Plenior* and Biblical Interpretation." In *Scripture, Tradition, and Interpretation*, edited by W. W. Gasque and W. S. LaSor, 260–77. Grand Rapids: Eerdmans, 1978.

Lindars, B. *New Testament Apologetic: The Doctrinal Significance of the Old Testament Quotations*. London: SCM, 1961.

———. "Place of the Old Testament in the Formation of New Testament Theology: Prolegomena." *New Testament Studies* 23 (1976): 59–66. See P. Borgen's response on 67–75.

Longenecker, R. N. *Biblical Exegesis in the Apostolic Period*. Grand Rapids: Eerdmans, 1975.

———. "Can We Reproduce the Exegesis of the New Testament?" *Tyndale Bulletin* 21 (1970): 3–38.

Longman, T. "The Divine Warrior: The New Testament Use of an Old Testament Motif." *Westminster Theological Journal* 44 (1982): 290–307.

Mánek, J. "Composite Quotations in the New Testament and Their Purpose." *Communio viatorum* 13 (1970): 181–88.

Manson, T. W. "The Argument from Prophecy." *Journal of Theological Studies* 46 (1945): 129–36.

Markus, R. A. "Presuppositions of the Typological Approach to Scripture." *Church Quarterly Review* 158 (1957): 442–51.

McCartney, D. G. "The New Testament's Use of the Old Testament." In *Inerrancy and Hermeneutic*, edited by H. M. Conn, 101–16. Grand Rapids: Baker, 1988.

———. "The New Testament Use of the Pentateuch: Implications for the Theonomic Movement." In *Theonomy: A Reformed Critique*, edited by W. S. Barker and W. R. Godfrey, 129–49. Grand Rapids: Zondervan, 1990.

Metzger, B. M. "The Formulas Introducing Quotations of Scripture in the New Testament and the Midrash." *Journal of Biblical Literature* 70 (1951): 297–307.

Miller, M. P. "Targum, Midrash, and the Use of the Old Testament in the New Testament." *Journal of Semitic Studies* 2 (1971): 29–82.

Moo, D. J. "The Problem of *Sensus Plenior*." In *Hermeneutics, Authority and Canon*, edited by D. A. Carson and J. D. Woodbridge, 179–211, plus footnotes on 397–405. Grand Rapids: Zondervan / Academie Books, 1986.

Moule, C. F. D. "Fulfillment-Words in the New Testament: Use and Abuse." *New Testament Studies* 14 (1968): 293–320.

Moyise, S. *Evoking Scripture: Seeing the Old Testament in the New*. London: T&T Clark / Continuum, 2008.

———. *The Old Testament in the New*. New York: Continuum, 2001.

———, ed. *The Old Testament in the New Testament: Essays in Honour of J. L. North*. Sheffield: Sheffield Academic Press, 2000.

Moyise, S., and M. J. J. Menken, eds. *Deuteronomy in the New Testament. The New Testament and the Scriptures of Israel*. Library of New Testament Studies 358. New York: T&T Clark / Continuum, 2010.

———. *Isaiah in the New Testament*. New York: T&T Clark / Continuum, 2005.

———. *The Psalms in the New Testament*. New York: T&T Clark / Continuum, 2004.

Nicole, R. R. "The New Testament Use of the Old Testament." In *The Right Doctrine from Wrong Texts? Essays on the Use of the Old Testament in the New*, edited by G. K. Beale, 13–28. Grand Rapids: Baker, 1994.

———. "Patrick Fairbairn and Biblical Hermeneutics as Related to the Quotations of the Old Testament in the New." In *Hermeneutics, Inerrancy, and the Bible*, Papers from ICBI Summit II, edited by E. D. Radmacher and R. D. Preus, 767–76. Grand Rapids: Zondervan / Academie Books, 1984. See responses by R. R. Youngblood on 779–88 and S. L. Johnson on 791–99.

Oesterreicher, M. M. *The Israel of God: On the Old Testament Roots of the Church's Faith*. Englewood Cliffs, NJ: Prentice-Hall, 1963.

*Osborne, G. R. "Type, Typology." In *International Standard Bible Encyclopedia, Revised*, 4:930–32. Grand Rapids: Eerdmans, 1988.

Packer, J. I. "Unfolding the Unity of Scripture Today." *Journal of the Evangelical Theological Society* 25 (1982): 409–14.

Patte, D. *Early Jewish Hermeneutic in Palestine*. Society of Biblical Literature Dissertation Series 22. Missoula, MT: Scholars Press, 1975.

Pickup, M. "New Testament Interpretation of the Old Testament: The Theological Rationale of Midrashic Exegesis." *Journal of the Evangelical Theological Society* 51 (2008): 353–81.

Porter, S. E. "Further Comments on the Use of the Old Testament in the New Testament." In *The Intertextuality of the Epistles: Explorations of Theory and Practice*, edited by T. L. Brodie, D. R. MacDonald, and S. E. Porter, 98–110. New Testament Monographs 16. Sheffield: Sheffield Phoenix, 2007. Though this article focuses on the use of the OT in Paul, it has broader relevance for the entire NT.

———, ed. *Hearing the Old Testament in the New Testament*. Grand Rapids: Eerdmans, 2006.

———. "The Use of the Old Testament in the New Testament: A Brief Comment on Method and Terminology." In *Early Christian Interpretation of the Scriptures of Israel: Investigation and Proposals*, edited by C. A. Evans and J. A. Sanders, 79–96. Journal for the Study of the New Testament: Supplement Series 148. Sheffield: JSOT Press, 1977.

Poythress, V. *The Shadow of Christ in the Law of Moses*. Brentwood, TN: Wolgemuth & Hyatt, 1991.

Rad, G. von. "Typological Interpretation of the Old Testament." *Interpretation* 15 (1961): 174–92.

Rendall, R. "Quotation in Scripture as an Index of Wider Reference." *Evangelical Quarterly* 36 (1964): 214–21.

Rohrs, W. R. "The Typological Use of the Old Testament in the New Testament." *Concordia Journal* 10 (1984): 204–16.

Sandmel, S. "Parallelomania." *Journal of Biblical Literature* 81 (1962): 1–13.

Shires, H. M. *Finding the Old Testament in the New*. Philadelphia: Westminster, 1974.

Silva, M. "The New Testament Use of the Old Testament: Text Form and Authority." In *Scripture and Truth*, edited by D. A. Carson and J. D. Woodbridge, 147–65, plus notes on 381–86. Grand Rapids: Zondervan, 1983.

Smart, J. D. *The Interpretation of Scripture*. Philadelphia: Westminster, 1961.

Smith, D. M., Jr. "The Use of the Old Testament in the New." In *The Use of the Old Testament in the New and Other Essays: Studies in Honor of William Franklin Stinespring*, edited by J. M. Efird, 3–65. Durham, NC: Duke University Press, 1972.

Snodgrass, K. "The Use of the Old Testament in the New." In *The Right Doctrine from the Wrong Texts? Essays on the Use of the Old Testament in the New*, edited by G. K. Beale, 29–51. Grand Rapids: Baker, 1994.

Sperber, A. "New Testament and Septuagint." *Journal of Biblical Literature* 59 (1940): 193–293.

Stek, J. H. "Biblical Typology Yesterday and Today." *Calvin Theological Journal* 5 (1970): 133–62.

Tasker, R. V. *The Old Testament in the New Testament*. Philadelphia: Westminster, 1947.

Vermes, G. "Jewish Literature and New Testament Exegesis: Reflections on Methodology." *Journal of Jewish Studies* 33 (1982): 361–76.

Waltke, B. K. "Is It Right to Read the New Testament into the Old?" *Christianity Today* 27, no. 13 (1983): 77.

Wilcox, M. "On Investigating the Use of the Old Testament in the New Testament." In *Text and Interpretation*, edited by E. Best, 231–43. Cambridge: Cambridge University Press, 1979.

Woollcombe, K. J. "The Biblical Origins and Patristic Development of Typology." In *Essays on Typology*, edited by G. W. Lampe and K. J. Woollcombe, 39–75. Studies in Biblical Theology 22. Naperville, IL: A. R. Allenson, 1957.

Zimmerli, W. "Promise and Fulfillment." In *Essays on Old Testament Hermeneutics*, edited by C. Westermann, 89–122. English ed. edited by J. L. Mays. Richmond: John Knox, 1963.

Books and Essays on the Gospels and Acts

Gospels and Acts in General

Doeve, J. W. *Jewish Hermeneutics in the Synoptic Gospels and Acts*. Assen: Van Gorcum, 1954.

*Evans, C. A. "Old Testament in the Gospels." In *Dictionary of Jesus and the Gospels*, edited by J. B. Green, S. McKnight, and I. H. Marshall, 579–90. Downers Grove, IL: InterVarsity, 1992.

———. *To See and Not Perceive: Isaiah 6.9–10 in Early Jewish and Christian Interpretation*. Journal for the Study of the Old Testament: Supplement Series 64. Sheffield: JSOT Press, 1989.

Evans, C. A., and W. R. Stegner, eds. *The Gospels and the Scriptures of Israel*. Journal for the Study of the New Testament: Supplement Series 104. Sheffield: JSOT Press, 1994.

France, R. T. *Jesus and the Old Testament: His Application of Old Testament Passages to Himself and His Mission*. London: Tyndale, 1971. Repr., Grand Rapids: Baker, 1982.

Hays, R. B. "Can the Gospels Teach Us How to Read the Old Testament?" *Pro ecclesia* 11 (2002): 402–18.

Kline, M. "The Old Testament Origins of the Gospel Genre." *Westminster Theological Journal* 38 (1975): 1–27.

Manson, T. W. "The Old Testament in the Teaching of Jesus." *Bulletin of the John Rylands Library* 34 (1951–52): 312–32.

Moo, D. J. *The Old Testament in the Gospel Passion Narratives*. Sheffield: Almond, 1983.

Moyise, S. *Jesus and Scripture: Studying the New Testament Use of the Old Testament*. Grand Rapids: Baker Academic, 2011.

*New, D. S. *Old Testament Quotations in the Synoptic Gospels, and the Two-Document Hypothesis*. Society of Biblical Literature Septuagint and Cognate Studies Series 37. Atlanta: Scholars Press, 1993.

O'Rourke, J. J. "Explicit Old Testament Citations in the Gospels." *Studia Montis Regii* 7 (1964): 37–60.

Thomas, K. J. "Torah Citations in the Synoptics." *New Testament Studies* 24 (1977): 85–96.

Matthew

Allison, D. C. *The New Moses: A Matthean Typology*. Minneapolis: Fortress, 1993.

Beale, G. K. "The Use of Hosea 11:1 in Matthew 2:15: One More Time." *JETS* [forthcoming].

Blomberg, C. "Matthew." In *Commentary on the New Testament Use of the Old Testament*, edited by G. K. Beale and D. A. Carson, 1–109. Grand Rapids: Baker Academic, 2007.

Carson, D. A. *Matthew*, vol. 1, *Chapters 1 through 12*. Expositor's Bible Commentary. Grand Rapids: Zondervan, 1995.

Eldridge, V. J. "Typology—the Key to Understanding Matthew's Formula Quotations?" *Colloquium* 15 (1982): 43–51.

France, R. T. "The Formula-Quotations of Matthew 2 and the Problem of Communication." In *The Right Doctrine from the Wrong Texts? Essays on the Use of the Old Testament in the New*, edited by G. K. Beale, 114–34. Grand Rapids: Baker, 1994.

Gundry, R. H. *The Use of the Old Testament in St. Matthew's Gospel*. Supplements to Novum Testamentum 18. Leiden: Brill, 1967.

Hartmann, L. "Scriptural Exegesis in the Gospel of Matthew and the Problem of Communication." In *L' évangile selon Matthieu: Rédaction et théologie*, edited by M. Didier, 132–52. Bibliotheca ephemeridum theologicarum lovaniensium 29. Gembloux: Duculot, 1972.

Hays, R. B. "The Gospel of Matthew: Reconfigured Torah." *Hervormde theologiese studies* 61 (2005): 169–90.

Hillyer, N. "Matthew's Use of the Old Testament." *Evangelical Quarterly* 36 (1964): 12–26.

Johnson, S. E. "The Biblical Quotations in Matthew." *Harvard Theological Review* 36 (1943): 135–53.

*Knowles, M. *Jeremiah in Matthew's Gospel: The Rejected Prophet Motif in Matthean Redaction*. Journal for the Study of the New Testament: Supplement Series 68. Sheffield: JSOT Press, 1993.

Luz, U. "Intertexts in the Gospel of Matthew." *Harvard Theological Review* 97 (2004): 119–37.

O'Rourke, J. J. "Explicit Old Testament Citations in the Gospels." *Studia Montis Regii* 7 (1964): 37–60.

———. "Fulfillment Texts in Matthew." *Catholic Biblical Quarterly* 24 (1962): 394–403.

Patte, D. *Early Jewish Hermeneutic in Palestine*. Society of Biblical Literature Dissertation Series 22. Missoula, MT: Scholars Press, 1975.

Soares Prabhu, G. M. *The Formula Quotations in the Infancy Narratives of Matthew: An Enquiry into the Tradition History of Mt. 1–2*. Analecta biblica 63. Rome: Pontifical Biblical Institute, 1976.

Stendahl, K. *The School of St. Matthew and Its Use of the Old Testament*. Acta seminarii neotestamentici upsaliensis 20. Lund: C. W. K. Gleerup, 1954.

Mark

Kee, H. C. "Function of Scriptural Quotations and Allusions in Mark 11–16." In *Jesus und Paulus: Festschrift für W. G. Kümmel zum 70. Geburtstag*, edited by E. E. Ellis and E. Gräßer, 165–88. Göttingen: Vandenhoeck & Ruprecht, 1975.

Markus, J. *The Way of the Lord: Christological Exegesis of the Old Testament in the Gospel of Mark*. Louisville: John Knox, 1992.

Mauser, U. *Christ in the Wilderness: The Wilderness Theme in the Second Gospel and Its Basis in the Biblical Tradition*. Studies in Biblical Theology 39. Naperville, IL: A. R. Allenson, 1963.

*Watts, R. E. *Isaiah's New Exodus in Mark*. Grand Rapids: Baker, 1997.

Luke–Acts

Bock, D. L. *Proclamation from Prophecy and Pattern: Lucan Old Testament Christology*. Journal for the Study of the New Testament: Supplement Series 12. Sheffield: JSOT Press, 1987.

Bruce, F. F. "Paul's Use of the Old Testament in Acts." In *Tradition and Interpretation in the Old Testament*, edited by G. F. Hawthorne with O. Betz, 71–79. Grand Rapids: Eerdmans, 1987.

Evans, C. A., and J. A. Sanders. *Luke and Scripture: The Function of Sacred Tradition in Luke–Acts*. Philadelphia: Fortress, 1993.

Goulder, M. D. *Type and History in Acts*. London: SPCK, 1964.

Kimball, C. A. *Jesus' Exposition of the Old Testament in Luke's Gospel*. Journal for the Study of the New Testament: Supplement Series 94. Sheffield: JSOT Press, 1994.

Mallen, P. *The Reading and Transformation of Isaiah in Luke–Acts*. Library of New Testament Studies. New York: T&T Clark / Continuum, 2008.

Manek, J. "New Exodus in the Books of Luke." *Novum Testamentum* 2 (1957): 8–23.

Moessner, D. P. *Lord of the Banquet*. Minneapolis: Fortress, 1989.

Pao, D. *Acts and the Isaianic New Exodus*. Wissenschaftliche Untersuchungen zum Neuen Testament 2/130. Tübingen: Mohr Siebeck, 2000.

Sanders, J. A. "Isaiah in Luke." *Interpretation* 36 (1982): 144–55.

John

Barrett, C. K. "The Old Testament in the Fourth Gospel." *Journal of Theological Studies* 48 (1947): 155–69.

Evans, C. A. "On the Quotation Formulas in the Fourth Gospel." *Biblische Zeitschrift* 26 (1982): 79–83.

Freed, E. D. *Old Testament Quotations in the Gospel of John*. Supplements to Novum Testamentum 11. Leiden: Brill, 1965.

Glasson, T. F. *Moses in the Fourth Gospel*. Studies in Biblical Theology 40. London: SCM, 1963.

Köstenberger, A. J. "John." In *Commentary on the New Testament Use of the Old Testament*, edited by G. K. Beale and D. A. Carson, 415–512. Grand Rapids: Baker Academic, 2007.

Meeks, W. A. *The Prophet-King: Moses Traditions and the Johannine Christology*. Leiden: Brill, 1967.

Reim, G. "Jesus as God in the Fourth Gospel: The Old Testament Background." *New Testament Studies* 30 (1984): 158–60.

Schuchard, B. G. *Scripture within Scripture: The Interrelationship of Form and Function in the Explicit Old Testament Citations in the Gospel of John*. Society of Biblical Literature Dissertation Series 133. Atlanta: Scholars Press, 1992.

Young, F. W. "Study of the Relation of Isaiah to the Fourth Gospel." *Zeitschrift für neutestamentliche Wissenschaft* 46 (1955): 215–33.

Paul

Aageson, J. W. *Written Also for Our Sake: Paul and the Art of Biblical Interpretation*. Louisville: John Knox, 1993.

Ellis, E. E. *Paul's Use of the Old Testament*. Edinburgh: Oliver & Boyd, 1957. Repr., Grand Rapids: Baker, 1981.

Evans, C. A. "Paul and the Hermeneutics of 'True Prophecy': A Study of Romans 9–11." *Biblica* 65 (1984): 560–70.

Evans, C. A., and J. A. Sanders, eds. *Paul and the Scriptures of Israel*. Journal for the Study of the New Testament: Supplement Series 83. Studies in Scripture in Early Judaism and Christianity 1. Sheffield: JSOT Press, 1993.

*Hafemann, S. J. *Paul, Moses, and the History of Israel: The Letter/Spirit Contrast and the Argument from Scripture in 2 Corinthians 3*. Wissenschaftliche Untersuchungen zum Neuen Testament 81. Tübingen: Mohr Siebeck, 1995.

*Hanson, A. T. *Studies on Paul's Technique and Theology*. Grand Rapids: Eerdmans, 1974.

Hays, R. B. *The Conversion of the Imagination: Paul as Interpreter of Israel's Scripture*. Grand Rapids: Eerdmans, 2005.

———. *Echoes of Scripture in the Letters of Paul*. New Haven: Yale University Press, 1989.

Jones, P. R. "The Apostle Paul: Second Moses to the New Covenant Community." In *God's Inerrant Word*, edited by J. Montgomery, 219–41. Minneapolis: Bethany Fellowship, 1974.

Koch, D.-A. *Die Schrift als Zeuge des Evangeliums: Untersuchungen zur Verwendung und zum Verständnis der Schrift bei Paulus*. Beiträge zur historischen Theologie 69. Tübingen: Mohr Siebeck, 1986.

Litwak, K. D. "Echoes of Scripture? A Critical Survey of Recent Works on Paul's Use of the Old Testament." *Currents in Biblical Research* 6 (1998): 260–88.

Malan, F. S. "The Use of the Old Testament in 1 Corinthians." *Neotestamentica* 14 (1981): 134–70.

Michel, O. *Paulus und seine Bibel*. Beiträge zur Forderung christlicher Theologie 2/18. Gütersloh: Bertelsmann, 1929.

Moritz, T. *A Profound Mystery: The Use of the Old Testament in Ephesians*. Leiden: Brill, 1996.

Moyise, S. *Paul and Scripture: Studying the New Testament Use of the Old Testament*. Grand Rapids: Baker Academic, 2010.

Piper, J. "Prolegomena to Understanding Romans 9:14–15: An Interpretation of Exodus 33:19." *Journal of the Evangelical Theological Society* 22 (1979): 203–16.

Porter, S. E. "Allusions and Echoes." In *As It Is Written: Studying Paul's Use of Scripture*, edited by S. E. Porter and C. D. Stanley, 29–40. SBL Symposium Series 50. Atlanta: Society of Biblical Literature, 2008.

Scott, J. M. *Adoption as Sons of God: An Exegetical Investigation into the Background of* Huiothesia *in the Pauline Corpus*. Wissenschaftliche Untersuchungen zum Neuen Testament 2/48. Tübingen: Mohr Siebeck, 1992.

*Silva, M. "Old Testament in Paul." In *Dictionary of Paul and His Letters*, edited by G. F. Hawthorne, R. P. Martin, and D. G. Reid, 630–42. Downers Grove, IL: InterVarsity, 1993.

*Stanley, C. D. *Arguing with Scripture: The Rhetoric of Quotations in the Letters of Paul*. New York: T&T Clark, 2004.

———. *Paul and the Language of Scripture: Citation Technique in the Pauline Epistles and Contemporary Literature*. Society for New Testament Studies Monograph Series 70. Cambridge: Cambridge University Press, 1993.

Tomson, P. J. *Paul and the Jewish Law: Halakha in the Letters of the Apostle to the Gentiles*. Compendia rerum Iudaicarum ad Novum Testamentum: Sect. 3, Jewish Traditions in Early Christian Literature 1. Minneapolis: Fortress, 1990.

Wagner, J. R. *Heralds of the Good News: Isaiah and Paul "in Concert" in the Letter to the Romans*. Boston: Brill, 2003.

Watson, F. *Paul and the Hermeneutics of Faith*. New York: T&T Clark / Continuum, 2004.

Wilcox, M. "Upon the Tree: Deuteronomy 21:22–23 in the New Testament." *Journal of Biblical Literature* 96 (1977): 85–99.

Wilk, F. *Die Bedeutung des Jesajabuches fur Paulus*. Forschungen zur Religion und Literatur des Alten und Neuen Testaments 179. Göttingen: Vandenhoeck & Ruprecht, 1998.

Wright, N. T. *The Climax of the Covenant: Christ and the Law in Pauline Theology*. Edinburgh: T&T Clark, 1991.

Hebrews

Barth, M. "The Old Testament in Hebrews: An Essay in Biblical Hermeneutics." In *Current Issues in New Testament Interpretation*, edited by W. Klassen and G. Snyder, 53–78. New York: Harper & Row, 1962.

Bateman, H. *Early Jewish Hermeneutics and Hebrews 1:5–13: The Impact of Early Jewish Exegesis on the Interpretation of a Significant New Testament Passage*. American University Studies 193. New York: P. Lang, 1997.

Caird, G. B. "Exegetical Method of the Epistle to the Hebrews." *Canadian Journal of Theology* 5 (1959): 44–51.

Childs, B. S. "Prophecy and Fulfillment: A Study of Contemporary Hermeneutics." *Interpretation* 12 (1958): 260–71.

Combrink, H. J. B. "Some Thoughts on the Old Testament Citations in the Epistle to the Hebrews." *Neotestamentica* 5 (1971): 22–36.

Guthrie, G. "Hebrews' Use of the Old Testament: Recent Trends in Research." *Currents in Biblical Research* 1 (2003): 271–94.

*———. "The Old Testament in Hebrews." In *Dictionary of the Later New Testament and Its Developments*, edited by R. P. Martin and P. H. Davids, 841–50. Downers Grove, IL: InterVarsity, 1997.

Hanson, A. T. "Christ in the Old Testament according to Hebrews." *Studia evangelica* 2 (1964): 393–407.

Howard, G. "Hebrews and the Old Testament Quotations." *Novum Testamentum* 10 (1968): 208–16.

Hughes, G. *Hebrews and Hermeneutics*. Society for New Testament Studies Monograph Series 36. Cambridge: Cambridge University Press, 1979.

Katz, P. "The Quotations from Deuteronomy in Hebrews." *Zeitschrift für die neutestamentliche Wissenshaft* 49 (1958): 213–23.

Kistemaker, S. *The Psalm Quotations in the Epistle to the Hebrews*. Amsterdam: van Soest, 1961.

McCullough, J. C. "The Old Testament Quotations in Hebrews." *New Testament Studies* 26 (1980): 363–79.

Rendall, R. "The Method of the Writer to the Hebrews in Using Old Testament Quotations." *Evangelical Quarterly* 27 (1955): 214–20.

Thomas, K. J. "The Old Testament Citations in Hebrews." *New Testament Studies* 11 (1964–65): 303–25.

General Epistles

*Charles, J. D. "Old Testament in General Epistles." In *Dictionary of the Later New Testament and Its Developments*, edited by R. P. Martin and P. H. Davids, 834–41. Downers Grove, IL: InterVarsity, 1997.

Johnson, L. T. "The Use of Leviticus 19 in the Letter of James." *Journal of Biblical Literature* 101 (1982): 391–401.

Revelation

Bauckham, R. *The Climax of Prophecy: Studies in the Book of Revelation.* Edinburgh: T&T Clark, 1993.

Beale, G. K. *The Book of Revelation.* New International Greek Testament Commentary. Grand Rapids: Eerdmans, 1999.

———. *John's Use of the Old Testament in Revelation.* Journal for the Study of the New Testament: Supplement Series 166. Sheffield: JSOT Press, 1998.

———. "The Old Testament Background of Rev 3.14." *New Testament Studies* 42 (1996): 133–52.

———. "The Origin of the Title 'King of Kings and Lord of Lords' in Revelation 17.14." *New Testament Studies* 31 (1985): 618–20.

———. *The Temple and the Church's Mission: A Biblical Theology of the Dwelling Place of God.* New Studies in Biblical Theology 17. Downers Grove, IL: InterVarsity, 2004.

———. *The Use of Daniel in Jewish Apocalyptic Literature and in the Revelation of St. John.* Lanham, MD: University Press of America, 1984.

Fekkes, J., III. *Isaiah and Prophetic Traditions in the Book of Revelation.* Journal for the Study of the New Testament: Supplement Series 93. Sheffield: JSOT Press, 1994.

Goulder, M. D. "The Apocalypse as an Annual Cycle of Prophecies." *New Testament Studies* 27 (1981): 342–67.

Jauhiainen, M. *The Use of Zechariah in Revelation.* Wissenschaftliche Untersuchungen zum Neuen Testament 2/199. Tübingen: Mohr Siebeck, 2005.

Mathewson, D. *A New Heaven and a New Earth.* Journal for the Study of the New Testament: Supplement Series 238. Sheffield: Sheffield Academic Press, 2003.

Michaels. J. R. "Old Testament in Revelation." In *Dictionary of the Later New Testament and Its Developments*, edited by R. P. Martin and P. H. Davids, 850–55. Downers Grove, IL: InterVarsity, 1997.

Moyise, S. "The Language of the Old Testament in the Apocalypse." *Journal for the Study of the New Testament* 76 (1999): 97–113.

———. *The Old Testament in the Book of Revelation.* Journal for the Study of the New Testament: Supplement Series 115. Sheffield: Sheffield Academic Press, 1995.

Ruis, J.-P. *Ezekiel in the Apocalypse: The Transformation of Prophetic Language in Revelation 16,17–19,10.* European University Studies. Series XXIII, vol. 376. New York: P. Lang, 1989.

Trudinger, P. "Some Observations Concerning the Text of the Old Testament in the Book of Revelation." *Journal of Theological Studies* 17 (1966): 82–88.

Author Index

Ancient Writings Index

Old Testament

Genesis

Exodus

Leviticus

Numbers

Deuteronomy

Joshua

Judges

John

Acts

Romans

1 Corinthians

2 Corinthians

Galatians